INVESTIGATING COUPLES

INVESTIGATING COUPLES

A Critical Analysis of
The Thin Man, The Avengers,
and *The X-Files*

by TOM SOTER

McFarland & Company, Inc., Publishers
Jefferson, North Carolina, and London

LIBRARY OF CONGRESS CATALOGUING-IN-PUBLICATION DATA

Soter, Tom, 1956–
    Investigating couples : a critical analysis of The Thin Man, The Avengers, and The X-Files / by Tom Soter.
    p. cm.
    Includes bibliographical references and index.

    ISBN-13: 978-0-7864-1123-8
    ISBN-10: 0-7864-1123-6
    (softcover : 50# alkaline paper) ∞

    1. Detective teams on television. 2. Detective and mystery television programs—History and criticism. 3. Detective teams in motion pictures. 4. Detective and mystery films—United States—History and critism. I. Title.
    PN1992.8.D48 S65 2002
    791.45'655—dc21   2001044929

British Library cataloguing data are available

©2002 Tom Soter. All rights reserved

No part of this book may be reproduced or transmitted in any form or by any means, electronic or mechanical, including photocopying or recording, or by any information storage and retrieval system, without permission in writing from the publisher.

Manufactured in the United States of America

Cover photograph: Myrna Loy, William Powell, and Asta in a publicity still for the *Thin Man* series

McFarland & Company, Inc., Publishers
    Box 611, Jefferson, North Carolina 28640
        www.mcfarlandpub.com

To my mother, Effie

Table of Contents

Acknowledgments	viii
Preface	1
1: The Detective	3
2: The Tough Guy	15
3: The Romantic	21
4: Ballad of a Thin Man	30
5: A Humorous Hitch	54
6: When a Man Became a Woman	63
7: M-Appeal	80
8: Trust No One	98
9: The Truth Is Out There	111
10: A Man and a Woman	125
Appendix 1: The Thin Man: *A Guide*	149
Appendix 2: The Avengers: *A Guide*	157
Appendix 3: The X-Files: *A Guide*	190
Chapter Notes	221
Bibliography	231
Index	237

Acknowledgments

As I put together this book, a number of people offered their assistance.

First, let me thank Honor Blackman and Patrick Macnee, who shared their memories and thoughts about *The Avengers* and other topics. Without their help, my work would have been much more difficult.

Let me also thank James Kotsilibas-Davis, who mentored me in my youth and who allowed me to quote from his excellent book about Myrna Loy.

Thanks also to Sandi Bushnell at DKPR, who supplied me with many *Avengers* DVDs, as well as introductions to Blackman and Macnee; to my brother Peter Soter and my friends Tom Sinclair and Karl Tiedemann, who all helped on the research front; to my other brother, Nick Soter, and his wife, Dora Miranda, who started me watching *The X-Files*; to my mother, Effie; and to my father, George, who introduced me to *The Thin Man* many, many years ago at Theater 80 St. Marks.

Thanks all!

Tom Soter
September 2001

Preface

The Thin Man was a detective series about a husband-and-wife detective team, Nick and Nora Charles. They drank a lot, traded quips, and were deeply in love.

The Avengers was a spy series about a man-and-woman detective team, John Steed and Emma Peel. They dressed stylishly, traded quips, and examined bizarre murders.

The X-Files was a science fiction series about a man-and-woman detective team, Fox Mulder and Dana Scully. They looked serious, traded theories, and examined extraterrestrials and bizarre occurrences.

Three different drama series, each a phenomenon of its time — the thirties, the sixties, the nineties — all highly successful in the critical and commercial arenas, and all three highly influential.

Beyond that, is there a connection?

To answer that, this book looks in detail at antecedents to each series, going into production detail, where necessary, and offering insights on the times, the people, and the places, often from people who were involved in the process.

Is there a connection? Well, as Fox Mulder is fond of saying, "The truth is out there."

1

The Detective

"Most readers are beset with a lot of problems they can't solve. When they try to relax, their minds keep gnawing over these problems and there is no solution. They pick up a mystery story, become completely absorbed in the problem, see the problem worked out to a final and just conclusion, turn out the light and go to sleep. If I have given millions that sort of relaxation, it is reward enough."
Erle Stanley Gardner[1]

"Hasty conclusion easy to make, like hole in water."
Charlie Chan (Warner Oland)[2]

The crime is perfect — and perfectly bizarre. A man is found dead in a locked room, without the possibility of murder. And yet he was murdered! So says the eccentric detective whose name could be Sherlock Holmes, Hercule Poirot, or Fox Mulder.

The bizarre, the unknown, and the inexplicable have always fascinated us. The legends of the Abominable Snowman, the Loch Ness Monster — even the so-called "second gunman" theory of the John F. Kennedy assassination — have left many saying, "The truth is out there."

Did George Reeves, TV's Superman, really kill himself? Was Mark David Chapman acting as a brainwashed hireling of the CIA when he shot John Lennon? Is there really a Santa Claus? The truth is out there.

Hollywood has long tapped into the fascination with the popular and the paranoid. Although TV's *The X-Files* and its imitators and sequels are only the latest manifestation of the trend, the story goes back even further, to the beginning of time, in fact, and the Bible's story of how God created the world in seven days. Seven days? How is that possible? And was there a talking serpent? Or a worldwide flood? The truth is out there.

Any mystery story always ends up with detectives. Some are amateur sleuths, others work for the police. Some are offbeat, others conventionally dry. If the public loves a mystery, then the public has also long had a fascination with sleuths—and it was the particular genius of *The Thin Man* movies to combine that fascination with gumshoes with a host of other public obsessions.

The first literary detectives were men and the first was an eccentric character named C. August Dupin who solved the "Murders in the Rue Morgue." Edgar Allan Poe was the author, and the story lays out all the conventions of the detective genre. Indeed, according to Jeff Siegel, in *The American Detective: An Illustrated History*, "Someone once analyzed 'Rue Morgue,' and discovered that Poe invented thirty-two conventions of the mystery story."[3]

There is the bizarre and brutal murder, with no apparent motive. In this case, an elderly woman and her daughter butchered in their Paris home: the mother's head severed by a razor blade, the younger woman thrust up a chimney, jammed up so forcefully that many men had to work together to pull her down.

There are the contradictory accounts of witnesses, laid out like a mathematical puzzle. All agree that two voices were heard: a Frenchman saying, "My God," and a second speaking in an indecipherable language that no one in a building which houses French, English, Spanish, and Italians can understand.

Then, too, there is the absence of motive, and the impotence and frustration of the police, who have no clue as to who did it. "A murder so mysterious, and so perplexing in all its particulars was never before committed in Paris—if indeed a murder has been committed at all," observes the local newspaper. "There is not, however, the shadow of a clew [sic] apparent."[4]

But the truth is out there, waiting for the right man to uncover it. In this case, it is Dupin, the amateur, armchair sleuth, who asserts that everything about the case is a clue. He is the classic detective of this type: a thinking machine who observes, reasons, and sees things that others miss, all the while explaining his motives to his "common man" associate, the narrator.

"We must not judge by the means," he says, "by this shell of examination. The Parisian police, so much extolled for acumen, are cunning but no more. There is no method in their proceedings, beyond the method of the moment."[5]

Dupin — like all the detectives of his ilk, both in literature and celluloid, leading right up to *The X-Files*' Fox Mulder and Dana Scully — sees things that others ignore. He goes to the site of the bizarre, savage murders (naturally, on the Rue Morgue, literally "Street of Corpses") and, with his associate, puts the clues together in a rational, ordered way.

Poe offers the detective as an intellectual superman, a man with a muscular brain and mental powers that go beyond mere mortals. "As the strong man exults in his physical ability, delighting in such exercises as call his muscles into action, so glories the analyst in the moral activity which *disentangles*," explains the narrator.[6]

In fact, the sleuth is the representative of a higher force — a righter of wrongs, but also a seeker of justice and truth — a justice and truth that are often not seen or not available to us in everyday life. Erle Stanley Gardner, a mystery writer in the 1920s who went on to create the classic lawyer-detective Perry Mason in 1933, once explained the appeal of such heroes and the stories in which they appeared. "Most readers are beset with a lot of problems they can't solve. When they try to relax, their minds keep gnawing over these problems and there is no solution. They pick up a mystery story, become completely absorbed in the problem, see the problem worked out to a final and just conclusion, turn out the light and go to sleep."[7]

Dupin is like a magician: he does not dirty his hands or spend much time canvassing the crime scene or witnesses as real police might. He talks volumes; in fact, "Rue Morgue" shows its age by its lack of action; it is more a monologue than a story. Dupin observes a great deal, and then, like the wizard he is, not only produces the solution — the murderer is a monkey — but also tricks the killer's owner into coming to him (Sherlock Holmes would later practice the same gimmick quite often). Dupin doesn't even break a sweat doing all this; in fact, he looks on the solution of the crime as a game, a contest between himself and the prefect of police. "I am satisfied with having defeated him in his own castle," he says at the conclusion, as though it were a chess match and not a murder investigation.[8]

Dupin set the pattern (the determined Sgt. Cuff in Wilkie Collins's 1860 novel *The Moonstone* was the second great detective), but it took Sir Arthur Conan Doyle's Sherlock Holmes to set the formula in stone. Holmes — almost infallible, certainly virtuous, amazingly eccentric — was to become a fixed point in the changing world of detective fiction.

Basil Rathbone and Nigel Bruce (left) as Sherlock Holmes and Doctor Watson. In many ways, super-sleuth Holmes is the chief prototype for Nick Charles, John Steed, and Fox Mulder: virtuous, eccentric, with keen powers of observation and almost super-human deductive abilities.

He was, in fan and follower Vincent Starrett's words, "the perfect sleuth,"[9] more popular than other heroes of the time because, like Dupin, he makes sense of the nonsensical ("You see but you do not observe"[10] he would often say by way of explanation). He is the hero who brings order where there is chaos, overcoming problems instead of letting them overcome him.

George Bernard Shaw called Holmes "a drug addict without a single admirable trait,"[11] yet Holmes's addiction to a seven percent solution of cocaine is hardly his most noteworthy characteristic. In fact, the drug addiction was a canny early move by Conan Doyle that made the character more human than Poe's Dupin, a thinking machine. Holmes had vices; he became bored; he loved flamboyance, presenting his solutions in as melodramatic a fashion as possible.

Holmes started many trends, and one of them was to be among the first fictional sleuths with a list of eccentricities. In the first mystery, *A Study in Scarlet* (1887), Holmes himself appears to be an enigma to his roommate, Dr. John H. Watson, who observes: "His ignorance was as remarkable as his knowledge. Of contemporary literature, philosophy, and politics, he appeared to know next to nothing. Upon my quoting Thomas Carlyle, he inquired in the naivest way who he might be and what he had done. My surprise reached a climax, however, when I found incidentally that he was ignorant of the Copernican Theory and of the composition of the Solar System. That any civilized human being in this nineteenth century should not be aware that the earth traveled around the sun appeared to be to me such an extraordinary fact that I could hardly realize it."[12]

Indeed: Holmes knows nothing of literature, philosophy, or astronomy, has a feeble grasp of politics, a practical understanding of geology, but a profound and accurate knowledge of human anatomy, chemistry, and sensational literature. He knows British law well.

Holmes explains his selective education to his friend: "I consider that a man's brain originally is like a little empty attic, and you have to stock it with such furniture as you choose. A fool takes in all the lumber of every sort that he comes across, so that the knowledge which might be useful to him gets crowded out, or at best is jumbled up with a lot of other things, so that he has difficulty in laying his hands on it. Now the skillful workman is very careful indeed as to what he takes into his brain attic. He will have nothing but the tools which may help him in doing his work."[13]

Holmes later gained more "impractical" knowledge, quoting literary types and politicos with ease (Doyle was not as consistent as his detective in following through on his stated theorems), but he remained an enchanting eccentric throughout his career. His violin playing became legendary, as did his thin face and flaring nostrils, the deerstalker cap (added by an illustrator), pipe, and distinctive expressions: "The game is afoot!" "You see, but you do not observe." "When you have eliminated all the possibilities, whatever remains, no matter how improbable, is the answer."

But, most of all, Holmes was dramatic and flamboyant, as in the famous exchange from the short mystery, "Silver Blaze":

"Is there any point to which you would wish to draw my attention?" one character asks Holmes.

"To the curious incident of the dog in the night-time."

"The dog did nothing in the night-time."
"That was the curious incident."[14]

Holmes was the sleuth par excellence, eccentric and unchallenged, an amateur who knew more than the professionals who practiced "the science" of deduction, not the improbable guesswork more common in literary (and real-life) criminal detection work at the time. The "Great Man," as his fans called him, rarely faltered in a series of short stories, which began appearing in *The Strand Magazine* in 1892. He was one of the first literary detectives to jump into multi-media, appearing on stage, in silent and sound movies, and in radio dramas.

Holmes's earliest film role combined the public fascination with the magic of the movies and its equal fascination with the magic of literary sleuthing. He appeared — oh so briefly — in *Sherlock Holmes Baffled*, a 1903 short which had more to do with technical trickery than the deductive powers of the Victorian-era detective. In it, an intruder in Holmes's flat literally "pops" in and out of the sleuth's grasp. Although more a means of showcasing camera gimmickry, the movie captures the essence of the genre's appeal: there are more things in heaven and earth than we can explain. A vanishing villain? Can Holmes find the answer?

It was tongue-in-cheek, magical, and had to deal with detection — sort of. Subsequent mystery movies carried on the literary tradition of Poe and Conan Doyle, even when the detectives couldn't talk. After his debut in 1903, Holmes himself appeared in a wide range of silent adventures — a long-running series starred Eille Norwood in the 1920s — but because these detectives were without sound, the stories relied more on the fantastic and the thriller aspect.

"The whole language and construction of the silent film worked against a figure who needed conversation and interrogation," noted William K. Everson in *The Detective in Film*.[15] "In the earlier days of film, the stress was on action or at least physical movement, often backed up by lengthy explanatory subtitles. In the twenties, when the movies rapidly achieved increasing sophistication, the pace slowed, meaning was expressed via visual subtleties, and the [sub]title was used less and less. Neither period made the detective an easy character to handle."

In fact, the early detective movies de-emphasized detection for cliff-hanger mysteries, often in serial cliffhanger form. *The Exploits of Elaine* (1915) features scientific criminologist Craig Kennedy (Arnold Daly) battling a master villain known as The Clutching Hand. Foreshadowing future super-sleuths of the big and small screen, Kennedy used deductions, intuitions, and scientific gadgets to track down The Hand. The villain also has his own super-weapons, including a death ray, a wristwatch that injects poison into its owner, and a suspended animation device.

There were also, surprisingly for the period, female sleuths. Ruth Roland appeared in the "Girl Detective" series in 1914-15. There was also the heroine of *The Penalty* (1920), a drama in which Lon Chaney plays Blizzard, a legless lunatic master criminal. According to Everson: "The heroine is a government detective who is to infiltrate Chaney's vice headquarters. A predecessor who tried it wound up in the river; she is warned by her superior that discovery will almost certainly mean death or (an ominous pause)—worse."[16]

Some of these detective adventures were serials, some were features, and all pushed the envelope with their outrageous adventures and ridiculously over-the-top gadgets used to murder people.

The absurd quality of such adventures was ripe for parody, of which Buster Keaton's *Sherlock Jr.* (1923) is a prime sample. In it, a young projectionist (Keaton) literally dreams of being a famous detective, Sherlock Jr., who solves the disappearance of a missing necklace. Keaton pokes fun at detective story traditions—when he "shadows" a man, he is so close to him and mimes him so perfectly that he could actually be his shadow—as well as spy movie/thriller conventions (a car chase, an exploding pool table ball).

There is also Stan Laurel and Oliver Hardy's two-reeler, *Do Detectives Think?* (1927). The movie combines comedy and slapstick with the detective/murder genre, in a way that anticipates both *The Thin Man* series and *The Avengers*. Laurel and Hardy aren't really detecting anything, of course; in fact, they're just a pair of high-class bodyguards for a man being threatened by a vicious killer.

But the movie shows how the genre, so ingrained in the public consciousness, was open to lampooning. Instead of the almost omniscient characters like Holmes and Dupin who know it all, we have two "detectives" who actually know less than we do. When they see a photo of an escaped killer in the newspaper, Hardy asks Laurel, "Where have we seen that face before?" not recognizing the butler (the killer in disguise) who just said "good night" to them moments before.

In the 1920s, novelists, too, began having fun with the absurdities of the genre, creating heroes who were flamboyant, slightly tongue-in-cheek, and operated outside the law. These "Gentlemen Outlaws" were more ingenious than police detectives and had colorful nicknames like "The Toff," "The Baron," "Nighthawk," and "Blackshirt." They also followed in the Robin Hood tradition: a well-bred, well-dressed hero helping the underdog against a muddled establishment.

One of the most famous of these was The Saint, who in the 1960s was linked with *The Avengers* on television. Often dubbed "The Robin Hood of Modern Crime," the character was an iconoclastic adventurer, whose credo, as expressed in the short story, "The Melancholy Journey of Mr. Teal," was straightforward: "To go rocketing around the world, doing everything that's utterly and gloriously mad — swaggering, swashbuckling, singing — showing all those dreary old dogs what can be done with life — not giving a damn for anyone — robbing the rich, helping the poor — plaguing the pompous, killing dragons, pulling policemen's legs."[17]

The Saint stories are fast-paced, intricately plotted, and highly unpredictable, dealing with stolen jewels, unexplained murders, and hair's breadth escapes. And they are all executed in a tongue-in-cheek style that readers of the thirties found uniquely brash (a typical Saintly rejoinder: "I hate to disappoint you — as the actress said to the bishop — but I really can't oblige you now"[18]).

The plots swing from action-packed boy's adventures to murder mysteries to psychological studies, all written in a distinctive, nonchalant air. In *The Saint's Getaway* (1932), for instance, Simon Templar, aka The Saint, intervenes in a sidewalk beating and is soon swept away in a rollicking saga involving multiple murders, torture, and jewel theft, as our hero dangles from speeding cars, moving trains, and castle windows. "The Story of a Dead Man," an early short story, finds Templar masquerading as a member of a notorious gang in a multi-layered mystery that keeps the reader guessing right up until the climax, when The Saint is trapped in a gas-filled dungeon. "The Unfortunate Financier," another short story, shows The Saint playing mind games with a con man who is too clever for his own good.

"When I start to plan a story," explained Saint creator Leslie Charteris in the 1960s, "the tests which they must meet to satisfy me, are (1) Is the story line conventional? If so, then how can it be twisted to outrage convention? (2) Is this character someone I can see and feel as flesh and blood, or is it a cardboard cut-out that I saw on some screen? If so, what does it need to make it different? I have always wanted to be an originator: let the others imitate me."[19]

Readers apparently loved Simon Templar's brand of insouciant adventure, with seven Saint books appearing in only two years. "The public of the grey, Depression-cowed early thirties needed The Saint so badly that nothing would have induced them *not* to believe in him," observed William Vivian Butler in *The Durable Desperadoes*. "Or to surrender that all-important illusion that maybe with the help of the right tailor, maybe by continually polishing up their drawling repartee, they might, if only for a moment or two, bring themselves to resemble him."[20]

"I was always sure that there was a solid place in escape literature for a rambunctious adventurer such as I dreamed up in my own youth, who really believed in the old-fashioned romantic ideals and was prepared to lay everything on the line to bring them to life," Charteris once explained.[21]

Not surprisingly, Hollywood soon came

Roger Moore as television's version of Simon Templar, aka The Saint. Known as "The Robin Hood of Modern Crime," the character possesses a devil-may-care attitude similar to that of Nick Charles in *The Thin Man*.

calling. Louis Hayward was the first cinematic Saint in *The Saint in New York* (1938), based on a Charteris novel that depicts Templar as a paid avenger, assassinating a series of criminals the law cannot touch. The character's dark side was considerably softened in subsequent motion pictures (the most well-known of which starred George Sanders) and radio series (one of which featured Vincent Price, who played The Saint as a gourmet whose greatest peeve was being interrupted while dining).

If The Saint spoofed the genre, Charlie Chan turned it on its head. In a time when literary and film sleuths were universally white males, usually erudite and upper crust, Oriental detective Chan was an amazing anomaly. He was Chinese and definitely middle-class. He was smarter than the white men and women around him. He may have been

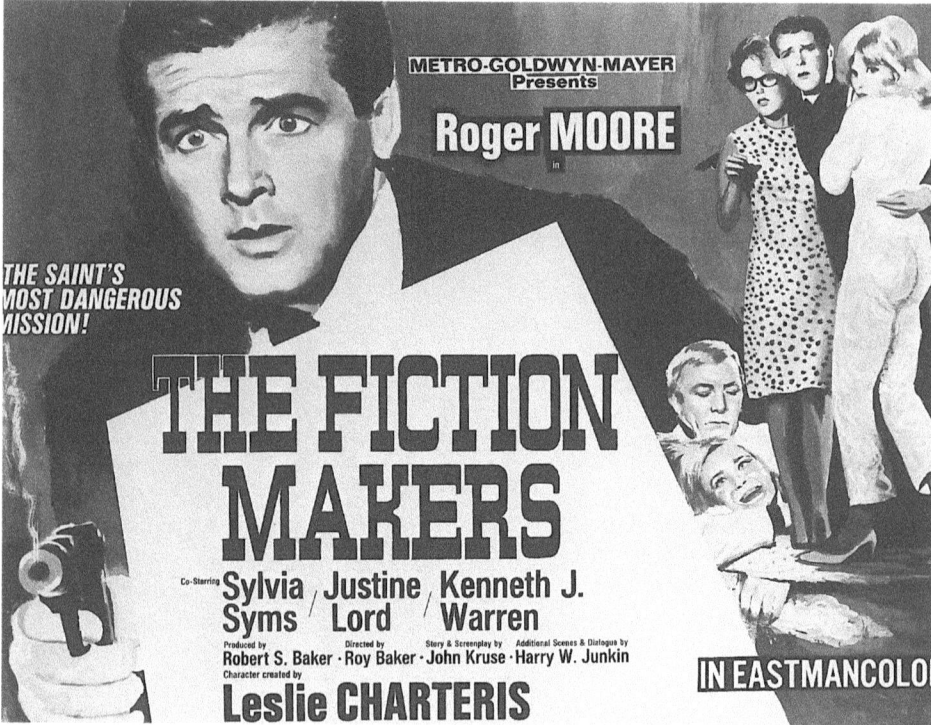

Poster for *The Fiction Makers*, a two-part episode of *The Saint* TV series that was released in Europe as a movie. Like Nick Charles, The Saint is a well-bred, well-dressed hero who helps the underdog against a muddled establishment.

"inscrutable," but, in that, he was no different from Holmes, Dupin, and many other sleuths who had gone before him. Yet he was also the first crack in the traditional detective role, clearing a pathway for the gender-bending that would eventually lead to *The Thin Man* and *The Avengers*.

Chan didn't spring full-blown from a Hollywood scriptwriter's brain but was the creation of American novelist Earl Derr Biggers (1884–1933), who wrote six Chan mysteries between 1925 and 1932 upon which 46 movies were built. Having an Oriental detective was highly unusual for the 1920s, when the norm was to depict the Chinese as exotic villains.

To put it in perspective: "Almost every Chinese or Asian character appearing before Chan's debut was an insidious devil, part of the Yellow Peril that hounded the west between the two world wars," writes Jeff

Siegel in *The American Detective.* "The most famous was Dr. Fu Manchu, a creation of Sax Rohmer, who was bent on world domination and the destruction of the Western way of life."[22]

Indeed, Biggers went out of his way to break conventions, proving to be a man ahead of his time who knew that the detective story had been parodied and pummeled and done to death. "Sinister and wicked Chinese are old stuff," the author once explained, "but an amiable Chinese on the side of law and order had never been used."[23]

His Chan stories are leisurely, intricate affairs, with the detective usually being underrated by those who first encounter him. Much as TV's rumpled police lieutenant Columbo did years later, Charlie plays on those lowered expectations to follow the tried-and-true detective mantra: observe and deduce.

Chan himself commented on the tunnel vision of America. In the novel, *Charlie Chan Carries On* (1930), he observes about the Chinese: "We are not highly valued in the United States, where we are appraised as laundrymen or maybe villains in the literature of the talkative films. You have a great country, rich and proud, and sure of itself. About the rest of the world — pardon me — it knows little and cares extremely less."[24]

The Chan adaptations began in 1926, with *The House Without a Key*, starring George Kuwa as the detective. Swedish actor Warner Oland took over the role in *Charlie Chan Carries On* (1931) and *The Black Camel* (1931). Since Holmes, sleuths were expected to have endearing eccentricities, and Charlie Chan was no different. Many of the Chan elements were unusual for the genre at that point: he was not a lone wolf but a family man (he had at least nine children). He was not physically fit or a man of action, but was portly and slow-moving. He delivered colorful aphorisms ("Alibi like dead fish, cannot stand test of time"; "Perfect crime, like perfect donut, often have hole"). And he was, frequently, only reluctantly drawn into a case.

The movies were also significant in cementing a pattern that would later become a formula of such genre movies, *The Thin Man* included. The early portion introduces the characters (all potential suspects in the murder-to-come, everyone with shady pasts and reasons to kill the victim-to-be), the middle portion features more murders, as the detective tracks down clues, usually aided by the comic relief: a none-too-bright assistant (in the Chans, an eager "Number One" or "Number Two" son; in the Holmes movies, Dr. Watson). Along the way, the sleuth must avoid various ingenious assassination attempts ("That was meant for us!" an assistant invariably says) while he also turns up more bodies.

Chan had imitators—Mr. Wong, Mr. Moto—and was in the forefront of a flood of sleuths who turned up in literature and films of the 1920s and 1930s: Nick Carter, Philo Vance, Ellery Queen, Perry Mason, Sam Spade, Nero Wolfe, and a certain martini-drinking, retired gumshoe named Nick Charles.

The Thin Man was about to be born.

2

The Tough Guy

"You can dish it out, but you can't take it."
　　　Enrico Bandello (Edward G. Robinson) in Little Caesar

With the onset of the Great Depression in 1929, not only did banks fail but so did the general public's faith in the system. Financially, the world was upside down; morally, it was, too, since Prohibition had made it a crime to drink gin or have a glass of wine. In this topsy-turvy world, gangsters became heroes. Or, as Robert Warshaw once put it, the gangster became "the no to the great American yes."[1]

Unlike the detective, the gangster did not have as long a lineage in popular consciousness. How could he? There were a few gangster movies (such as D.W. Griffith's *The Musketeers of Pig Alley* in 1912, developed following a scandal about corrupt city officials) but it took politics and public policy to make the gangster into a viable film figure. When Congress passed the Eighteenth Amendment to the Constitution in 1920, prohibiting the manufacture and sale of alcohol, it unleashed a criminal industry almost overnight: bootlegging. There was big money to be made in liquor and, if the government had lost its collective mind, the criminal was there to take advantage of that.

The public glamorized the gangster. In a world without a center, when the whole system seemed askew, he was out for individual rights, taking what he wanted because no one was going to give it to him. In literature, F. Scott Fitzgerald's *The Great Gatsby* (1925) pictured the glamor that could result from a life of crime: Gatsby, a former bootlegger, is charming, suave, mysterious—and fabulously wealthy. In films, *Underworld* (1927), a silent picture, depicted the tough guy (George

Bancroft) as hero and painted him as essentially a romantic figure — a rough character who still does the "right" thing, sacrificing himself so that his girl and best friend can get married.

The romance had its basis in reality. Gangsters were in the news constantly, and no one was bigger news than Al Capone. In the 1920s, he was the criminal to catch. Flamboyant and daring, the mobster was a larger-than-life figure to those who knew him and even more so to those who didn't. When his brother, Frank, was killed in a battle with the police, Al Capone threw a lavish funeral. The flowers, provided by racketeer florist Dion O'Banion, cost $20,000 (the big funeral scene also appeared in a number of later gangster movies).

According to historian Marilyn Bardsley, Capone was not unique: ostentatious and unusual gangsters were the norm. She cited the criminal Dion O'Banion "who had a burgeoning bootlegging and florist business ... [he had] ... a perennial-boy likability [who] ... never acted tough. His habit of calling even enemies 'swell fellow' mirrored an ingrained cheeriness and courtesy. He chronically beamed at the world; it amounted to a fixed grin, belied only by unblinkingly cold blue eyes. He was an indefatigable handshaker and backslapper, though never at the same time: at least one hand stayed free to go for one of the three gun pockets tailored into his clothes.

"O'Banion was known for bizarre behavior which included gunning down a man in front of crowds of people for the flimsiest of reasons and then killing a man after meeting him at Capone's Four Deuces."[2]

Such activities were tailor-made for Hollywood. It is no surprise, then, that the powerhouse genre of early talkies was the gangster picture. *Little Caesar* (1930), starring Edward G. Robinson, and *The Public Enemy* (1931), starring James Cagney, depicted the gangster as a warped hero, an Everyman who fought his way against the system — the ultimate outsider who stuck it to The Man.

Mervyn LeRoy's *Little Caesar* was the first great gangster movie. It depicts the rise and fall of "Little Caesar" Enrico Bandello (Robinson), a man who works his way to the top of the Chicago mob. His catchphrase to those he deposes is telling of the character's — and the movie's — point of view: "You can dish it out, but you can't take it." Rico is constantly dishing it out to those who "can't take it," softy bosses, partners who break, underlings who flee in terror. The moral of the story is to get ahead you have to be tough.

Significantly, although Rico is a violent, heartless man who pursues money, he is less interested in power than the trappings that money can bring: the clothes, the plush office, the cigars. He has been pushed around and, unsentimentally, cynically, he proceeds apace, pushing his way to the top. "You're finished, see?" he says to gangster after gangster in what became a much-parodied sneer.

In the end, however, he himself is finished by the very sentiment he despises: he can't do what he needs to do and shoot his best friend, Joe (Douglas Fairbanks Jr.), who is about to inform on him. And because of that sentimental feeling, his world collapses around him. "This is what I get for liking a guy too much," he says when it's obvious that he is finished. And so, like a Roman candle, Rico burns brightly and quickly, before being extinguished.

Rico is typical of most of the gangsters in the crime movies of the early thirties: he is a surface tough guy, swaggering and powerful, until the end when an impulsive act brings him to an end. Robinson is terrific as Rico, bringing to his toughness an edge of insecurity. The seeds of his destruction can be seen in the scene he plays with "Big Boy" (Sidney Blackmer), the head of the gang, who calls him to his office to promote him. Rico is as wound-up as a kid at an exam, jumpy but swaggering at the same time, uncomfortable with the trappings of power yet longing for them nonetheless. He is a fish out of water who ultimately drowns.

The movie owes everything to Robinson's unsentimental performance, which critic Phil Hardy noted is "undercut by the miscasting of Fairbanks as Rico's childhood friend whose breakaway to pursue a career as a dancer (and to marry ...) is seen as the ultimate betrayal by Robinson. Blandly played by Fairbanks and obviously reared in an entirely different world, the character makes nonsense of Rico's disastrous weakness, when, clearly motivated by an inextricable mixture of homosexual attraction and childhood nostalgia, he cannot bring himself to shoot his old friend."[3]

Tommy Powers (James Cagney) is cut from a similar cloth in the seminal early gangster movie, *The Public Enemy*. Shot in a semi-documentary style, it purportedly shows the genesis, rise, and fall of street tough Powers. The story starts with Powers as a boy, and he's shown to be an early no-good, literally tripping up his best friend's sister with a piece of string, simply for the pleasure of causing trouble. His early thievery develops into grand larceny, bootlegging, and, finally, murder for profit, for revenge, and for pleasure.

This is the tough guy as pure evil, suffering from, in Hardy's words, "sexual inadequacy. The grapefruit he smashes in [Mae] Clarke's face suggests misogyny, while [Jean] Harlow's consolingly cradling arms hint at a mother complex."[4]

Yet Powers is both unsympathetic and, at the same time, admirable: he takes what he wants when he wants it (women, power, booze), and never accepts "no" as an answer. He is an equal-opportunity heavy, slapping women and men about with equal gusto. Indeed: he picks up a woman (Clarke), and dumps her after a time because she nags him too much, trying to control him. Commitment is unheard of in Powers' world; instant gratification is the M.O. Nowhere is Powers' disdain for convention better seen than in the famous scene where he pushes the grapefruit in Clarke's face after she harangues him about his life.

But there is something about the character that Depression-era crowds would warm to: Powers has an almost Biblical code of behavior. He honors his mother above all else, won't lift a hand against his upright, hard-working (and insulting) brother, Mike (Donald Cook), and seeks an eye for an eye against anyone who betrays him or his friends: he shoots the horse that kills his boss, and guns down the gangland leader who kills his best friend.

"Where Rico Bandello was presented as an unmitigated rat," observed Hardy, " ... Tom Powers is a hero in light disguise ... he is a free-booting spirit exulting in the freedom of action as a gangster which enables him to beat the Depression (and to win audience approval)."[5]

The violence is handled discreetly, offstage, but its aftermath is treated brutally. Tommy kills a childhood mentor with glee (the hood who betrayed him dies singing a favorite tune of Powers at the piano).

The movie also shows how Powers is swept away by the glitter, the booze, the women, and the high life. He is *The Thin Man*'s Nick Charles without irony, without humor, without a moral center. And audiences were thrilled by such exploits. After all, it was "The Man" who had brought the country low with the Depression.

The Howard Hawks–directed *Scarface, Shame of a Nation* (1932) presented the gangster as a powerful, near psychotic social climber. According to Todd McCarthy, in *Howard Hawks: The Grey Fox of Hollywood*, some of the story was taken from the career of Al Capone. "The film's magnificent opening scene, in which fat-cat mobster 'Big Louie' Costillo is rubbed out in a phone booth after an all-night party, was based on the killing of Chicago racketeer 'Big Jim' Colosimo by Capone and Johnny Torrio in an effort to take over the Chicago underworld."[6] There were similar parallels throughout the movie.

In *Scarface*, Paul Muni plays the violent, animalistic Tony Camonte, up-and-coming gunsel for a mob boss. Tony takes what he wants, although the one thing he really wants but can't have is his sister, Cesca (Ann Dvorak). The erotic subtext between Cesca and Tony, who sees red whenever Cesca is with another man, isn't very "sub." Ultimately, when he kills someone to protect her, he ends up destroying himself.

The movie is harsh, violent, and full of dramatic visual flourishes. The messages are thick: the gangsters are powerful, but in the end, it is we, the public, who give them the power they have by glorifying them and not enforcing the laws. These are savage gangsters, with Hawks's brilliant, off-screen killings and shadowy lighting making them seem even more violent.

Hardy called it "a kind of satanic opera, orchestrated on the one hand by the bizarre strain of black humor running throughout the film as an ape gradually becomes humanized (or an ignorant immigrant becomes integrated with the American dream), and on the other by an almost precious dilettantism (with the doom of each succeeding victim heralded by a cross either painted with light or formed by trellises, street signs, and shadows)."[7]

Manhattan Melodrama (1934) added a new touch to the gangster movie: the flamboyant but good-naturedly sympathetic bad guy (Clark Gable). Incidentally the first pairing of *The Thin Man*'s William Powell and Myrna Loy, the story is hokey, a tale of two boyhood pals (Powell and Gable) who grow up to be on opposite sides of the law. It mirrors the semi-documentary, hard-edged style of *The Public Enemy* for a while, but, this being an MGM and not a Warners picture, finally succumbs to sentimentality. (The movie gained notoriety as the last film seen by "Public Enemy No. 1" John Dillinger before he was shot down in an alley behind the movie theater; he reportedly had a yen for Loy.)

The gangster cycle culminated with *High Sierra* (1941), a terrific movie, starring Humphrey Bogart as Roy "Mad Dog" Earle, a tough guy with a sentimental side. In the story, Earle has just been released from prison after eight years—in a pardon engineered by his old boss—so that he can stage a bank heist. But the plot is secondary to the ideas and the characters. Although he is tough and a convicted killer, Earle represents an older, no-nonsense kind of professional, a man who holds loyalty and dependability above all else. He is faithful to his boss even after the old man dies, and only kills when he's left no choice (even in the robbery, he wounds, rather than kills, a guard). He is a man who grew up on a farm and is looking to "crash out"—i.e., be free of prison, of convention, of the fear and loathing that he inspires in others. That sort of "crashing out" of convention had become a staple of both *The Thin Man* series and the screwball comedies of the 1930s.

Unlike Rico in *Little Caesar* or Tommy in *The Public Enemy*, Earle is a man searching for peace, not power, for an ideal woman to share his life with, not someone to slap around. Although it's never explicitly stated, the viewer gets the sense that Earle was forced into his criminal life by necessity, not desire (he talks about wanting the simpler life of his youth; certainly the dream of everyone as he grows older). He thinks he's found it in Velma (Joan Leslie), a club-footed girl with whom he falls in love. Her outer deformity mirrors his inner one, and he hopes that by fixing her he can fix himself; that he can hitch himself to someone "respectable"—virgin, untouched by his rough life—and somehow cleanse himself.

It is a false hope. For Roy Earle is doomed: a walking anachronism, a dinosaur in a fast-paced time of undependable people and fickle females. The only one who sticks by him is Marie (Ida Lupino), a product of an abused childhood who sees in him "the real thing," a kindred spirit also hoping to "crash out." But Earle is cursed. That curse is underlined when he is befriended by the little dog, Pard, who represents friendship as bad luck. Everyone who had become friendly with the dog has died—and Roy is no exception. The message is clear: to be in love, to be sentimental, or to make friends is to be weak. And weakness is death.

Bogart's Earle is a departure from gangsters past, bringing an edge of menace but also a sensible and sentimental side—humanizing traits which ultimately bring him down. In fact, *High Sierra* was a turning point in the gangster movie, much as *The Thin Man* was in the detective film: it blended genres, adding romance to what had been a passionless tough guy business. It carries on the idea of the gangster film but transforms it, blending in the poetry of tragedy. "You're spiraling towards death," one character says, comparing him to real-life gangster John Dillinger. Another observer says that Earle has a "rendezvous with death."

Gangsters would feature prominently in the works of many detective and mystery novelists of the time. In fact, the romanticized gangsters of the 1920s and 1930s played a crucial role in the development of *The Thin Man*.

3

The Romantic

"Now, it isn't that I don't like you, Susan, because, after all, in moments of quiet, I'm strangely drawn to you, but — well, there haven't been any quiet moments."
David (Cary Grant) in Bringing Up Baby

The Thin Man, like *The Avengers* and *The X-Files*, appropriated many disparate genres. But it owed one of its greatest debts to the screwball comedy. Pace was everything in screwballs, but so was the Screwball Woman. This was the type, best personified by Carole Lombard, who was beautiful, bright, and befuddled, talking in paragraphs, not sentences, with barely a breath between words. The hero would ask her one thing and she would answer a dozen — usually going off on tangents you never knew existed.

A typical screwball monologue? Try the one Irene (Lombard) delivers to Godfrey (William Powell), the man she loves, in *My Man Godfrey* (1936). Although Godfrey attempts to reply to some of her statements, he never gets a chance, as Irene flits from idea to idea, almost as quickly as it takes to blink an eye.

"You're more than a butler. You're the first protégé I ever had," she says. " ... Like Carlo ... He's mother's protégé. It's awfully nice, Carlo having a sponsor because he doesn't have to work and gets time for his practicing but then he never does and that makes a difference ... Do you play anything, Godfrey? Oh, I don't mean games or things like that, I mean the piano and things like that ... Oh, it doesn't really make any difference. I just thought I'd ask. It's funny how some things make you think of other things."

Like the gangster films of the period, screwball comedies were a reaction against hard times, and were best known for their beautiful, batty women whose fast speech and zany actions conceal a brainy purpose (usually to ensnare a man) but are equally noteworthy for their outlandish plots, their sentimental cynicism, and, in film historian Elizabeth Kendall's words, their use of "the heroine to articulate the good impulses at the bottom of the American soul, and [their use of] the heroine's romance with a charming but psychologically underdeveloped young man to dramatize a rapprochement between the good and the more negligent impulses. Put another way, Depression romantic comedies responded to their audience's loss of faith by making a virtue of personality traits usually thought of as feminine — a moral subtlety, an unashamed belief in the validity of emotions."[1]

The heyday of these comedies was from the mid–1930s through the mid–1940s, when crisis and change in American life left people feeling as dizzy (from an economic depression and a world war) as the befuddled heroes listening to those wacky screwball girls.

The modern romantic comedy began inauspiciously enough with Frank Capra's low-budget *It Happened One Night* (1934), to which the movie version of *The Thin Man* owes a great deal. It was a big hit, but no one had much faith in it when it was first shopped around: co-stars Clark Gable and Claudette Colbert bad-mouthed it; Capra himself thought more of his earlier *Lady for a Day* (1933); and Hollywood insiders predicted disaster. Its surprising success, however — best picture, best director, best screenplay, best actor, and best actress Oscars and a big box office take — led to a rash of romantic comedies of the screwball variety.

It Happened One Night is a wonderful romance featuring a marvelous face-off between sparring lovers Gable and Colbert, a pair initially as mismatched (but ultimately as perfectly matched) as Nick and Nora Charles are in *The Thin Man*: he's rough-and-tumble, a man's man with integrity, smarts, and a know-it-all manner (and a good sense of humor to boot); she's bright, beautiful, spoiled, and smug — but also a match for him in the verbal quips department. Director Capra's populist touch is wonderfully in evidence (helped by a superb Robert Riskin script), with clever dialogue, a fast pace, and great chemistry between Gable and Colbert.

The movie also set the stage for what was to become the "Capra picture," which had a degree of influence on *The Thin Man* series. Screenwriter Riskin gave the director a focus he had lacked in previous movies (such as *Dirigible*, 1931, or *American Madness*, 1932) and the two of them collaborated, in one way or another, on over a dozen movies. "We vibrated to the same tuning fork," Capra once said of his partner.² Added an observer who knew them both: "Frank provided the schmaltz and Bob provided the acid. It was an unbeatable combination. What they had together was better than what either of them had separately."³

The Capra-Riskin formula usually involved a number of elements: naturalistic performances, superb supporting characters, a hearty serving of sentiment and good horse sense, witty dialogue, and a basic plot in which a Christ-like innocent goes up against an entrenched system that nearly destroys him. The protagonist, becoming wiser in the ways of the world, would escape defeat by the love of a woman and the help of the little people. In the process, his virtue is redeemed and deepened by the experience. As the novelist Graham Greene put it, the director's favorite theme was "goodness and simplicity manhandled in a deeply selfish and brutal world."⁴

Capra used the techniques of film — lighting, cutting, actor's expressions — terrifically well. "[There are] moments or scenes that descriptions of the characters or summaries of the plot of the movie leave out," wrote Ray Carney in *American Vision: The Films of Frank Capra*. "They are scenes or fleeting moments within scenes in which perhaps nothing is happening socially — moments, for instance, when characters simply sit still and are silent; when they look at each other but do not speak; when music swells on the soundtrack, or the rhythm of the editing changes, or a special lighting effect is employed, even though nothing is apparently happening in terms of the advancement of the plot or the dialogue spoken. Such moments, when the social situations of the characters or the lines they speak *cease* to express the meaning of a scene, are frequently the most important ones in Capra's movies."⁵

Through such films as *Lady for a Day, It Happened One Night*, and *You Can't Take It with You* (1938), Capra became known as a proponent of the common man, downtrodden in real life by the Depression. But, as Joseph McBride pointed out in *Frank Capra: The Catastrophe of Success*, the irony is that Capra himself was a conservative Republican and fan of the dictator Mussolini, and he voted against Franklin Roosevelt four times because he was afraid the Democrat would redistribute the director's wealth, much as his own Mr. Deeds wants to do at the end of *Mr. Deeds Goes to Town* (1936).

"Like the popular artist he was, Capra was being led by his audience," observed McBride. "*They* were demanding reform, *they* were demanding social welfare programs and redistribution of wealth, *they* were angry at the shortsightedness and greed of big business and the Republican party. The sense of brotherhood and compassion that came from Riskin's writing and began to open up the narrow vision of Capra's work brought him into closer contact with his audience, giving his work a deeper and more popular resonance, putting him in touch with a sense of community for which he previously had little feeling."[6]

Capra was also successful because he had the savvy and good sense to partner with collaborators who would increase his strengths as a cinematic storyteller, from cameraman Joseph Walker's sophisticated lighting techniques to screenwriter Riskin's clever characters, construction, and dialogue. "Capra in the prime of his career liked to surround himself with colleagues who were not yes men, and his ability to listen to and absorb such a range of viewpoints ... [contributed] to the complexity of his films," wrote McBride.[7]

Capra himself was excellent with actors, saying once, "I am interested most in characterizations. The people must be real."[8] He achieved that reality through careful preparation. "If the scene called for it, he used two cameras, three cameras," Capra actor James Stewart told McBride. "The cameras were there, but he didn't move them all over so that you were conscious of them moving all the time.... You became not conscious of where the camera *was* exactly; you forgot about the camera." In so doing, "he was capable of getting things on the screen and telling a story on the screen so that it got beyond directing, beyond acting, beyond writing, as far as the audience was concerned. It got above the movie itself; it appeared to the audience as a real experience, as something actually happening that they were viewing, and he had the cameras picking it up."[9]

Capra's choice of leads—his favorites were Stewart, Gary Cooper, and Barbara Stanwyck—is also indicative of his shrewdness. "Each of them brought to a role almost the opposite of the 'star quality,'" wrote Carney. "They represent a vacancy, blankness, or indefiniteness that ... is exactly right for Capra's investigations of the achievement of identity.... They are figures of desire or inarticulate idealism searching for a cause to follow, a leader to embrace, or a satisfactory form of personal expression."[10]

Capra's screwball comedy techniques were taken up by other romantic comedies. Those movies would generally feature what could be called the "Classic Plot," starting with the boy meeting the girl in a situation guaranteed to make one or both of them dislike the other. In

Bringing Up Baby, for instance, Susan and David meet in a comic battle over who owns a golf ball and a car (She: "Your ball, your car. Is there anything in the world that doesn't belong to you?"). *Top Hat* (1935), a musical with screwball comedy elements, finds Jerry (Fred Astaire) dancing so loudly in the room above Dale (Ginger Rogers) that she angrily confronts him. (He: "Every once in a while I suddenly find myself dancing." She: "I suppose it's some kind of affliction.")

In these comedies, there is a heroine who is either smarter than the guy, daffier than the guy, or colder than the guy. In the course of the movie, she will sequentially despise him (but still get entangled in his affairs), come to admire him (even as she fights with him), and finally realize she loves him. In the process, she will also change from spoiled or cold or daffy to concerned or warm or slightly less daffy.

Then there's the hero. He's either a surface cynic, using a wisecrack to cover his feelings (Colbert to Gable in *It Happened One Night*: "Your ego is absolutely colossal." Gable: "Yeah. Not bad. How's yours?"), or else hopelessly repressed and befuddled. In the first instance, the heroine brings out the romantic in the hero, as he comes to realize that there's more to her than he thought. In the second case, the hero realizes that there is more to life than being straitlaced.

The battle is another key element, for as Susan puts it in *Bringing Up Baby*: "The love impulse in the man frequently reveals itself in terms of conflict." There's the other classic ingredient: the almost childlike nature of the heroine, who constantly defies convention and thereby helps unstuff the hero's shirt. There's a child inside of all of us, say these movies, repressed by the constraints of society. To be slightly crazy and in love is to be imaginatively free.

The unlikely pair will find themselves thrown together, however, and would then face various obstacles to their true love. The most popular plot finds the man or woman already engaged to someone else, whom the audience (but not the character) could see is a terrible mismatch for that person. In *Holiday* (1938), a romantic comedy with screwball touches, Cary Grant's Johnny Case is a free-spirited soul who meets a kindred sort in Linda Seton (Katharine Hepburn), the sister of Julia (Doris Nolan), the woman he thinks he wants to marry. But he sees only Julia's surface beauty and charm, not the inner, conservative side to her. In fact, she wants to control him, suppress him, and make him worship at the altar of capitalism. Typically, in these sorts of romances, those in love don't realize they love the wrong person until it's almost too late.

The pair also come from different worlds. In *Pat and Mike* (1952),

Pat (Katharine Hepburn) is about to marry a man (Aldo Ray) who is inappropriate for her. She meets Mike (Spencer Tracy), whom she initially dislikes and mistrusts. He is rough-and-tumble while she is oh-so-elegant. Of course, they fall in love.

There are also, typically, a galaxy of wise, witty, and zany supporting characters. These can include eccentrics like the divorce detective (Edgar Kennedy) in *Unfaithfully Yours* (1948) who becomes passionate about classical music ("No one handles Handel the way you handle Handel! And your Delius! Delirious!") or the wealthy hot dog manufacturer (Robert Dudley) in *The Palm Beach Story* (1942) who doesn't hear well, but speaks to the point: "I invented the Texas Wienie. Lay off them — you'll live longer."

There is also, inevitably, the Grand Misunderstanding, which leads to the Final Reconciliation. In *Swing Time* (1936), Penny (Ginger Rogers) thinks that Lucky (Fred Astaire) is two-timing her, and only resolves the confusion in the last moments.

The comedies were immeasurably helped by the wonderful romantic pairings, those couples with a unique chemistry who returned again and again, because the audiences did: sexy sophisticates William Powell and Myrna Loy (13 appearances), the "he gives her class, she gives him sex" team of Fred Astaire and Ginger Rogers, and the "tough guy and the lady" duo of Spencer Tracy and Katharine Hepburn. There were others, of course, but these were the top duos.

Howard Hawks's *Twentieth Century* (1934), an early screwball comedy/romance from a script by Ben Hecht and Charles MacArthur (authors of the much-filmed play, *The Front Page*), features two marvelously hammy performances by John Barrymore and Carole Lombard as a pair of over-the-top characters: the Svengali-like Broadway director Oscar Jaffe and the monster he has created, egotistical star Lily Garland. What makes it all palatable and more than just a cartoon is the love that Oscar and Lily really share for each other. But the comedy also comes from the fact that they love themselves — and performing — even more. Nothing is real for either of them, unless it has been written (Jaffe constantly comments on moments in life by comparing them to scenes or dialogue in a play).

What Hawks brought to the screwball was his brand of fast-talking characters and breakneck pace: everything is clipped and frenetic, larger-than-life with an undercurrent of sentiment and a layer of bemusement. Actors are like children, says Hawks, but so are the people who get involved with them — even Jaffe's two loyal assistants (Walter Connolly, Roscoe Karns) put up with him because they seem to enjoy the thrill of life-on-the-edge. It is all amusing because of its absurdity. That same sort of distancing — the awareness that life can be silly and fun if you enjoy yourself — was applied to *The Thin Man* with remarkable results.

The romance formula and the mismatched couplings lasted right up until the Rock Hudson–Doris Day comedies of the late 1950s and early 1960s. Those movies added a bizarre subtext not seen in the classic period, whose lack of clear-cut morality was a precursor of the James Bond movie series and *The Avengers*. *Pillow Talk* (1959), for instance, seems to be a frothy bedroom farce about an amoral playboy (Hudson) who takes on another identity — a naive Texan — to woo a woman who can't stand his real personality (Day). But because it lacks the light touch and moral center of the greatest romances, the movie comes across as an exploration of deeply disturbed people who lie, cheat, and betray each other with abandon.

Hudson's playboy, Brad Allen, is possibly the most despicable leading man ever seen in a light comedy: he manipulates perky working woman Jan Morrow (Day) into falling in love with him and almost sleeps with her. The single working woman is painted as unnatural; so, too, is marriage. Allen constantly talks about the dangers of domestication, while his wimpy best friend (Tony Randall) marries too often and too quickly, and is depicted as a mama's boy who sees a therapist and might just be a closet homosexual.

Pillow Talk and the other Hudson-Day spoofs were huge successes, but also the last gasp of the traditional romantic comedy formula. By the late sixties, the genre had been transformed. Romance was out; rebellion and sexual revolution were in. Films like *The Graduate* (1967) celebrated youth and rebellion, not convention, while the easy-loving James Bond adventures put the final nail in the coffin of old-fashioned romance.

The man who helped bring back and also change the idea of the romantic comedy was, of all people, that unromantic nebbish, Woody Allen. The pinnacle of the Allen oeuvre, *Annie Hall* (1977), is the story of Alvy Singer (dubbed "a real Jew" by one character) and Annie Hall (Diane Keaton), a whitebread neurotic who learns, loves, and, finally, leaves Alvy. Allen's film is a meditation on the impermanence of life and love, of how everything changes, but the memory lingers on.

The film is brilliantly constructed as a comic reminiscence, starting off with Allen's to-the-camera statement, "I broke up with Annie this week," and leading, by degrees from the middle, to the beginning, and then before the beginning of the relationship. Along the way, we learn about Alvy's obsessions, about his kindness and cruelty, his selfishness and his sexuality.

The difference between this and the romantic comedies of the earlier era is its obsession with "me, myself, and I." Everything is reflected from the prism of Alvy's consciousness, giving the movie a point-of-view that is at alternate times romantic, comic, and selfishly melancholy. But it is always terribly insightful and more realistic than most of the classic romances ever were.

Allen's neuroses took flower among recent filmmakers who further transformed the romantic comedy: In *The Real Blonde* (1997), writer-director Tom DiCillo brilliantly skewers the obsessions, neuroses, and self-centeredness of actors and other media, while also presenting a funny, sad, and maddeningly real portrait of men and women trying to connect. The story focuses on Joe (Matthew Modine), a struggling actor with no career but a lot of attitude, and his girlfriend Mary (Catherine Keener), a make-up artist who has a hidden hostility towards men. Crossing in and out of their lives are a soap opera actor (Maxwell Caulfield), an airhead model (Bridgette Wilson), a tough-talking talent scout (Kathleen Turner), an exploitative photographer (Marlo Thomas), and a horny shrink (Buck Henry). DiCillo has a keen understanding of his character's needs, frustrations, and fantasies. Indeed, as the soap star searches for his ideal, a real blonde, DiCillo makes it clear that the world is not about seeking perfection but settling for imperfection. He is savvy enough to know that you can't always get what you want but should just look out for what you need.

Other recent romantic comedies, however, simply ape the forms of the past. *A Life Less Ordinary* (1997), for instance, is a "madcap" comedy that's strong on the mad part but lacking much comedy. The movie is peopled with types, not characters, with Ewan McGregor playing an inept kidnapper, Cameron Diaz a spoiled rich girl, and Holly Hunter a foul-mouthed angel who must get the two of them together.

Then there's *Runaway Bride* (1999), a TV sitcom version of the great screwball comedies of the thirties, especially *It Happened One Night*, with Richard Gere in the Gable role of the cynical reporter and Julia Roberts in the Colbert part of the spoiled, willful runaway bride, immature and unsure of what she wants from a man. The movie is by-the-numbers, though, with Gere and Roberts hating each other for the first third, discovering and then respecting each other in the middle, and falling in love in the final section. Everything comes out of the pop-psyche world of television sitcoms: she runs because the men she's going to marry don't know her. Yet how could they? She doesn't know herself. The story is meant to be a light-hearted voyage of self-discovery but instead comes across as a smug journey of self-congratulation by the filmmakers who seem to be so satisfied with how clever they are (and how rich they'll be by reuniting the box office hit team of Gere and Roberts from *Pretty Woman*).

Nonetheless, the best of the new crop bring romance back with gusto, such as *Notting Hill* (1999), a charming, if unlikely, love story about (British) boy meeting (Hollywood movie star) girl, losing her over misunderstanding No. 1, finding her again, then losing her again over bigger misunderstanding No. 2, finding her again, rejecting her, and then finding her for all time. It follows the romantic comedy formula, but the saga is made palatable by the chemistry between Hugh Grant and Roberts (who has just the right mixture of toughness and vulnerability to make the part work).

Some say it's no surprise that romance in the movies has returned. With uncertainty in the world, people search for the safety of convention. "When we're in a period of turmoil, there's an unconscious reaction by people to want to go back to a more structured time," noted Robert R. Butterworth, a Los Angeles–based clinical psychologist. "When in doubt, people tend to go towards stability."[11] And that could mean the stability of romantic movie conventions.

Yet there's more to it than that. For movie love is the best sort of love, the kind that lasts forever, in a never-never world of eternal bliss, and happily-ever-after moments, like that wonderful moment in *The Lady Eve* (1941), when love is triumphant and Eve (Barbara Stanwyck) exclaims to her lover (Henry Fonda): "Why didn't you take me in your arms that day on the boat? Why did we have to go through all this nonsense? Don't you know you're the only man I ever loved, you big fathead? Don't you know I couldn't look at another man if I wanted to? Don't you know I waited all my life for you ... you big mug?"

Romance, gangsters, and detection all came together, gloriously, in *The Thin Man*.

4

Ballad of a Thin Man

"We had no idea whether this kind of comedy would go. It had two unprecedented elements that scared the hell out of the whole studio: they were having fun with murder, and they were a married couple who acted with total sophistication."
Samuel Marx, former head of the MGM story department[1]

The Thin Man, filmed in under a month in 1934, was an unusual movie for its time. Besides being breezy and entertaining, it set standards and trends that would reverberate well into the 1990s and beyond. For the first time in a major sound picture, a man and woman were equal partners with equal intelligence. They were not unmarried young people meeting and discovering affection, but a savvy, world-wise couple who could poke fun at each other because they were so much in love. It featured a middle-aged leading man, combined three genres that were rarely joined, and was a smash hit. On television, years later, it indirectly influenced both *The Avengers* and *The X-Files*, also groundbreaking works on their own.

No one could have foreseen any of that when director W.S. (Woody) Van Dyke first came up with the idea of filming *The Thin Man*, a crime novel by Dashiell Hammett. The Great Depression was in full force, unemployment and bread lines were everywhere, and few would have expected a book about a boozy detective and his wealthy wife to have popular appeal. But it did.

The novel sprang from the typewriter of Hammett, a former Pinkerton detective. The author drew some of its background from his own eclectic life. He had been born Samuel Dashiell Hammett in

St. Mary's County, Maryland, on May 27, 1894. After dropping out of the Baltimore Polytechnic Institute as a teenager, Hammett went into the army ambulance corps during World War I. By 1919, however, he had contracted a pulmonary condition (which would affect him until his death in 1961). That illness eventually led to his discharge.

Although he was hospitalized with tuberculosis in 1920, Hammett had improved enough to move to San Francisco in 1921 with his former nurse, Josephine Anna Dolan, whom he had married the year before. Partly because of his illness, the young man was restless and unfocused, working as a clerk, stevedore, advertising manager, and, finally and most significantly for his future career, as a private detective for the well-known Pinkerton Detective Agency.

At this point, *The Thin Man* may have already been taking shape in his mind. As a detective, Hammett found himself involved in some unusual cases: the bizarre theft of a Ferris wheel and the regular surveillance of gambler Nick Arnstein (the same Arnstein who later figured in the play and movie *Funny Girl* [1968]). He also worked for the defending attorneys in the notorious Fatty Arbuckle case in which a young woman died a few days after a party in Arbuckle's rooms.

But detective work wasn't paying the bills. So, by 1923, unable to support his wife and two daughters, Hammett turned to writing for the burgeoning pulp magazine market. And, when he did, he wrote about what he knew best: crime and detection.

The pulp magazines were to 1920s audiences what television is today: entertainment for the masses. They took their name from the paper on which they were printed. As Tony Goodstone explained in his book, *The Pulps*: "In 1896, publisher Frank Munsey, believing that a story was more important that the paper it was printed on, changed *The Argosy* from a boy's magazine to an all-fiction magazine with untrimmed, rough wood-pulp pages ... measuring approximately seven-by-ten inches and half-an-inch thick. He had created the first 'Pulp.' Before failing circulation ... killed them off in 1953, the Pulps had divided, amoebae-like, into ... hundreds of titles, and furnished inexpensive reading, escape from social oppression and hope for the future for tens of millions of readers."[2]

The pulps featured cowboys and criminals, inventors and ingenues, detectives and delinquents. That noble savage, Tarzan of the Apes, made his first appearance in 1912 in a pulp, as did Nick Carter, detective, a highly romanticized version of a private eye. The pulps dealt in archetypes and genres, as indicated by their titles: *Sport Story Magazine*, *Love*

Story, Gangster Stories, Mammoth Adventure, Railroad Stories, Dare-Devil Aces. The writing was breezy, and the emphasis was on action and romance.

Hammett's pulp-writing, however, was different. He brought a gritty, hard edge of realism to his pieces which made them stand out from the pack. It was no accident, either. As critic William L. DeAndrea noted, the writer's first stories appeared under the pseudonym Peter Collinson, which is "a symbol of the detachment and alienation that abounds in his writing. In the underworld slang of the day, a Peter Collins was a nobody; the pen name announced the writer to those in the know as nobody's son."[3]

Hammett drew on what he had learned as a sleuth, and imbued his writing with the suffering he must have felt from his tubercular condition. He perfected what became known as the "hard-boiled detective" and the genre that went with it, noted for terse writing, excessive violence, and believable characters.

"The term *hard-boiled* has been around since World War I," noted mystery writer/historian Max Allen Collins. "...it was an adjective applied to the tough drill sergeants who made men out of boys and soldiers out of civilians. When the war ended, those soldiers turned back into civilians, popularizing the term *hard-boiled* into something referring to any person, or action, that reflected a tough, unsentimental point of view."[4]

The hard-boiled novelists used the language of the streets and their characters were not gentlemen but gangsters, crooked cops, and tough detectives. The earliest practitioners—like Carroll John Daly with his creation, the two-fisted, gun-shooting detective Race Williams—were heavy on violence, light on mystery and any kind of literary aspirations.

Hammett had more style and also played around with detective story tradition. The writer worked "against familiar conventions of detective literature," critic John M. Reilly observed. "A wry remark such as 'I know a forger who left his wife because she had learned to smoke cigarettes while he was serving a term in prison' diminishes the categorical morality of crime literature, and other comments on the inadequacy of fingerprints as clues or the number of unsolved cases in a detective's files disparage all accounts of infallible detective procedures."[5]

Hammett also tried to deglamorize crime. The writer "took murder out of the Venetian vase and dropped it into the alley, explained fellow crime writer Raymond Chandler in an essay, "The Simple Art of Murder." "He wrote ... for people with a sharp, aggressive attitude to life. They were not afraid of the seamy side of things; they lived there. Violence did not dismay them; it was right down their street. Hammett gave murder back to the kind of people that commit it for reasons, not just to provide a corpse; and with the means at hand, not with hand-wrought dueling pistols, curare, and tropical fish."[6]

In 1923, Hammett began publishing his tales of the "Continental Op" ("op" being an abbreviation for "operative") in *Black Mask*, a pulp. From 1922 to 1933, he published five novels, two novelettes, and dozens of short stories. He was prolific out of necessity: he had a family to feed. The author began drinking during this period, and admitted later that his chronic alcohol problem may have had something to do with the writer's block he eventually developed. After 1934, although he constantly hammered out bits and pieces of novels and stories, he published nothing new.

By the late 1920s, Hammett had also fallen in love with Lillian Hellman, an aspiring playwright who would become his lover and constant companion for the rest of his life. As with much of his writing, Hammett used his relationship with Hellman as the starting point for *The Thin Man*.

The Thin Man was the last novel Hammett published in his lifetime, and unlike his previous works, it is a mystery with elements of black comedy. Like his other novels, however, it does feature an assortment of slightly unsavory characters, including a nymphomaniac liar and a doped-up Italian gangster. What makes it noteworthy, though, are its protagonists: Nick Charles, a lazy, retired gumshoe, and Nora, his wealthy wife, who—between parties and bouts of drinking—manage to solve a complicated, slightly sordid mystery.

The story had been percolating in the writer's mind for some time. In 1930, a few years before *The Thin Man* found its publisher, Hammett had produced a 65-page draft of an unfinished novel (also called *The Thin Man*). Set in San Francisco (the later book took place in New York), it starred a private detective named John Guild (he was turned into a police sergeant in the final version). In 1942, when Hammett sold the typescript of the unfinished novel, he recalled the reason why the book was not finished:

"By the time I had written these 65 pages my publisher and I agreed that it might be wise to postpone the publication of *The Glass Key*—scheduled for the fall—until the following spring. This meant that *The Thin Man* could not be published until the fall of 1931. So—having plenty of time—I put these 65 pages aside and went to Hollywood for a year.

One thing and/or another intervening after that, I didn't return to work on the story until a couple of more years had passed — and then I found it easier, or at least generally more satisfactory, to keep only the basic idea of the plot and otherwise to start anew. Some of the incidents in this original version I later used in *After the Thin Man*, a motion picture sequel. But, except for that and for the use of the characters' names Guild and Wynant, this unfinished manuscript has a clear claim to virginity."[7]

The finished novel is both typical and atypical Hammett. It has the unsavory realism and pace of his earlier stories but — in Nick and Nora Charles — also features a streak of romance that had been missing from his previous tales.

The book also explores familiar Hammett issues. In John M. Reilly's words, the writer replaces "the mystery puzzle and idealized heroes of earlier detective fiction with themes that codify a modern sense of urban disorder. He achieves this ... by creation of a milieu of pervasive corruption ... the socially reputable are as criminal as the gangsters with whom they often collaborate." Additionally, "Nick Charles [may affect] sophistication [but is] ... a masked figure.... Beneath the tough and cool face ... we sense a vulnerability that becomes justification for wariness and a disposition to violence."[8]

The fictional Charles marriage — the couple flirts with other characters and banters good-naturedly with each other — was based on Hammett's love affair with Hellman. Besides their healthy respect for each other's intelligence, Hammett and Hellman shared a plot point that would become key in the book and in all six *Thin Man* movies: Nick's reluctance to get involved in a new case. "I used to nag him to go back to work as a detective," Hellman admitted in 1969. "He'd grow very angry at the idea."[9] Yet the device gives the story unusual tension. Unlike other fictional detectives, who relish the challenge of a mystery, Nick would just as soon have a few drinks with his wife as get involved in any more crime.

The novel was a huge bestseller. Depression-era audiences were both caught up in the mystery and in the Charleses' personae. It soon came to the attention of W.S. Van Dyke, a contract director at the MGM studios in the 1930s. Not known as a genre man, Van Dyke was attracted not to the story per se but to the characters. The book, he noted some time later, showed "the first example of the possibilities of happy, mature romance. There had been so many stories, novels, and screenplays about puppy love that audiences sickened of the overdose. Romances among mature people are as old as the universe itself, but apparently they had been obscured by the petting parties of the flaming youth on the screen."[10]

Van Dyke had the novel on his mind when he directed *Manhattan Melodrama*, the 1934 MGM crime drama which starred three contract players: Clark Gable, Myrna Loy, and William Powell. As discussed earlier, Gable and Powell play boyhood chums who end up on the opposite sides of the law. Although Loy appears as Gable's woman (as she does in a number of later movies), it is the chemistry with Powell that is immediately apparent.

"The Gable character put me up to jumping into a car occupied by the Powell character," Loy recalled in 1982. "Van Dyke never introduced us, probably because he assumed we already knew each other. It was a night scene on the back lot and it was raining. I was supposed to open the door and get in and sit down beside Powell, which I did. I looked at him, and he looked at me and said, 'Miss Loy, I presume.' Right from the start, there was that marvelous thing between us."[11] The easy rapport between Loy and Powell reminded the director of Nick and Nora.

Van Dyke then approached MGM studio head Louis B. Mayer with the idea of using the pair in a film version of Hammett's mystery. Mayer was astounded, since both actors had primarily played heavies: Loy in some 47 movies as either a vamp or — because of her almond-shaped eyes — a sinister Oriental. (She had most recently played Fu Manchu's daughter in 1932's *The Mask of Fu Manchu*.) As for the dapper, mustached Powell, even though he had starred as detective Philo Vance in four successful features, Mayer felt that he was better suited to villainy and, at 42, not young enough to make the transition to leading man.

By this point, Powell himself probably agreed. Born in Pittsburgh in June 1892, he had begun his acting career in high school, where he played Captain Absolute in Sheridan's *The Rivals*. His father urged him to be a lawyer, but after a few weeks of studying law, he quit the University of Kansas in 1911. The stage was in his blood.

Powell then took a step as unusual as Hammett's plunge into realistic pulp writing: he wrote a 23-page letter to a wealthy aunt, explaining why he wanted to be an actor and asking for a loan of $1,400, to be paid back at six percent interest. Impressed by his daring, the aunt gave him half that (and Powell did pay it back), which he used to enrole in New York's Academy of Dramatic Arts.

By 1920, the actor was receiving critical kudos for his part in a romantic play *Spanish Love*. That led to his movie debut in 1922's *Sher-*

lock Holmes, starring John Barrymore as the great detective. In silent movies, he was often seen as a villainous supporting player; in *Romola*, 1924, he marries Lillian Gish and then seduces Dorothy Gish; in *Beau Geste*, 1926, he is an Italian thief who commits suicide), culminating in Josef von Sternberg's *The Last Command* (1928), for which he received great praise for portraying a cruel film director.

What silent movies couldn't capture, however, was Powell's eloquent, precisely phrased diction. That, combined with his razor-thin mustache and smooth manner, cemented his image as a well-mannered cad or criminal. The one exception was the series of four Philo Vance detective movies, starting with *The Canary Murder Case* (1929), which showcased the complex plotting but not the screwball humor of *The Thin Man* series. "Vance made a mint of money for the studio and did well by yours truly also," Powell noted once.[12]

By the early 1930s, he had been at both Paramount and Warners, where he made a variety of pictures mostly as villains. In 1934, he signed on with MGM. His first MGM feature was *Manhattan Melodrama*, his 50th film and Loy's 48th.

Of Welsh descent, Loy was born in Montana as Myrna Williams on August 2, 1905. Her father named her Myrna after a railroad water stop that caught his fancy. From an early age, she had a distinctive look. At public school in Los Angeles, where she and her mother moved after her father died in the flu epidemic of 1918, Loy's beauty caught the eye of one of her teachers. He used her as the model for a statue called "Aspiration," which stands in the schoolyard to this day.

Later labeled Hollywood's "Perfect Wife," Loy started off as a bad girl, again because of her appearance. As the trade paper *Variety* noted in its review of her appearance in *Cave Man* (1926): "She looks like one of the best vamp bets yet revealed. She is tall, has a provocative face, and one of those fancy looking haircuts which is a lot of hohokus but makes an impression."[13] In her autobiography, Loy herself noted: "I was a dancer and could slink, so they fostered this exotic, sexy image."[14]

At 18, she joined the chorus at Grauman's Chinese Theater in Los Angeles. By 1925, she had made her film debut as an extra in *Pretty Ladies* (1925). She screen-tested with Rudolph Valentino (but later admitted that the test was "awful"), and then, as Myrna Loy (the name was suggested by a poet friend of hers), appeared as an extra in the silent version of *Ben-Hur* (1925). That role, as a "hedonist," led to a variety of exotic seductresses: as a Chinese girl who escapes a slave ring in *Crimson City* (1928); as Yasmini of India in John Ford's *The Black Watch*

(1929); as the daughter of the title character in *Mask of Fu Manchu*— she called that character "a sadistic nymphomaniac"[15]— and as an occultist from Java seeking revenge for racism in *Thirteen Women* (1932). She was also in *The Jazz Singer* (1927), the first talkie.

"Interviewers often assume that I had a miserable time playing all those evil creatures, all those women with knives in their teeth," she recalled in her autobiography. "Not at all. I can't say that things came easily—it took a long, long time to find my real niche—but those roles were fun to play, despite their unreality."[16]

Loy began getting more sympathetic parts in two Van Dyke pictures: a whore with a heart of gold in *Penthouse* (1933), and a "lady" in *The Prizefighter and the Lady* (1933); she was also sweet as Coco in *Topaze* (1933), opposite John Barrymore. (It was at about this time that the rumors began about Loy being the favorite actress of gangster John Dillinger, who was shot to death in 1934 outside a Chicago theater where he had just seen *Manhattan Melodrama*.)

What captured viewers was Loy's integrity, which was a part of her real-life persona. "In those days," colleague Betty Black told biographer James Kotsilibas-Davis, "a lot of girls I knew were sleeping their way to the top. Myrna was never interested in getting a part that way. Naturally, as a young girl, she had many offers of desirable parts if she'd sleep with somebody. But no, Myrna wanted a part because she had earned it."[17]

Van Dyke was adamant about casting Powell and Loy in *The Thin Man*. "I loved it," recalled Loy in her autobiography. "I'd fired an occasional quip, but my roles had been very straight up to that point. When I discussed it with Woody, however, a problem had developed. Mayer considered me wrong for the part.... There was no precedent for casting me. Oh, they had a terrible battle!"[18]

He finally obtained Mayer's approval by guaranteeing to complete the picture in two weeks on a minuscule budget (Loy recalled that, normally, it would take two months to shoot such a movie). The compact schedule suited the director, who had earned the nickname "One-Take" Van Dyke. Because of his methods, the San Diego–born director averaged three films a year for 25 years. "He was held in some awe for the speed at which he worked and for his ability to complete a film against the odds," observed David Thomson in *A Biographical Dictionary of Film*.[19] And, against the odds, Van Dyke helped invent a new genre: the screwball mystery.

"Actors are bound to lose their fire if they do scenes over and over,"

Van Dyke once observed about his working methods. "It's that fire that brings life to the screen." (As Loy put it many years later: "He wanted spontaneity and speed insured it."[20])

Spontaneity was certainly required for Loy's first appearance in the movie. Swamped with an armful of Christmas packages, she is dragged on camera by the Charleses' terrier, Asta, who manages to trip her right at Powell's feet. As Loy recalled in her autobiography: "Woody asked me, 'Can you fall?' I said, 'I never worked for Mack Sennett but I'm a dancer.' He said, 'You just trip yourself and go right down.' He put a mark on the floor where I was to land and then I just did it without any rehearsal. I hit the mark with my chin."[21] True to his reputation, Van Dyke got it in one take, while Loy later marveled that she hadn't broken her neck.

The director's pace allowed little time for rehearsal. Powell, for one, complained when it came time to unravel the crime. The denouement involved pages and pages of script — virtually a monologue — and at one point he got up and said, "I don't know what I'm talking about."[22] Equally trying were long takes in a sequence that required the actors to feign eating a dinner of rapidly putrefying oysters.

Van Dyke was decisive about what he wanted in the screenplay. He worked closely with screenwriters Frances Goodrich and Albert Hackett, a husband-and-wife team who later penned *It's a Wonderful Life* (1946) for director Frank Capra. The Hacketts wrote "films of consistently high quality and remarkable range,"[23] noted critic Mark Rowland, who interviewed the pair. Besides *The Thin Man*, they wrote everything from musicals (Nelson Eddy and Jeanette MacDonald in *Naughty Marietta*, 1935, and *Rose Marie*, 1936, both for Van Dyke; *Easter Parade*, 1948, *Seven Brides for Seven Brothers*, 1954) to westerns (*The Virginian*, 1946) and social issue dramas (*The Diary of Anne Frank*, 1959).

Their versatility was important in the genre-bending, groundbreaking world of the first *Thin Man* movie. Like Van Dyke, who could cast against type with Powell and Loy, the writers had to be able to combine a mystery with a comedy and not make the transitions jarring. And their director was equally versatile: he had directed adventure movies, westerns, and musical comedy-romances.

The Hacketts' screenplay was the team's first major success and owed a lot to Van Dyke's influence. He had them tailor the movie — which they wrote in just three weeks — to the personalities of Powell and Loy, emphasizing the relationship over the mystery. "It is the bantering, almost shockingly modern relationship between Nick and Nora ... that gives the series its charm," wrote a critic in 1982. "In fact, their attempts to conceal the true depth of their love for each other under a self-protecting veneer of light-hearted semi-indifference seems far more typical of relationships of the 1980s than of the 1930s."[24]

The couple was different in other ways. "Nick and Nora, unlike other movie couples, never have to court or to break up and then come together again," observed film critic James Harvey. "All those plot things needed at the very least to keep a movie going are taken care of in the *Thin Man* series by the 'case.' And the low level of energy and inspiration of these mystery plots allows the two stars to be comfortably, even happily, uninvolved with them as they are with the murders themselves. Nick and Nora are untouched by action; they're involved in a state of being."[25]

Van Dyke and his team made significant changes in the tone — but not the conception — of the characters. Hammett's original Nora is a tough-talking, more-or-less equal partner, almost as smart as Nick. Yet she is hardly as interesting as she would become on screen. As reconceived for Loy, she becomes a world-wise innocent, a 29-year-old heiress projecting a knowledgeable naiveté that charms her more-knowing husband. Powell's Nick is different from his novelistic counterpart, as well. Not the sarcastic gumshoe of the book, he is a slightly smug, constantly inebriated amateur detective, more Boston gentleman than New York shamus—a gentleman, albeit with shady connections, whose ability to laugh at himself and others makes him more accessible than the original character.

"Van Dyke had encouraged [Powell] to alter lines and business to make him feel natural," Powell biographer Charles Francisco noted, "and he would later admit that Nick Charles was closer to the real Bill Powell than any role he had ever played."[26]

"The match was perfect," said critic David Thomson, "two slender sophisticates, smiling haughtily at each other through a mist of wisecracks. They were not the Nick and Nora Charles that Dashiell Hammett had in mind, but that did not prevent them from making one of the most enjoyed screen marriages in *The Thin Man*."[27]

Nick and Nora competed in mock battles that "embody a witty fastidiousness," observed James Harvey. "The characteristic Nick-and-Nora joke is one ... where we're reminded of all the familiar possibilities in a familiar situation, only to find them rejected for something lighter, richer, funnier."[28]

Powell and Loy give the movie a comic center the book lacks, and

Myrna Loy, William Powell, and Asta in a publicity still for a *Thin Man* movie: the series bends genres by mixing elegant comedy with traditional mystery conventions.

their light touch makes the violent goings-on palatable, an idea picked up years later by *The Avengers*. "It proved," wrote Van Dyke in 1936, "that murder mysteries on the screen did not necessarily have to be morbid nightmares; with sparkling wisecrackery ... a murder mystery can be turned into a pleasing, laughable entertainment and still retain every element of first-class baffling mystery."[29]

In the interests of entertainment, Van Dyke insisted on eight Powell-Loy romantic scenes, usually involving affectionate bantering hinting at deeper feelings. The director also chose to play up the dog, Asta — a bit player in the novel — as a symbol of the Charleses' iconoclastic playfulness. The terrier accompanies them almost everywhere, eating clues, chasing policemen, and generally wreaking havoc. A number of different dogs played Asta over the years. The first, named Skippy, bit Loy at one point, causing their relationship to be, in her words, "a bit strained."[30]

The opening credits to the movie itself are superimposed over a shot of *The Thin Man* novel's dust jacket, which is adorned with a picture of Dashiell Hammett, looking suitably jaunty. After the credits, we see an atmospheric shot of the shadow of a man working in a factory. The figure is Clyde Wynant (Edward Ellis), a tall thin man and an eccentric inventor (and the title character), who owns the factory. He also has an explosive temper. When he is interrupted in his work by his assistant, Tom, he accidentally drops what he is working on. Turning on Tom, he fires him. Later, we see that he is kind-hearted and absent-minded, because he forgets about firing Tom and rehires him ("Forget it, forget it," he says impatiently when Tom says, "You fired me.").

Tom has come to announce that Wynant's daughter, Dorothy, has arrived. Dorothy is beautiful, sweet, and loving, and is played by young MGM starlet Maureen O'Sullivan in her most winning manner (two years before this, she had played Jane in the first Johnny Weissmuller Tarzan picture). The father and daughter obviously have a close bond, and Dorothy introduces her dad to the man she plans to marry, Tommy (Henry Wadsworth).

Here's where the first bit of mystery enters the tale: Wynant says that he is leaving town on unspecified business — a new, secret invention. But he promises to be back at Christmas, three months hence, for his daughter's wedding. The idea that the Wynants are a bit "cuckoo" is also introduced: Dorothy's eccentric younger brother is discussed as being "as cuckoo as the rest of us." A crucial fact shows up at this point: Wynant says that his leg has been hurting because of his old war wound.

This entire sequence does not appear in the book. The Hacketts have taken the back story and dramatized it, making some significant changes. Clyde and especially Dorothy Wynant have been significantly softened. Clyde is made into a bit of a curmudgeon, absent-minded with a slight air of lunacy about him. Dorothy is a loving daughter — with a romantic life — and not the slightly drunken, slightly wild girl of the novel.

MacCaulay (Porter Hall), the Wynant's lawyer, arrives by cab. The first real joke of the movie occurs here, in the throwaway style that the series frequently employs: MacCaulay, a stuffed-shirt type, complains to the driver that he drove too fast and recklessly, and that because of that, he will get no tip. The cabbie, who hands the attorney his change, replies, "Don't worry, brother, I already took it!" and drives off. The pompous prig has been punctured by the brash "little guy."

Wynant tells MacCaulay of his plans, but refuses to divulge where he is going. The inventor goes to get some stock certificates from his office, and we are introduced to his bookkeeper, Tanner, another suspect. Wynant finds that the certificates are missing and suspects Julia Wolf, his mistress, of taking them.

We next see Julia (Natalie Moorhead) on the phone. She is a curvy, platinum blonde, well-dressed in a well-appointed apartment. A few feet from her sits Joe Morelli (Edward Brophy), a bald, squat tough guy, who is reading a magazine. Wynant walks into the apartment and Joe curtly says, "You're in the wrong place, buddy."

Morelli leaves, however, when he realizes that Wynant is "the boyfriend." Wynant asks, accusingly, who Morelli is. Just an old friend, Julia replies. Then an argument ensues over the missing stocks, wherein we see Wynant's darker, more threatening side. In the middle of their conversation she gets a phone call from Nunheim (Harold Huber); Wynant picks up the phone and Nunheim hangs up.

"What are you going to do?" asks Julia, fearfully.

Wynant's only reply is a grim smile. He walks off into the night, a tall thin shadow.

The opening sequence is very ingeniously structured in the style of the best mysteries. It cleanly offers a collection of future suspects—Tanner, Morelli, MacCaulay, Nunheim, Julia—as well as a man they all have reason to fear and or hate: Wynant.

The next sequence begins three months later, during the Christmas season. We find Dorothy and her fiancé dancing at an elegant restaurant; then we see a man shaking a martini mixer in time to the music. It is done with flippant elegance. So is the first comment by this character, Nick Charles, a dapper gentleman with a pencil-thin mustache: "The important thing is rhythm. Always have rhythm in your shaking. A dry martini you always shake to waltz time."

And so we are introduced into another aspect of *The Thin Man*'s world: the casual elegance and the mocking approach to alcohol and the high life.

Dorothy notices Nick at the bar and has a playful exchange with him; he is slightly inebriated, but as we are soon to learn, that is partly a pose and hardly an impediment to his powers of observation. We discover that Nick had met Dorothy years ago when she was a little girl and he was a detective working for her father. We have gone from style to substance again: the back story is smoothly inserted with dialogue lifted directly from the book. Dorothy is looking for Wynant; he had promised to return by Christmas, but no one has heard from him. Nick says he has been in San Francisco for four years, since his marriage, and has given up detecting—a constant theme in the series. He recalls Wynant fondly: "He was a great guy, but screwy."

The camera cuts to a point-of-view shot of a dog-owner being pulled into the restaurant by a frantic wire-haired terrier. We then see the owner: an elegantly dressed, beautiful young woman, loaded down with packages. She is pulled into the restaurant and trips, and after falling quips, "Women and children first, boys."

It is Nora Charles—and it is also one of the great entrances in cinema. Nora has been using Asta, the frantic dog, to hop from bar to bar in search of her husband, Nick. "Hello, sugar," Nick says casually.

"Pretty girl," says Nora, as Dorothy walks off.

"Yes, she's a very nice type," says Nick, staring at Nora.

"You got a type?"

"Only you, darling. Lanky brunettes with wicked jaws."

"Who is she?"

"Oh, darling. I was hoping I wouldn't have to answer that."

"Come on."

"Well, Dorothy is really my daughter. You see, it was spring in Venice and I was so young and I didn't know what I was doing. We're all like that on my father's side."

"By the way, how is your father's side?"

"Oh, it's much better, thanks, and yours?"

"Hey, how many drinks have you had?"

"This will make six martinis."

"Alright." She turns to the waiter. "Will you bring me five more martinis? Line them up right here."

The next scene shows the slight superiority Nick will maintain over Nora throughout the series. After the drinking, it is the morning after and Mr. Charles is none the worse for wear. Mrs. Charles, however, is prostrate with a headache. The couple have a visitor to their hotel room: it is MacCaulay, who has come to see if Nick knows where Wynant is. He also asks about Mimi, Wynant's ex-wife and Dorothy's mother. Nick reiterates that he is not a detective and has been managing Nora's money. He is not interested in mysteries anymore. This is a far cry from Powell's role as Philo Vance, where he investigated crimes out of curiosity and for the challenge of solving them.

As MacCaulay gets a phone call — from Wynant — Nick and Nora playfully make faces at each other in a bit of business that shows how much childish fun they have with each other, even after four years of marriage. MacCaulay now calls Mimi to reassure her over Wynant's safety. We move to the home of Mimi (Minna Gombell), a platinum blonde who is obviously vain about her looks and has a nervous, shrill manner. She argues with Dorothy, and with her teenage son, Gilbert (William Henry), who dresses like an adult and talks about Freud and mother. We are also introduced to Mimi's second husband, Chris Jorgenson (Cesar Romero), an obviously shady character (and another of the movie's many suspects).

Searching for Wynant, Mimi goes to Julia Wolf's apartment; we get a glimpse of Nunheim lurking in the hallways. Mimi finds Julia dead. Startled, Mimi still has enough sense to take something from the dead woman's hand and put it in her bag.

A series of cinematic "wipes" flip the story along, showing how various characters react to Julia's death: Nunheim and a blonde, Morelli, the police. Lt. John Guild (Nat Pendleton), a not-so-bright police detective, is introduced cross-examining MacCaulay about what Wynant and Julia fought about. The scene ends with the medical examiner pointing out something "interesting."

There is a fade-in to Mimi telling her daughter, son, and husband about what she saw. Gilbert is very interested in clues, in whether there was blood, and asks if Mimi killed her. She wants to speak to Chris alone but is interrupted by the doorbell. The police arrive as Jorgenson sneaks out the back door. The police question her, asking if she saw anything in Julia's hand because the medical examiner feels that someone had forced open her fingers. After the police leave, we see what Mimi took: a piece of jewelry belonging to Wynant.

The scene switches to the Charleses' hotel suite; there is a party underway — a collection of Nora's friends, the sophisticates, and Nick's pals, street toughs — comic versions of the gangsters found in *The Public Enemy* and *Little Caesar*. Both types represent the blending of the upper and lower classes of society that is a hallmark of the series. Nick is serving martinis. "Those were the good old days," someone is saying, as he passes out drinks. "Don't kid yourself," replies Nick. "These are the good old days."

Through it all, Asta lies on the floor, watching the undertakings with great suspicion. Nora answers the door; a thuggish character is there who announces that Nick is a nice guy who sent him up the river once. Nora keeps asking if Nick was a good detective.

A policeman is at the party, listening to a radio report about the Wynant murder mystery. He suggests Nick get involved, but the ex-detective is determined to stay out of it. "I'm a gentleman now," he notes (which, of course, is an ironic comment on gentleman detectives like Philo Vance or The Saint).

Everyone tries to draw Nick into the investigation: reporters come by because they think he's involved. He deflects questions with flip remarks about being on a bender (later in the story, he says the case is "interfering" with his drinking). Finally, Nora gets him alone in the kitchen and says she'd like him to take the case. He refuses; saying he's already working on a case — of Scotch. She asks if he is holding her drink — rye — he gulps it down. Yes, that's rye.

The movie picks up the theme of the book that Nick Charles is a reluctant sleuth, uninterested in using his great talent and more interested in having a good time. In that way, some have said that he parallels his creator, Hammett, who, once successful, stopped using his talent for writing and began drinking heavily instead.

Dorothy shows up at the party; Nick takes her into a back room, and she draws a pistol from her bag. He easily and casually disarms her. She confesses to Julia's murder, although after Nick asks her a few pointed questions and receives unbelievable answers, it is obvious she is lying to protect her father.

Dorothy then breaks down sobbing and is in Nick's arms when Nora suddenly enters. It shows the nature of the Charleses' trust and maturity — despite their childlike game-playing — that Nora is not suspicious or angry. He scrunches up his face at her over Dorothy's shoulder; Nora scrunches hers back.

For the first time, Nick expresses interest in the case. He tells Nora to keep Dorothy in the room, away from the reporters — who may believe her false confession — and says he's going to investigate her story. Nick is not drawn in by curiosity but by a damsel in distress.

Mimi suddenly shows up at the door, followed by Gilbert. She wants Nick to help her find Wynant but Nick declines. When Mimi hears that Dorothy is there, she goes to her daughter and slaps her, which angers Nora, who cracks, "Too bad you didn't bring your whip."

A series of quick shots show toughs at the party, singing and goofing off, and the sequence ends with Nora saying, "Oh, Nicky, I love you because you know such lovely people."

The scene switches to Nick and Nora in their beds, with Nora trying to get her husband to look further into the case. There is a knock at the door. It is Morelli, who wants to see Nick. He comes into the bedroom aiming a gun. "Put that gun away," says Nick from bed. "My wife doesn't care but I'm a very timid fellow."

Morelli, a parody of gangster types in *Little Caesar*, talks about "that dirty little Nunheim" who put the finger on him. Nick denies knowing anything ("You're peddling your fish in the wrong market"). In the midst of this, the police arrive and Nick slugs Nora to get her out of the line

William Powell and Myrna Loy in *The Thin Man*, the first and best installment in the series.

of fire; he is shot but he tackles Morelli. Nora comes to, angrily saying she wanted to see Nick "take" him.

The police had been staking out Nick and Nora's suite; they want to know what he knows. A search ("What's that man doing in my drawers?" cracks Nora) reveals Dorothy's gun. The sequence ends with a semi-reversal: Nora is glad Nick isn't on the case, to which he replies: "On it? I'm in it. They think I did it." Nora's reply: "Well, didn't you?" He throws a pillow at her.

The next scene — fairly famous as a symbol of the series — finds the Charleses celebrating Christmas. Nick is lying on his back on the couch, like a young boy, contorting his body into various positions as he shoots ornaments off the Christmas tree with an air pistol. Nora watches tolerantly nearby, sitting in a fur coat, which is obviously her Christmas present. He takes aim over his shoulder and misses the ornament and hits the window. He asks her if she is hot in the coat, and although she is sweltering, she says it looks too nice to take off.

They talk about the case, which they've read all about. MacCaulay shows up, he shows Nick a cable he got from Wynant asking Nick to take the case. While they are talking, MacCaulay gets a call from the police saying that Wynant committed suicide in Allentown, Pennsylvania.

After MacCaulay leaves, Nick decides, finally, to plunge into the investigation, saying he has a hunch Wynant didn't do it — and that he's tired of being pushed around. The Charleses meet Lt. Guild outside their hotel; he tells them the suicide was a false alarm, and Nick agrees to work with the police. Guild says he is on the way to see Nunheim, an informant. Nick — in a bow to 1930s sexism — doesn't want Nora along, so he tricks her into a cab and sends it to Grant's Tomb.

The next scene finds Nick and Guild at Nunheim's. The stool pigeon gets into a domestic spat with his brassy wife, Marion (Gertrude Short), who is furious at her man for working with the police. A comic scene ensues in which she throws pots and pans at Nunheim — a variation in reverse on the domestic spat/grapefruit scene in *The Public Enemy*. Then, she exits with her bags, and Nunheim pleads with Guild to let him go after her. Nunheim says he has some information in the back room; he goes there and shuts the door.

Nick, meantime, has stopped blowing smoke rings from his chair to pick up the phone and dial a number. "Who're you calling?" asks Guild. "The police," Nick replies, realizing that Nunheim has fled down the fire escape. This is significantly different from the book. There, Guild makes the call; here, the casual Nick is one step ahead of everyone.

We next find Nunheim talking on the phone, speaking with someone about the murder. He says he needs $5,000 more or else he'll reveal all to the police. He arranges a meeting; the next scene finds him getting shot by an off-camera assailant. That is followed by a sequence at the morgue, in which Guild tells Nick that Nunheim was shot with the same gun that killed Julia Wolf. Wynant is on the loose.

Nora phones and the movie dips again into comedy. "How'd you like Grant's Tomb?" Nick asks. "It's lovely; I'm having a copy made for you," she replies. She then tells Nick that she is at Mimi's and that Jorgenson has disappeared.

The scene cuts to Mimi's. Mimi tells Nick that she has proof of Wynant's guilt: Wynant's watch chain. Dorothy runs away and cries, telling her fiancé to forget about her because she and her whole family are crazy. Meantime, Guild is certain that Wynant killed both Julia and Nunheim. Nick is dubious.

We now see a montage — including newspaper headlines, policemen on the phones—concerning the search for Wynant. A shadow of a thin man is superimposed walking across the images.

After that, we rejoin Nick, who is in a hat and raincoat and tells Nora he is taking Asta for a walk. She discovers he is going to Wynant's factory to look around. She tells him to be careful, and reveals her fears in banter. She: "Go ahead, see if I care. But I think it's a dirty trick to bring me all the way to New York just to make a widow of me." He: "You wouldn't be a widow long." She: "You bet I wouldn't." He: "Not with all your money."

Beneath the surface wisecracks, we see a deep love, when Nora runs to Nick and embraces him, one of the few times emotion is expressed clearly and honestly. Because of that it is both a touching and emotionally rich scene, punctuated by a wisecrack (of course) directed at Asta: "You take care of him, or you'll never wag that tail again."

At the closed factory, Nick, with Asta's help, discovers the remains of a body buried beneath the cement. He also searches the rest of the property and surprises Tanner (Cyril Thornton), the bookkeeper, who— it turns out — is a former criminal Nick had sent to prison. Tanner tells Nick that Julia Wolf took the stocks. Tanner came back to the factory that night to replace money he himself had stolen so that Wynant would not come after him.

Nick calls the police. They arrive and dig up the body. Judging from the clothes, it seems to be the corpse of a 250-pound man. From the initial "R" on the belt buckle, Guild surmises that it is the remains of a man named Rosebriem, a mysterious figure who had threatened to kill Wynant years before. He deduces that Wynant killed Julia and Nunheim because both had discovered the body. Nick is dubious and goes to the morgue with the coroner, admitting he is "very curious" about the body. An examination reveals shrapnel in the corpse's leg.

Another montage of newspaper headlines follows, as we are shown the police searching for Wynant. Clever visuals include a fisherman's net spread over a map of the United States, with a superimposed shadow of the thin man.

The next sequence begins with the Charleses posing for photographers, who ask what will happen next. Nick replies that he and the wife will be heading back to California to "rest up from this vacation." After the newspaper people leave, Nora admits to being unhappy. "I give you three murders and you're still not satisfied," Nick quips, and then reveals — in an offhand manner that belies its importance — that the remains of the body just discovered were none other than those of Wynant.

Nick explains — under duress, since Nora holds his drink at arm's length from him until he explains — that he was suspicious because the clothes were "very carefully preserved and the body was just as carefully destroyed.... The murderer was counting on one thing: all skeletons look alike." Nick remembered that Wynant had a piece of shrapnel in his shin and when he saw that at the coroner's, he had all the proof he needed. He had been dead for two months, so he couldn't have committed the murders.

In a significant departure from the book and a nod to mystery movie convention, Nick says he's going to get the murderer by gathering all the suspects together at a formal dinner party. He will explain all the clues, and in the process, hope someone makes a slip and reveals himself (or herself) to be the killer.

The party itself is a comic take on the classic Charlie Chan convention of gathering the usual suspects, with rough-talking cops dressed up as waiters and guests — both high- and low-class — escorted to the party by policemen. "You know," Nora says as more guests are brought in, "you're a great help to a hostess. I wish I had you at all my dinner parties."

The humorous touches continue in the prelude to the grand finale: police-waiters ordering guests to have cocktails, indignant guests complaining that they had tickets to the theater ("Nicky's putting on a show of his own"), and so on. Dorothy arrives drunk, with a strange man, closer in character to her novelistic counterpart; Jorgenson turns up with his first wife.

The dinner begins and Nick announces that Wynant is not the murderer, that he actually saw him recently. Mimi quickly chimes in that she saw Wynant, too, and describes what he was wearing. This revelation is interrupted by Nora saying, "Waiter, will you serve the nuts." Pause. "I mean, will you serve the guests the nuts."

Nick reveals that Wynant is dead; Dorothy bursts into tears, Tommy slugs the man she was with and an unperturbed Nora gives him a chair saying, "Tommy, Tommy, you sit here."

"The murderer is right in this room, sitting at this table," Nick says, and after a pause. "You may serve the fish." The technique is typical of the series, which constantly bends convention, dropping in humor during moments of high drama. "Nice food, isn't it?" Nick says in an aside to Nora, who replies: "Yes, it's the best dinner I ever listened to."

Nick runs through all the suspects, and gets them to piece together the different elements of the puzzle: Morelli admits that Julia was cheating on Wynant, aided and abetted by someone else. The inventor sought out his mistress' conspirator, confronted him, and was killed for his efforts.

Throughout this monologue, Nick breaks off to address the suspects by name which startles them — and us — into thinking he is about to accuse them of being the killer. But it is only misdirection, as he asks them whether they want more wine or food.

The murderer "planned the whole thing beautifully." He closed up the shop, communicated with MacCaulay, and then buried Wynant's body with the fat man's clothes. By keeping up the myth of Wynant being alive, he and Julia Wolf could still collect money. When the murderer heard that Mimi was going to see Julia, however, he panicked, thinking Julia might reveal his identity. So, exit Julia. Wynant's watch chain was planted to point suspicion at him.

Nunheim, who was having an affair with Julia, happened to be in the hallway, heard the shots, and actually saw the murderer. Nunheim was paid off once, but, when he got greedy, was killed off, too.

There was a weak link in the chain of evidence against Wynant, however. The murderer had made him seem alive by using telegrams and phone calls but no one had ever seen him. So, says Nick, the killer paid Mimi to say she had seen Wynant. When Mimi denies that, Nick points out that Mimi was disinherited when she remarried. But now, with the revelation that Jorgenson is a bigamist — he had never gotten a divorce from his first wife — it turns out that Mimi is still married to Wynant. She stands to inherit the whole estate.

Realizing that she will be next in line on the murderer's hit list, Mimi breaks down and fingers the killer, who pulls out a pistol. Nick is too quick for him, however, and slugs him. "What do you want me to do?" Nick says to Guild. "Wrap him up in cellophane?"

"Nicky, he might have killed you. Oh, I'm glad you're not a detective!" cries Nora. Nick's jaw drops.

The final scenes take place on a train bound for San Francisco. Nick, Nora, Dorothy, and Tommy are toasting the end of the case. Nick and Nora then retire to their room where Nora says she will put Asta in the bottom bunk with her. "Oh yeah?" says Nick, as he puts Asta on the top bunk and embraces her. The camera stays on Asta, who covers his eyes with his paws. Then there is a cut to the phallic symbol of the train speeding along the tracks to the strains of "California, Here I Come."

The Thin Man was shot in 14 days, with two days left over for retakes. It went on to earn over $2 million in its first release, as well as Academy Award nominations for best picture, best actor, and best screenplay. Not surprisingly, it also made Powell and Loy stars.

The Thin Man may have been an unexpected hit, but its success was linked directly to Powell and Loy. Their characters, wrote film historian William K. Everson, "satisfied a kind of wish fulfillment from audiences in those rather grim days in that they solved the depression by completely ignoring it rather than by offering patronizing platitudes or artificial solutions. The Charleses were obviously wealthy people unaffected by the depression; audiences might envy their way of life, but they didn't *resent* it because Nick and Nora never stressed their wealth and certainly never squandered it."[31]

"... From [our] very first scene, a curious thing passed between us, a feeling of rhythm, complete understanding, an instinct for how one could bring out the best in the other," Loy noted in her autobiography. "In all our work together you can see this strange — I don't know what ... a kind of rapport. It wasn't conscious."[32]

"When we did a scene together, we forgot acting technique, camera angles, and microphones. We were just two people in perfect harmony," agreed Powell. "Many times I've played with an actress who seemed to be separated from me by a plate-glass window; there was no contact at all. But Myrna, unlike some actresses who think only of themselves, has the happy faculty of being able to listen while the other fellow says his lines. She has the give and take of acting that brings out the best."[33]

Their technique, Loy told Joseph Hurley, "wasn't a conscious thing.

If you heard us talking in a room, you'd hear the same thing. He'd tease me a little, and there was a sort of blending which seemed to please people. Bill is naturally a witty man; he doesn't have to have lines."[34]

The two shot 13 more movies over 13 years and became linked together in the public mind. As Hurley reported: "When they registered at the St. Francis Hotel in San Francisco, where the second movie in the [*Thin Man*] chain was doing location work, the management automatically booked them into a single, elegant suite, assuming they were husband and wife offscreen, as well as on."[35] After Powell died in 1984, Loy said: "I never enjoyed my work more than when I worked with William Powell."[36]

The Thin Man was groundbreaking in combining genres—comedy and mystery—and in painting a woman as a more equal (though not completely equal) partner with a man. Much as Honor Blackman and Diana Rigg would do on *The Avengers* in the early sixties, *The Thin Man* demonstrated that a woman could be as witty and intelligent as a man.

The Thin Man also showed a couple in perfect sync. As Loy biographer Karyn Kay noted: "Under the protective umbrella of a respectable, upper-class marriage, Nick and Nora share the fun of fast living—a

William Powell, Asta, and Myrna Loy. "I never enjoyed my work more than when I worked with William Powell," Loy said once.

lifestyle usually reserved in the cinema for singles. They are partygoers and steady imbibers, but Nick and Nora drink together and go home together. Despite banter about infidelity and promiscuity, Nick and Nora enjoy a lusciously sensuous but definitely monogamous relationship.... They are the perfect couple in the perfect marriage. They did the outrageous—they enjoyed each other as man and wife."[37]

"We attended the first preview in fear and trembling," said Samuel Marx, former head of the MGM story department. "The executives went down to Huntington Park ... I'd bought this sprightly detective story for $14,000, and we had no idea whether this kind of comedy would go. It had two unprecedented elements that scared the hell out of the whole studio: they were having fun with murder, and they were a married couple who acted with total sophistication.

"I can only tell you that it was a night of great jubilation on the Huntington Park sidewalk after that preview. The whole thing broke with tradition in several ways, yet it looked like a smash. That first preview was a thermometer that told us how much heat this team was generating. They had a chemistry that came out of Myrna Loy and William Powell, plus the characters of Nick and Nora Charles. It was automatic that you would now continue to put them together. The reaction was so great and it never stopped."[38]

5

A Humorous Hitch

> " ... there is much in *The Avengers* that came from my long admiration of Hitchcock. He too used the unexpected setting, and his villains were always charming or unexpected: a dentist, a fisherman, and so on..."
>
> Brian Clemens[1]

By combining and poking fun at different genres, *The Thin Man* changed the way filmmakers conceived of genre. Mysteries no longer had to be serious affairs; they could contain comedy and romance. And romances themselves no longer had to be soapy and sentimental, they could have the hard edge of the screwball comedy.

In the post–*Thin Man* world, things were different. And in the pre–*Avengers* universe of the 1930s, 1940s, and 1950s, the groundwork was laid for even more genre-bending by the works of Alfred Hitchcock and the craftsmen at the Ealing Film Studios.

"There is much in *The Avengers* that came from my long admiration of Hitchcock," Brian Clemens, a writer, producer, and guiding force behind *The Avengers* admitted once (quoted in Carraze and Putheaud). "He too used the unexpected setting, and his villains were always charming or unexpected: a dentist, a fisherman, and so on."

The detective genre was shaken up by the British-born Hitchcock, who was one of the first to see the potential in combining genres. The director added comedy to the suspense film in his programmer, *Number Seventeen* (1932), a thriller with comic touches, and then went full force with *The Man Who Knew Too Much* (1934), a movie which pokes fun at murder and mayhem in a way few had done in a serious movie before.

5. A Humorous Hitch

The so-called "Master of Suspense" had a humble beginning: he was born August 13, 1899, in Leytonstone, England, the son of a working-class greengrocer. As a Catholic sent to a Jesuit school, the boy quickly learned two lessons which helped him in his later career: fear authority and be fascinated by the forbidden fruits of sin and sex.

The young man studied to be an engineer but eventually ended up designing title cards for the more glamorous world of silent movies. Entranced by filmmaking, Hitchcock worked on every job he could, learning about lighting, editing, set design, and script construction.

His first movie was shot in Germany in 1925, yet it was his third picture, *The Lodger* (1926) which made his reputation and helped define his later movies. Besides employing his favorite theme of the innocent man suspected of a heinous crime, the silent film showcased the 27-year-old director's dazzling technique. When the killer strikes, for instance, all the viewer sees are five images cut together in rapid succession: a girl screaming; a street woman looking up from her stoop; a cat jumping off a garbage can; a policeman running; and a masked figure walking into the fog. It is stunning in its simplicity—and as jarring as anything in *Halloween* (1978) or *Friday the 13th* (1980).

The Thirty-Nine Steps (1935) went even further, combining laughs and adventure in a style that was later appropriated by the James Bond pictures. These were canny moves: the comic touches—dark or otherwise—helped make the more serious (and sometimes grisly) elements acceptable while widening the scope of the director's appeal.

The Thirty-Nine Steps also contains the thriller elements of such great silent serials as *The Exploits of Elaine*: the dashing (both literally and figuratively) hero, the icy but secretly passionate blonde, the suave villain, the MacGuffin (a plot device that gets the action going), and the chase, based on a series of slightly implausible but completely believable (in the context of the movie) events. The hero here is Richard Hannay (Robert Donat), falsely accused of murder. He's on the run from both the police and the villains—a foreign spy ring—as he tries to clear his name. There are great visuals, great characters, great setpieces, and, above all, great technique.

Technique became a hallmark of Hitchcock, from a constantly roving camera in the legendary "one-take" movie *Rope* (1948), to his 78 edits in 45 seconds for the *Psycho* (1960) shower scene. "Hitchcock began his career as a director at the height of what he always called the Golden Age of film," explained William Rothman in *Hitchcock: The Murderous Gaze*. "The great directors of the German cinema ... were achieving unprecedented expressive effects with camera movement, set design, and lighting.... [French directors] were experimenting with subjective devices and other formal innovations.... Hitchcock started with a clear sense of film's traditions and a conviction that film was an art."[2]

"Making a film means, first of all, to tell a story," Hitchcock himself said in *Hitchcock*. " ... The next factor is the technique of filmmaking, and in this connection, I am against virtuosity for its own sake. Technique should enrich the action. One doesn't set the camera at a certain angle just because the cameraman happens to be enthusiastic about that spot. The only thing that matters is whether the installation of the camera at a given angle is going to give the scene its maximum impact."[3]

To that end, the director experimented with sound in *Blackmail* (1929), the first British talking picture. Here, he cleverly played with how characters listen. A woman who has stabbed a man repeatedly notices the word "knife" in a mundane breakfast conversation, and, to show her growing sense of guilt, that is soon the only intelligible word she ultimately hears, as the dialogue gradually turns into gibberish.

As mentioned, the director also added comedy to the suspense film, an unusual step in the thirties. He played on the conventions of the genre, including humor that came not out of the situations but out of the relationships. When *The Lady Vanishes* (1938) combined comedy with suspense, it employed the techniques and tricks that Hitchcock had picked up in the preceding dozen years. The story is a whodunit and a whydunit, a spy story about an elderly woman who vanishes on a train. It's that simple. But it isn't. Hitchcock fills the story with a host of diverse minor players, including two who could be seen as role models for characters in *The Avengers*: the comedy team of Basil Radford and Naunton Wayne as two proper Englishmen obsessed with cricket scores.

Foreshadowing *The Avengers*, the movie also features a pair of male and female detectives, Gilbert and Iris (Michael Redgrave and Margaret Lockwood), talented but free-spirited amateur sleuths who must solve the inexplicable disappearance of the woman who apparently did not exist. Gilbert and Iris banter and bicker like Fred Astaire and Ginger Rogers, but—also like Astaire and Rogers—end up falling in love by helping each other solve the puzzle. Hitchcock exploited another element of the mystery story which helped increase its popularity: the mystery of relationships, of the way people who initially dislike each other can fall in love. The sexual tension in *The Lady Vanishes* and subsequent Hitchcock thrillers bubbles up and transforms the tale into something much greater, that is ultimately more universal and more affecting than the average thriller.

In fact, Hitchcock — like W.S. Van Dyke with *The Thin Man*— realized that thrills and comedy alone were not enough to make a successful movie. It needed romance. So, while most of his films are nominally about suspense, they are also about lovers who discover the depth of their feelings through a hair-raising adventure.

In *Rear Window* (1954), the hero fears marriage to a beautiful woman with whom he is involved. Perversely, the dangers the couple face investigating a brutal killing are what finally brings them closer together. James Stewart plays L.B. "Jeff" Jeffries, a photographer hobbled with a broken leg who takes to watching the people in the apartments across the alley. They all turn out to be, in cinematic style, reflections of the character's hopes, desires, and fears about marriage to Lisa (Grace Kelly), the beautiful clothes buyer with whom he's involved. He sees examples of the nagging wife, the loving wife, the emasculating wife. As the movie progresses, Jeff and Lisa both think they have discovered a murder and perversely, and typically for Hitchcock, investigating the crime is what brings them closer together.

"Within the world of a Hitchcock film," explained William Rothman in *Hitchcock: The Murderous Gaze*, "the nature and relationships of love, murder, sexuality, marriage ... are at issue."[4] Or as film director François Truffaut put it: " ... in Hitchcock's cinema ... to make love and to die are one and the same."[5]

Hitchcock developed these themes in his formative, British-based years during the thirties. By the 1940s and 1950s, he was working in America. It was there that his movies became even richer and more complex, dealing with issues of love and trust (*Notorious*, 1946), homosexual longing (*Strangers on a Train*, 1951), transference of guilt (*The Wrong Man*, 1957), and obsessive, destructive passion (*Vertigo*, 1958).

Many argue that it was the Catholic in Hitchcock who introduced morality into the subtext of many of his greatest movies. *Shadow of a Doubt* (1943), to name just one, explores the ideas of evil disguised as innocence and innocence perverted by evil. Teresa Wright plays Charley, namesake of her Uncle Charlie (Joseph Cotten), who is a murderer wanted by the police. Charley's dilemma: does she turn in the man she has worshipped for years or let him go? It is a horrible choice since Uncle Charlie is charming, loving, and gracious — the perfect gentleman yet also the perfect embodiment of villainy.

By cloaking such themes in the thriller genre, Hitchcock ensured his popularity and also helped — in another genre-bending move — change the way critics viewed suspense movies. A film such as *Silence of the Lambs* (1991) could never have won an Oscar or have been treated seriously if Hitchcock hadn't led the way. Indeed: with Hitch, entertainment and art became one, as the director drew the viewers into a dreamily plausible world which quickly became a nightmare.

"I try to put in my films ... what Poe put in his stories," Hitchcock said once, "a perfectly unbelievable story recounted to readers with such a hallucinatory logic that one has the impression that this same story can happen to you tomorrow."[6]

As his image solidified during his career, Hitchcock never stepped too far out of character, disguising his important filmmaking aspirations behind the mask of a popular entertainer. Always the showman, Hitch was transformed into the most recognizable director in the world when he began offering droll introductions to the long-running *Alfred Hitchcock Presents* TV series in 1957.

Nonetheless, the "Master of Suspense" moniker became a trap. The director soon became increasingly more worried about topping himself (he once quipped that the things which scared him the most were little children, policemen, high places, and the idea that "my next picture won't be as good as the last one"[7]). *Psycho* (1960) may have been a financial smash, but after the relative failure of *Marnie* (1964), he didn't know where to go. Restricted by his image, fears, and studio from the kind of experimentation he had attempted in his prime, the director stagnated.

Yet the greengrocer's son eventually had the last laugh. Once derided as a "simple" director of "thrillers," Alfred Hitchcock finally became much, much more. By the time of his death in 1980, he had been knighted, feted, and revered by younger filmmakers, critical institutions, and the public at large as a cinematic genius. Since then, the word "Hitchcockian" has become an adjective to describe any number of films. Hitch's term "The MacGuffin"— to describe a meaningless plot device that starts the action rolling — has entered the popular lexicon. And, for many, his movies have become exemplars of what moviemaking is all about: passion, audience involvement, visual beauty, and technical virtuosity. Or, in a phrase, pure cinema. And, as we will see, Alfred Hitchcock's work had a significant influence on both *The Avengers* and *The X-Files*.

"Hitchcock's most profound subject and achievement," critic David Thomson once wrote, "is the juxtaposition of sanity and insanity, of bourgeois ordinariness and criminal outrage.... Hitchcock became a way of defining film."[8]

Something similar can be said about the Ealing Film Studios, which, through a series of blackly comic films produced in the late 1940s and 1950s, was equally influential on *The Avengers* and, to a lesser extent, on *The X-Files*. The plot of an Ealing classic, *Kind Hearts and Coronets* (1949), is typically dark. Because his mother married beneath her social station in the proud, wealthy Ascoyne D'Ascoyne family, Louis Mazzini (Dennis Price) has been banished from the family's inner circle and into poverty. Nonetheless, he is still ninth in line to inherit the dukedom — so he soon begins systematically murdering the eight relatives who stand in his way.

What could be described as a grim drama about a dangerous psychopath, instead becomes one of the grandest comedies of all time, in which murder is treated as casually as mustard on a sandwich. "He seemed a very pleasant fellow," Mazzini notes about one of his intended victims, "and I regretted that our acquaintanceship must be so short."

Kind Hearts is one of a handful of British comedies made over forty years ago by Ealing Films, a small British studio that shot low-budget movies with a quasi-documentary look. And although Ealing went out of business in 1959, the company's influence — particularly for what have become known as "The Ealing Comedies" — has been far-reaching, affecting everything from *The Avengers* and *Monty Python's Flying Circus* to such movies as *Nuns on the Run* (1990), *Get Shorty* (1995), and *The Englishman Who Went Up a Hill But Came Down a Mountain* (1995). All have a touch of Ealing about them.

The studio's legacy was most noticeable in 1988's *A Fish Called Wanda*, a $200 million hit directed by former Ealing director Charles Crichton which starred John Cleese and Michael Palin from *Monty Python*, and Jamie Lee Curtis and Kevin Kline. "You could call *A Fish Called Wanda* an Ealing comedy that's been time-warped into a world recovering from the impact of *Monty Python's Flying Circus*," wrote the *New York Times*' Benedict Nightingale.[9]

But what exactly is an "Ealing" picture? The studio itself began in the 1920s and produced everything from weepy melodramas and costume dramas to tales of the supernatural (such as the classic *Dead of Night*, 1946), but to many, the company was defined by four comedies made between 1949 and 1955: *Kind Hearts and Coronets*, *The Lavender Hill Mob* (1951), *The Man in the White Suit* (1951), and *The Ladykillers* (1955). All starred Alec Guinness, and all featured an offbeat and at times darkly comic sensibility that was particularly British, but also particularly Ealing.

"These movies had an even-tempered, genteel nuttiness," wrote Terence Rafferty in *The New Yorker* magazine in 1988. "Even when they dealt with murder, as they frequently did, they maintained a placid and unsurprised tone — which was, of course, the source of most of the humor."[10]

Ealing comedies, which owed some of their popularity to England's post–World War II depression, combined farce with good manners and death with good taste in their depiction of quirky battles against convention. "Everything about Ealing was defiantly small, and glorified the small at the expense of the big, the conventional, the pompous," observed Peter Ustinov in *Forever Ealing*.[11] The films, noted David Shipman in *The Story of Cinema*, are "insular ... in the best sense, with a sharp eye for the foibles of the British."[12] (In fact, the same has often been said about *The Avengers*.)

Each of the comedies, most of which were produced on small budgets and earned large profits, involved eccentric individuals who pursued wild dreams of wealth, knowledge, or power. *The Lavender Hill Mob*, directed by Ealing house director Charles Crichton (who later directed episodes of *The Avengers* and came out of retirement to direct *A Fish Called Wanda*), features a timid bank clerk (Guinness) putting together a daring robbery of the Bank of England. *The Man in the White Suit* paints an ironic portrait of labor and management combined against a naive inventor (Guinness) who has devised a fabric that never wears out — and would thus put both sides out of business.

The Ealing method, noted George Perry in *Forever Ealing*, was to throw a small group of disparate characters in a situation of adversity and show how they cope. That is the case in *The Ladykillers*, which finds an oddball gang of bank robbers (including Guinness and Peter Sellers), hiding out in an old lady's rooming house, pretending to be an amateur chamber orchestra. (The movie is the chief inspiration for *A Fish Called Wanda*, another film about a robbery that is peopled with eccentric characters.) When she gets wise to their scheme, they try to kill her — but end up killing each other instead. "Like all the Ealing comedies," observed David Shipman, "its keynote is a coy irony."[13]

But it is *Kind Hearts and Coronets*, a black comedy with no equal, that is the greatest and perhaps most influential of Ealing's output. The movie is both a satire of British snobbery and a celebration of it, with Dennis Price as the proud, arrogant, and murderous relation to the upper-crust D'Ascoyne family. In the course of the story, one simultaneously admires and is appalled by Price, a Briton who is eminently proper, even in the way he kills.

The movie's main *tour de force* comes in the casting of Alec Guinness as all eight victims. Whether he is playing doddering priest, snobbish duke, fresh-faced photographer, or women's rights advocate Lady Agatha D'Ascoyne, Guinness is superbly different — and comically brilliant — in each role. "I was invited to play four of the victims," Guinness told the *New York Times* in 1984. "... I sent back a telegram that said, 'I see no point in playing four parts. How about me playing eight?' To my astonishment, they agreed."[14]

The movie is aided immeasurably by the wonderfully literate script, another Ealing quality (and one which was certainly an influence on such comedic groups as Beyond the Fringe). Director Robert Hamer admitted in 1952 that he wanted to make a movie that used "this English language, which I love, in a more varied and, to me, more interesting way than I had previously had the chance of doing in a film."[15] The movie's elegant narration by Price is one of its many charms ("It is so difficult to make a neat job of killing people with whom one is not on friendly terms").

Guinness, who began in theater, had appeared in only a few films before 1949, most notably *Oliver Twist* (1948) as Fagin. "I longed to do absurd and clownish things," he admitted in *Who's Who in Comedy*. "Buster Keaton and Stan Laurel were my heroes."[16] Ealing gave him the chance to be both funny and a movie star, beginning with *Kind Hearts*. "There weren't many sophisticated comedies then, certainly not black comedies," he noted in 1984. "And I think *Kind Hearts* opened the gate to quite a lot of black comedy."[17]

In fact, the studio's influence can clearly be seen in many later movies. Not only did its zany comedies, poking fun at British mores, open the way for such satirists as the Monty Python group, but the movies also created a new cinematic language. For instance, the casual way death is discussed in Alfred Hitchcock's *The Trouble with Harry* (1955), a farce about a corpse who keeps being buried and unburied, could have come right out of an Ealing picture: "After you've dug him up," says the prim elderly woman about the body, "I'll make you some hot chocolate." *Get Shorty*, too, could be a modern Ealing comedy. The saga of a New Jersey gangster (John Travolta) mixing it up with eccentric stars, producers, and killers in Hollywood, the movie has the same blackly comedic look at life, death, and ambition that typified Ealing.

Ealing comedies could best be described as realistic fantasies, with unusual events taking place in a meticulously believable setting, noted Perry in *Forever Ealing*. That quality can be seen throughout *The Avengers*, and also in such recent movies as *Fierce Creatures* (1997) and *The Englishman Who Went Up a Hill But Came Down a Mountain*. In *Fierce Creatures*, the *Wanda* follow-up, a small, idyllic English zoo is taken over by a large multinational corporation, and the story depicts the eccentrics versus the executives who try to change the zoo. *Englishman* is the whimsical tale of disparate Welsh townsfolk joining together in a wild quest: making a much-admired hill 1,000-feet high so that it will be listed on a surveyor's map as a mountain.

Ealing-style movies include farcical elements, and often a slightly dark, iconoclastic tone. *Clockwise* (1985), an adventure of comic anarchy, shows how the best-laid plans can go ridiculously awry because of the comic obtuseness of the lead character (John Cleese). Similarly, *Nuns on the Run*, about two inept gunmen on the lam (Eric Idle and Robbie Coltrane), hiding out as nuns in a convent, is both silly and gently satirical in the best Ealing manner. "Con men sell life insurance," says one of the gangsters, "the church sells after-life insurance."

Above all, Ealing movies and their successors take a polite, civilized attitude towards the absurd, the unusual, and the outlandish. *The Missionary* (1982) offers Michael Palin as a shy, well-meaning missionary to London's prostitutes who becomes a howling success because of his sexual prowess. The story is done with a light touch, and Palin makes the retiring priest both innocent and wise, a worthy successor to characters played by Guinness. The movie also features a butler who constantly gets lost escorting guests in a multi-roomed mansion ("He really is the most disastrous butler," observes his employer, who nonetheless admits that he cannot fire him because "he's been here for 25 years").

Ealing movies and their offspring are about comic movie-making at its best, a cinema where civilized cruelty is commonplace and comic invention top-notch. Indeed, the films are wonderful because they are so wonderfully dark. "Comedy that doesn't have [a cruel] streak is essentially mediocre, safe, and uninteresting," John Cleese observed in a *Cleese Encounters*, a biography in which he linked *A Fish Called Wanda* to the tradition of Ealing. "The question then, is it really cruel?... When Tom is run over by Jerry on a steamroller you laugh, but you don't think, 'God, that poor cat must have suffered dreadfully.' ... Intelligent people understand that they can laugh at an idea that would not be funny in real life."[18]

6

When a Man Became a Woman

"To me the great secret of *The Avengers* is the knowledge that woman can not only keep it going with men, but can top men, and can rescue men, and they can treat men as their friend and equal without emasculating them. There's too much made of the male-masculine thing, I think."

Patrick Macnee[1]

The Avengers, as we know it, came about because of an actors' strike. An actors' strike that led to a groundbreaking partnership that changed the way television looked at men and women, much as *The Thin Man* did in movies.

It all started with Howard Thomas. It was 1960 and Alfred Hitchcock's *North by Northwest* (1959) was a box-office hit on the big screen, while Ian Fleming's James Bond thrillers were just taking off on the printed page. Thomas, managing director of Britain's ABC television network, later admitted that he felt it was time to develop an escapist adventure series in the Hitchcock-Bond vein for British television. To do that, he turned to Sydney Newman, the head of drama at ABC. Newman was an apt choice, since he had a range of experience: he had created the highbrow anthology series, *Armchair Theatre*, and also the more lowbrow *Doctor Who*, a children's science fiction program.

For inspiration, Newman looked at Hitchcock's films and, closer to home, a recent police show called *Police Surgeon* which had featured a young actor named Ian Hendry. Although the half-hour series had lasted just 13 weeks, viewer surveys showed that Hendry was well-liked and Newman thought he could structure a series around him.

"This had to be different: melodramatic, an action-adventure-thriller with a sense of humor," recalled the producer. "I felt that I could capitalize on the current, literary popularity of the John Le Carre/Ian Fleming genre and send it up. Why not make fun of the whole 'spy' nonsense?... However, a series based on one character, shot live every week, would be too great a burden on [Hendry]. I needed a second character. To contrast Hendry's integrity and his physical presence, I thought of teaming him with an undercover agent, an MI5 type, someone he wouldn't approve of. Someone amoral, suave, and brainy, who wouldn't deign to dirty himself by physically fighting, preferring a silenced gun or a sword-cane. Sparks would fly between them."[2]

Working with Leonard White, *Police Surgeon*'s co-producer, Newman took a few elements from the former series—for instance, Hendry again played a doctor involved with crime—but otherwise developed a series that was quite unusual. The initial episode was a far cry from what would come later. In it, Hendry plays Dr. David Keel, a young doctor who is about to get married. Through a terrible misunderstanding, Keel's fianceé is killed by drug smugglers and Keel, ravaged by grief, vows revenge. He becomes involved with a shadowy undercover man named John Steed, who helps him capture the killers and "bring them to book."

Steed was played by Patrick Macnee, a man well-suited for the part. Born in 1922 to an upper-class English household, the actor was brought up with "good manners"—but also learned quickly to appreciate and sympathize with the bizarre. At an early age, his mother left his father, an alcoholic racehorse trainer, and took the young boy to live with her lesbian lover. Known as Uncle Evelyn, the lover, paid for Patrick's schooling at Eton.

"What was eminent about that bringing-up is that a man was not allowed in the house at all," Macnee said later. "They had to come in through the back door. All the people who worked on the farm were never allowed in the house. I think they allowed the men once a year for pheasant shooting in September. Now, I took it for granted that I lived with lesbians. I didn't even know what lesbians were. I just didn't see any men, that's all. But I didn't grow up homosexual because I'm not homosexual. I can't take any credit for that. I just like women."[3]

At public school, Macnee developed an interest in acting. After five years at Eton, the Macnee family had a run of bad luck, and their finances dwindled. On the advice of the actress Margaret Rawlings, he applied to

Webber-Douglas drama school in South Kensington and won a scholarship. He stayed for a short time and then moved into repertory theater. He found a variety of roles and also met his first wife, Barbara Douglas, during a run of *Little Women*.

In 1941, he joined the navy, where he was part of Eighth Gunboat Flotilla at Dartmouth. Discharged in 1947, Macnee returned to the theater and raised a family (a son and daughter) and also obtained small roles in films, among them Laurence Olivier's *Hamlet* (1948). In search of work, he went to Canada where he built a reputation on television. (He appeared in a live American TV version of *A Night to Remember* in 1956, about which he noted: "We made the Titanic go down in a fish tank."[4]) He had trouble finding jobs, and eventually took an associate producer position in England on *The Valiant Years*, a documentary series based on Winston Churchill's memoirs. When the producer of that program was suddenly fired, Macnee took over.

Newman had worked with Macnee in the past and when he was preparing *The Avengers*, thought of him for the Steed role: a "George Sanders" type, slightly mysterious, slightly shady, and oh-so-elegant. (The producer even wanted Macnee to wear a Sanders-like moustache, but the actor refused.)

Macnee and Newman met. "Over dinner Leonard mentioned a series he was working on," Macnee recalled in *Blind in One Ear*, his autobiography. "It was called *Police Surgeon*. It hadn't made the ratings, but whenever its star Ian Hendry appeared, women cuddled their television sets. The television bosses had decided to reshape the show. That reshaping would include changing the title from *Police Surgeon* to *The Avengers*, as well as introducing a sidekick for Ian."[5]

Macnee agreed to co-star. Yet for a series that would become known for its light-hearted approach to murder, the first season of *The Avengers* was certainly gritty and hard-hitting. "Hot Snow," the initial episode, was dark, realistic, and, because it was shot on videotape and live-on-camera, very stagy. Its subject matter was most un*Avengers*-like, dealing with drug-smugglers (a hot button issue), bereavement, and the seedy underside of British crime. "... that first episode was played as though it was something by Graham Greene," recalled Macnee,[6] who also said: "... the series began as something of a male-dominated show, with the late Ian Hendry and I [sic] swaggering around London in grubby, Gestapo-style, tightly-belted raincoats, the ubiquitous cigarette drooping from our lips.... Much of our early location work was done around the sleazier parts of London's West End. In those early days, our wardrobe seemed to consist of one dirty mac apiece. As Ian and I jumped over the walls and hid in the alleyways of Soho, we surely resembled a couple of dirty old men on the run from police officers who'd just raided a strip joint. In fact, we were the ones chasing criminals."[7]

The only existing episode from that first season, "The Frighteners," supports Macnee's view. The teleplay, by Berkely Mather (who received co-credit on the *Dr. No* screenplay one year later), is an odd affair, low-key, realistic, and worth examining in detail, partly because it is so different from what was to come.

The opening titles in "The Frighteners" consist of line art of Hendry and Macnee that looks like it has been drawn on crumpled pieces of paper; the theme music is not the familiar Laurie Johnson pop theme but a monotonous jazz tune by Johnny Dankwoth. Macnee is second-billed.

The story starts with an exterior filmed shot of an office building; the scene then switches to inside, where a secretary takes a memo to Sir Thomas Weller (Stratford Johns), a nervous, balding man behind a desk (the camera jiggles slightly in one of the flubs typical of the live-on-tape technique). He tells her to leave and then gets on the phone and talks angrily to someone about "that nuisance abatement problem. Deal with it as we arranged. I want him frightened good and hard."

The image switches to film footage of an outdoor market and we see two tough-looking characters (as they appear so does a superimposed title, "The Frighteners"). They enter a butcher shop, and go past the butcher to a secret doorway. Once inside, they report to another fat man — a second-rate Sydney Greenstreet — who is called The Deacon (Willoughby Goddard).The sequence is shot with film noirish lighting and in tight close-ups that give atmosphere while disguising the cheapness of the sets.

"The style [of the show] was an enforced accident — simple economics," writer-producer Brian Clemens said once. "A lot of its evolution was due to the very limited budget. Because they didn't really have any sets — say a general store and a few loaves and fishes — and director Peter Hammond ... turned those loaves and fishes into multitudinous and stimulating foreground shots."[8]

The Deacon is affable and almost casual as he gives a photo of a young, good-looking man to the shorter of the two thugs, Moxon (Philip Locke). "There's your pigeon," he says, telling them to give the man a "routine massage." Slowly, Moxon puts on a set of brass knuckles as The Deacon gives him details. After they leave, the last shot — typical of director Hammond's style — is of The Deacon on the phone, photographed through the bars of a bird cage containing a parrot.

The scene dissolves to a cab interior. Steed is inside. He greets Dr. Keel and tells him about a "massage contractor" who beats "the daylights out of his customers." In an aside, Steed notes dryly, "But the therapeutic value to the patient is debatable."

The next sequence begins in Chelsea. A restaurant is the setting, again with an oddly tilted angle. A man is talking angrily into a telephone to a pretty young blonde at the other end, Marilin Weller (Dawn Beret), who is making excuses, saying she can't come because "he hasn't left." Suddenly, a hand reaches over from offscreen and disconnects the call. She looks to her right; the camera pulls back to reveal Sir Thomas Weller standing next to her.

So far, the episode has carefully laid out its main characters. Now it's time for the action. The scene dissolves to a tight shot on the boots of a cockney flower lady from whom Steed is buying a flower. It is the sort of stylistic touch that will become characteristic of Steed: he is on a job, but is still thinking about his appearance ("You're a gay old thing," comments an amused Keel).

Steed tells Keel that there is going to be a "demonstration" in the area. The scene shifts to a man ringing the bell of an apartment building; the camera zooms in on the address: "No. 27," and that action, along with the musical "sting" tells us that the address is significant. Nonetheless, the story is confusing, far too complex and deliberately paced for its own good.

The Deacon's men are seen discussing their job, which will take place at "No. 27." A policeman walks by on what is the most surrealistic street set this side of a Beckett play or *The Cabinet of Dr. Caligari* (1919), the German expressionist film. On another street corner, again dimly lit and obviously artificial (there is hardly an attempt at reality), Jeremy de Willoughby (Philip Gilbert), the man from The Deacon's photo, appears, followed by another man in a police uniform. Keel and Steed appear, and the latter confers with the officer.

The thugs are now putting nylon stockings over their heads in preparation for their job. Back at No. 27, de Willoughby is walking into a trap: the thugs attack, warning him to "stay away from the girl." Then, Steed and Keel arrive and make short work of the bad guys. One of them runs away; and then Steed suggests to Keel that they take de Willoughby and the remaining thug, Moxon, to the doctor's surgery.

The next sequence opens up in Keel's surgery. Steed, alone with

Moxon, ends his interrogation by pulling out a straight-edged razor blade. "What are you going to do with that?" asks Moxon. "Just give you a shave," replies the agent with a chilly smile.

Meanwhile, Keel is treating de Willoughby, who refuses to go to the police but won't say why. There is more oddly angled camerawork as the two have a conversation; de Willoughby gets dressed and looks at himself in the mirror. As he does so, he talks to Keel who is offscreen but seen in the mirror's reflection. Their conversation is interrupted by a strangled cry from the back room. Keel rushes in and Moxon is calling out, "Keep him away, he's bonkers!" Steed explains to the doctor that he's using "gentle psychology" to get answers, and then shows a flash of anger when he tells Keel that "we're literally at rock bottom in this case."

They soon find that de Willoughby has used the interruption as an opportunity to escape. Steed takes off after him. Keel returns to the back office and warns Moxon that without proper care of his "broken vertebrae" in his neck, he will die. Keel makes a bargain: he will get him to a properly equipped hospital if Moxon takes Keel to The Deacon.

The scene shifts to de Willoughby at the front door of his apartment. He is soon seen talking to Nigel (David Andrews) about de Willoughby's debts. De Willoughby is revealed to be a cad and bounder who only wants to marry Marilin Weller for her money (he refers to her as that "little slut"). Steed is listening outside.

Meanwhile, Keel has worked his way into The Deacon's secret lair. Once there, he menaces The Deacon and Moxon with a syringe supposedly filled with hydrochloric acid, which he threatens to squirt in The Deacon's face if he makes a false move. The Deacon reveals that his wealthy patron is Sir Thomas Weller. Keel and Steed confer on the phone and arrange to meet. On leaving, Keel is forced to squirt The Deacon, who tries to attack. By the time the villain realizes that the liquid is harmless, Keel has left.

In the taxi once again, Steed reprimands Keel for taking unnecessary risks. Keel says that Steed wanted the information, and now he has it. Replies Steed: "So Keels rush in where Steeds and angels fear to tread."

The next scene has The Deacon demanding payment from Sir Thomas, who refuses to pay. The Deacon threatens to get even, as he calmly sips some brandy. "Old brandies like this should never be drunk in haste," he remarks.

In the meantime, Steed has broken into The Deacon's headquarters and, joined by the police, lies in wait. Back at Weller's office, Keel has arrived and criticizes Sir Thomas for hiring The Deacon to beat up de

Willoughby. Sir Thomas becomes angry. As Keel leaves, he remarks, "You want a doctor's advice, you should watch your blood pressure."

De Willoughby is talking with Marilin. Sir Thomas is about to send her away, so she must see him. Meanwhile, de Willoughby is visited by Keel, who offers to help him and Marilin elope. Back at the butcher shop, The Deacon is telling Moxon that he plans to kill both Sir Thomas and Keel ("We have to make an example of Sir Thomas"), when Steed and the police jump out of the shadows and arrest them with the evidence of their crimes in hand. The sequence ends with Steed asking the parrot for advice on the races.

The final chapter finds Keel and de Willoughby at Keel's apartment. They are waiting for Steed, who is pretending to work for an escort service and will bring Marilin to the house. De Willoughby and Marilin are reunited. Keel brings in a bottle of wine. It is a short-lived reunion, however. A cockney woman arrives saying she is Jeremy's mother. He denies it but she describes a "childhood" scar on de Willoughby's left shoulder. When he is shown to have the scar, the girl leaves in tears, her lover exposed as not a nice upper class boy but a social-climbing bounder. Steed then tells de Willoughby to disappear and never approach Marilin again or Steed will reveal all the "dirt" he has gathered on him.

In the last scene, "mom" is revealed to be an actress employed by Steed and Keel ("Gone and never called me mother," she laughs); she knew about the scar because Keel had seen it when he treated de Willoughby. "Never was ten quid better earned," Keel says. Steed and the woman share a drink as she tells him, "I've known David for years."

"The Frighteners," typical of the first season, is an intricately plotted episode to be sure, but also fairly conventional, mixing a crime plot with something out of Victorian romances (the class-crossing bounder!). Talky and studio-bound, with only Macnee's Steed at all quirky, the series comes across as a stilted crime melodrama, nowhere near as original or stylish as what was being done on film with *Danger Man* or across the ocean in the U.S.

Without a major actor's strike that occurred in 1961, it may have just ended there. But the walkout went on for months, shutting down *The Avengers* after 26 videotaped episodes had been completed. When production was about to resume, Hendry announced that he would not be returning, hoping instead for a career in films. Macnee later admitted that he was devastated by the decision, insisting that Hendry was the reason for any success the series enjoyed.

But Newman was undaunted and decided to go ahead with an

unusual idea: replace Hendry with a woman. In doing that, he encountered a great deal of opposition from the corporate hierarchy, which felt that the public would not accept a woman as an equal to a man.

Leonard White wanted Honor Blackman for the part. In a scenario that paralleled W.S. Van Dyke's situation on the first *Thin Man* movie, White faced complaints from Newman and others who felt that Blackman was completely unsuitable for the part, since, until then, she had played vapid wives and a variety of other colorless characters. Newman argued that Blackman was saccharine and too genteel for the role. He wanted Nyree Dawn Porter.

"It is true that being a natural blonde — my very first cutting in any newspaper said, 'A peaches-and-cream complexion,' and all that kind of stuff— I was very typically British, which implied, I'm afraid in those days, not spunky," recalled Blackman recently. "So, yes, probably, it was a surprise [when they chose me]."[9]

The actress was ripe for a change of pace, primarily because she was becoming very frustrated by such typecasting. She felt that she had long ago been pigeonholed by producers like Newman and longed to do something different, something closer to who she was in real life. She was born in the East End of London in 1926 and, she noted, "though I didn't live there, my parents were both the nearest thing to cockneys, really. On my fifteenth birthday, my father said to me, 'Would you like a bicycle or would you like to learn to speak like a lady?' Because in those days, accents were important — over here, you know how class-conscious we are — and certain accents weren't acceptable. Now, you're more acceptable with an accent than speaking as I do. Anyway, I knew what my father wanted me to answer. So, I said I'd like elocution lessons.

"And I had the most marvelous teacher who was so inspiring and so lovely and she gave me scenes from plays and poetry to learn to practice my vowels on, as opposed to 'How now, brown cow,' and I got hooked and she thought I had talent, and I went to drama school and that's how the whole thing happened. It was really pure chance."[10]

The character Blackman would ultimately play in *The Avengers* was named Cathy Gale and was modeled on a number of women who had inspired Newman: the anthropologist Margaret Mead, Margaret Bourke-White, a well-known *Life* magazine photographer who took on dangerous assignments; his own wife; and a woman he had heard about in Kenya. According to Macnee, at the time of the Mau Mau insurrection in Kenya, Newman had "read of a redoubtable lady whose farm had been besieged by native insurgents."[11]

"What knocked me out was the woman," Newman later explained. "She was a well-set, once pretty woman of about forty, wearing slacks and a bush jacket. On her back was her baby in a papoose-like bag, but strapped around her waist was a bullet-studded belt with an enormous pistol in a holster. A baby beside a pistol!... She gave me the answer to the Hendry casting problem.... Why shouldn't Hendry's role be played by a woman, I thought. God knows, women were, in life, doing incredible things."[12]

That collection of strong-willed, forceful women was combined into Catherine Gale (gale force, get it?), a woman who had lost her husband and children in the Mau Mau rebellion. An anthropologist, Mrs. Gale gets involved when John Steed consults her.

"At the beginning, when I went to talk to them about it, Sydney Newman's first idea was to have somebody a little like Margaret Mead, the anthropologist," Blackman said. "Then he had this quaint idea that she should — I didn't know this till afterwards — that she should be somebody with a withered arm, which it would have been rather difficult to look for somebody like that, I would have thought."[13]

Honor Blackman as Mrs. Cathy Gale. The strong-willed, independent character was modeled on a number of women: the anthropologist Margaret Mead; Margaret Bourke-White, a well-known *Life* magazine photographer who went on dangerous assignments; the producer's wife; and a brave woman who fought in a revolution in Kenya.

Blackman and Macnee immediately hit it off. "One look at Honor and it was tricky concentrating on anything else," said Macnee. "Possessing a magnificent bust and the lithe hips of a boy scout, Honor was also blessed with an English rose complexion, superbly chiseled bones, and honey blonde hair."[14]

Because of his background, Macnee found it easy to get along with her. "I never thought about it," the actor said. "But growing up, all I knew were women. So when women — Honor Blackman used to take hours putting her make-up on, or Diana Rigg — it didn't faze me at all. I asked Honor Blackman when she went and played with Sean Connery in the Bond film [1964's *Goldfinger*], she said, 'Oh, he wouldn't let me get away with a thing.' Implying that I let her get away with almost everything, which I did."[15]

There were changes made in the series besides the addition of a female lead. Macnee was asked to alter his character. The producers felt that the flamboyant real-life Macnee was a great deal more interesting than the drab Steed. Newman asked Macnee to change his style of dress. "He knew me very well and was puzzled that I, a man of such extraordinary imagination, should opt to wear such boring clothes for my role as Steed," Macnee said in his autobiography. "What the devil did he mean? John Steed was more than a part to me, he was an extension of myself. And that 'self' had been shaped by eighteenth- and nineteenth-century influences.... My clothes were elegant but in such a conventional way as to make them thoroughly uninteresting. Steed's daring conduct had to be complemented by his clothes. I decided that Sydney was right."[16]

As the actor told *Avengers* historian Dave Rogers: "The character of John Steed was created purely as a name, as an opposite type to the rather steady doctor. At first, you never quite knew if he was good or evil. He was a shadowy sort of character who emerged through windows with a pistol and impeccable brolly.... I took the veneer of Bond for Steed, without using the core."[17]

The actor said he refused to lift any traits from the literary James Bond. "We were before the Bond films," he noted. "Somebody gave me a Bond book [at the time the series began] and said, 'I think this will help you with your character.' I read it and found it, as I always have, totally repulsive. Bond is a repulsive man. A sadist. He's completely upper-class, frightfully snobbish. He's exactly like Ian Fleming was. Ian died of drink and tobacco just like that, way before his time. No, Bond is totally reprehensible to me."[18]

Macnee, instead, decided to "dandify" the character, making him more eccentric than 007, a parody of the British gentleman spy as portrayed in Hitchcock's thrillers by Robert Donat in *The Thirty-Nine Steps* and Michael Redgrave in *The Lady Vanishes*. And, as with producer Leonard White's ideas for Cathy Gale, the actor took inspiration from real life and cinema in the creation of the new Steed, lifting fancy outfits from his memories of his father, the extra-polite manner of speaking from a military commander he had known, the slightly foppish attitude from both the Scarlet Pimpernel ("daringly snatching prisoners from the guillotine"); and "Ralph Richardson in *Q Planes* [1939], in which he played a man who carried a stick, wore a homburg hat, and was a Scotland Yard detective."[19]

He admitted that he also "thought of the Regency days — the most flamboyant, sartorially, for men — and I imagined Steed in waisted jackets and embroidered waistcoats ... the point about Steed was that he led a fantasy life — a hero dressed like a junior cabinet minister, an old Etonian whose most lethal weapon was the hallmark of the English gentleman — a furled umbrella."[20] Macnee was eventually nominated as one of the ten best dressed men in world, and Pierre Cardin and Hardy Amies invited him to join them in a partnership to design men's clothes.

Mrs. Gale's clothing was at the other extreme. If Steed was a man of the past, Cathy was the woman of the future. Most date *The Avengers*' initial success to the first episode in which Mrs. Gale appeared in a black leather outfit. Indeed, it is a memorable image: clad from head-to-toe in black leather which offset her blonde hair, Blackman set both men and women drooling. Noted Blackman at the time: "These clothes couldn't be more perfect for Cathy. I don't think I've ever had a professional wardrobe which has helped me capture the essence of a character so completely."[21]

The leather, Macnee recalled, "gave a charge to people, particularly when they saw it on Honor's soft, female frame. Lit and oiled, it can be a second skin, and hugely erotic. At the time, it was seen as something frightfully naughty ... we suggested bondage. We implied everything on that show, but mainly we used humor. Without humor, none of it would have worked."[22]

The costuming came about at Macnee's suggestion. In his autobiography, he recalled the advice given by an old "Etonian chum": "If the show continued to run, he suggested, a strong injection of black leather and more than a hint of sexual deviation would arouse a population still shackled by Victorian morality and hurtle *The Avengers* into the ratings.

For myself, the last thing I wanted was a series designed to appeal to every kink in the country, and I treated this suggestion as nothing more than the fantasies of another pervert."[23]

The leather costuming actually came about to solve a practical problem. Initially, there was a great deal of talk about how Mrs. Gale would fight. At first, the writers thought about giving her a pistol that she would carry in her handbag. That was awkward, however, since she had to stop the action to take out the gun. It was then decided that she would employ judo. The problem with that was that she either ripped her pants when throwing people or revealed her underwear when her skirt was blown up during a stunt. Leather was a master stroke, both practically and aesthetically. Practically, it meant no more rips. Aesthetically, it created a visual contrast between Steed, the 18th century man, and Mrs. Gale, the 21st century woman.

Their relationship was defined early on as one of mutual respect, tempered by Mrs. Gale's dislike of Steed's unscrupulous methods. She was the "know-it-all" to whom Steed came for assistance; he was the man with the mission. "To me the great secret of *The Avengers* is the knowledge that woman can not only keep it going with men but can top men, and can rescue men, and they can treat men as their friend and equal without emasculating them," Macnee said. "There's too much made of the male-masculine thing, I think."[24]

There was also an undercurrent of sexual tension that helped fuel the series' great popularity. "... we decided to put the partnership of the two characters upon a strictly formal basis," Macnee observed in his autobiography. "We would refer to each other as 'Mrs. Gale' and 'Steed.' Why did men and women always have to end up between the sheets? The bosses were appalled, once again. This kind of relationship would not be commercial.... Sydney and Leonard backed us to the hilt, insisting that Honor play a female version of Ian's role."[25]

In Blackman's view, the big question of whether or not she and Steed would ever sleep together — or even kiss — was a major element in *The Avengers'* popularity. If they had become lovers, she felt, the tension would have been lost. "I was a very proper person [as Mrs. Gale] and I was a widow, and he was always trying to make sexual advances, so I think if there's any suspicion, that's what it came from," Blackman said. "I think if you smell suspicion, that's what it was, because Mrs. Gale used to get very cross with him because of his advances. That was half the titillation. And you wondered if he would get her off her high horse, really. I think if they turned into lovers, it would have been lost. I did a

[TV] series here called *The Upper Hand* [in America, it was remade as the Tony Danza sitcom *Who's the Boss?*] and it was 'Will she? Won't she? Will they? Won't they?' And then they got married. And it died. It's pointless, isn't it? We all like the chase; we don't want to win. We might like to win, but it's not exciting for the viewer once we've overcome."[26]

But, the actress also noted that the well-adjusted Cathy Gale was in many respects pure fantasy: "No one could be so brainy and remote and physical and sexy and untouchable and wear leather and high boots and be perfectly normal as well."[27]

Initially, the series kept its focus on crime-related stories. White used leftover scripts from the Hendry period for the first set of shows, substituting Mrs. Gale for Dr. Keel. But when it came time to write new installments, the writers found it difficult to create dialogue for Cathy. Although she was meant to be the equal of Steed, her dialogue did not sound right.

"When we started, the writers were so unused to writing for a woman of intelligence who was the partner, so to speak, in a series, of a man and who didn't take a back seat and didn't run around at his direction," she recalled. "So they set about writing the sort of dialogue that the little woman at home or at the kitchen sink or whatever would say. And it was very frustrating and I and Patrick and Leonard, our producer, and the various directors we had, we spent our times saying, 'Oh, that's not right,' and I'd say, 'Oh, I'd never say that,' and Patrick would say, 'She'd never say that.' So we pulled it to pieces quite a lot and it was very frustrating. So I said, 'Just tell them to write it for a man. When I deliver it nobody will think it's male dialogue.'"[28]

As the series progressed, the more outlandish plots—episodes with an unusual twist or turn on the cliché—became the more popular ones. Steed and Mrs. Gale went from investigating blackmail rings and smugglers to exposing magicians who dealt in the occult and assassins who used a charm school as a cover. Cathy's black leather got her into a motorcycle gang, Steed's rarely seen superior operated out of a meat locker, and the series became more popular than ever.

"It was originally a very straightforward scene, on paper," explained director Jonathan Alwyn about a sequence in "The Outside-In Man." "We said, 'This is boring; Steed having to go to see this guy's secretary, whatever, and be ushered into the back room.' So we decided to change all that. I said, 'Why don't we call the secretary Miss Brisket and instead of him going through to his superior's office, we have him shown into the meat-hanging area?'"[29]

"Quite where the tongue-in-cheek came from, I don't know," added writer Richard Bates. "I think this was probably a series of accidents. Patrick Macnee had and still has a very strong sense of humor and a very good turn of dialogue. Once we'd become attuned to that, the writers and I were able to write very successfully for the Steed character in particular."[30]

The outlandish twist was becoming one of the calling cards of these early *Avengers*, which took visual cues from director Fritz Lang (*Metropolis*, 1927) and other German expressionist directors. The camera angles were carefully devised to hide the low-budget sets while the moody, noir lighting was devised to make the most of the videotape technology that limited the scope of the stories.

Just as important in the Blackman seasons were the fights. "I was warned that I might have to do judo," she recalled. "And I said, 'Well if that's so I'll have to be taught, because I don't know anything about it.'"[31] Blackman learned judo and was actually able to throw her opponents. Having a woman able to best a man in hand-to-hand combat added to the program's mystique and to Blackman's popularity. But it also led to a number of difficulties.

The producers wanted more fights. Yet judo is complicated to shoot because, outside of a person being thrown, not a great deal happens. To capture it properly, there had to be complicated camera setups. "Certainly, the judo was frightfully difficult because if you've got any sense you're doing judo on the mat," Blackman said. "But if you're doing it on the cement floor, I mean it is a nightmare and my spine can bear witness to that because they always used to include at least one stomach throw. You take hold of a guy's lapels, and you put your foot on his diaphragm, and you drop onto the floor on your bottom if you've got any sense, and then you roll over backwards. And when he's over your head not when he's on it, otherwise he lands on your head, then you get him over your head and then you kick. It's the only dramatic judo throw.

"Judo isn't exciting," she added. "Somebody has to use force on you in order for you to throw them. If they don't [actually] attack you, it's frightfully difficult. And that was one of my problems because you'd have awfully nice, kind actors … who would think, 'Oh I can't thrash her, and I won't do anything with force.' Some actually sagged as I got near them. It was like picking up a sack of potatoes! And they thought they were helping. It was a nightmare."[32]

Blackman recalled the most notorious fight, in which she actually knocked out a stunt man who also happened to be a professional wrestler named Jackie Pallo. "He was a very, very well-known wrestler, who was much better known after I finished with him. It was bad luck, really, because in the second year, the fights had become so popular that they wanted at least two of them in each episode. They tried to push in three but it really got too ridiculous because in the first year we only had five cameras altogether — and one was always on the credits, so there were only four cameras moving. That was the skill of the directors in those days. They had to work it all out who took which shot so that the cables didn't all get tangled up because you ran from one set to the next, changing your clothes as you went.

"With judo, because it isn't dramatic, you really had to have a camera on hands, on faces, and one on the legs, and one at long distance. It's sort of close-up, medium shot, long shot sort of thing. So they decided in the second year, which really surprised me, that they would shoot the fight the night before the transmission, which is all very clever but if I died or had been injured, we wouldn't have had a show.

"But still, when Jackie Pallo, this wrestler, who was lovely, I must say, we had this graveyard set up in the studio and there was a freshly dug grave in it and we have to have this fight and this last piece is I'm standing up on a little grassy knoll sort of thing, and he comes running around at sort of foot level, and I'm supposed to kick him away. And if you're decent, you put your foot on somebody's face and then kick. But on this particular occasion, it was the fifth time that we had started shooting it and the cameras didn't get the shot.

"This is the agony. We were exhausted. The camera didn't get whatever shot it wanted. Then you started again. Then Camera 3 didn't get it. So we started again. We were really knocked out. This was the fifth time. And after the kick, he runs around the grassy knoll and we fight for a shovel that's waiting by the grave. Then I let go of the shovel and he falls in the grave. He ran around the grassy knoll, and I went to go for the shovel and I remembered, 'I've got to kick him.' So I turned around and I booted him in the face. And, as I watched, his nose split open, his eyes went absolutely cross, and you could see he was unconscious, really. But he still managed to run around the thing. Honestly, actors are amazing. And we fought for this shovel and he fell back in the grave. I let go. And he was out for seven and a half minutes. I was walking around the grave sobbing, saying, 'I'll never fight again.' I was terrified."[33]

Such incidents were typical of live TV and added to the excitement of the show's early years. "The point is live television is live television,"

Macnee said. "I did that in New York in the fifties and you're not at your best, let's face it. You're sort of tentative, you're nervous.... When you have to do a series like *The Avengers* which, for four years was live, you really had to be on your toes. And I think if you're on your toes, your brain works better, and I think what I did show in that show for all those years was a brain and [that I was] a sort of alert person."[34]

"There were no retakes," Blackman added. "If somebody died in front of the camera, you stepped over them and took their lines. It really was a nightmare. I must say, that was one thing about Patrick. Sometimes, he used to wing it. And he would always, miraculously, get back to your cue. It was quite extraordinary. You'd think, 'Now where's he gone now? Will I ever be able to answer the sentences made?' And then he'd always come back to his cue. He was quite amazing like that. I'm a very solid performer. I like to know what I'm doing. And certainly if you're working with someone like Patrick who flies occasionally, it's as well that one of us is the substantial person."[35]

The Avengers, as it developed in the Macnee-Blackman years, was unique. It was a spy show in a time when spies were increasingly coming into vogue (the first James Bond movie, *Dr. No*, appeared in 1962), but it was also the first series to recognize what would become a major social issue of the 1960s: women's liberation. Bond treated women as sex objects, the *Playboy* magazine mentality in full flower. Steed, however, treated women as partners, as people to be appreciated and respected.

It was a crucial difference, and one which resonated with the public. Blackman recalled the response she got, both positive (from women) and negative (from many men, who, she thought, felt threatened). Blackman herself delighted in the role, since she had long been typecast. "I can't tell you how liberating it was," she said. "I mean I had gotten so bored [playing demure types]—actually I had just started playing murderesses and things—but I had had such a long haul in the sweet English rose department. It was a breath of fresh air coming to her and it was huge fun. What was lovely about it was that the applause one got from women—I mean the amount of fan mail there was that was 'Good on you,' 'Keep it up,' and 'Well done.'"[36]

She found a different sort of typecasting after she left *The Avengers*, in which she was offered more violent femme fatale roles, both on screen and on stage. "It took a while to grow out of that. But then if you make a success in anything, it always happens. I made a great success at that [sexy mother] character in *The Upper Hand*.... Since then, people have always tried to cast me as the glamorous, sexy, mother who misbehaves all the time. Indeed, I'm about to be one of those sorts of ladies again. It's quite extraordinary. They always do that in this profession. You play a nurse and before you can turn around, you're playing nurses forever, so on and so forth."[37]

Like *The Thin Man*, *The Avengers* in this period featured a pair of protagonists who bantered (slightly) while investigating crimes. However, Steed, unlike Nick Charles, was not a reluctant detective — he was actually the instigator, the Nora role — and it was Mrs. Gale who was the reluctant gumshoe, and, ironically, the smarter and more domineering of the two. "Honor's [Cathy Gale character] was slightly bossy," Macnee recalled. "She is [bossy] as an actress [too]. I love her dearly, but bossy is her middle name."[38]

Macnee said the flip-flopping of traditional roles was intentional. Steed was the reactor; Mrs. Gale, the one with the detailed knowledge of scientific issues. Steed is like a schoolboy, a playful gentleman with a hard edge beneath the surface, a silk suit covering a steely interior. "As it went on, and Patrick did his wonderful stuff of fighting with his umbrella and so on and never really giving anybody a thorough sock in the jaw," Blackman recalled. "And he spent his time saying [to me], 'Oh, darling, you'll hurt yourself, don't do that. Do what I do.' Really, in a way, I took over the male role. And Patrick was very balletic in his fighting."[39]

7

M-Appeal

"... Suddenly, it was a woman who had the capacity for doing everything that a man can do, and that's what made the character so extraordinary."

Diana Rigg[1]

"... the women were representative, in a comic strip sort of form, of women coming into their own. It was also very stylishly directed and the people who worked on it happened to be extraordinary. All those people contrived to make a show that was way ahead of its time..."

Patrick Macnee[2]

By 1966, *The Avengers* had a worldwide audience of over thirty million viewers in forty countries. Between 1961 and 1969, it spent a total of one-hundred-and-three weeks as one of the top twenty series in Britain, and in 1967, its peak year, it was the third most-watched program of the year, on the top ten chart for twenty-three weeks. And that success continued, unabated, into the 1990s, when the series was called the most profitable British export of all time.

The Avengers struck a chord in the way *The Thin Man* never did. While *The Thin Man* presented the character of an intelligent woman, Nora Charles was conventional in that she was still considered "the girl." For the first time, *The Avengers* showed that a woman could be equal, even superior, to a man.

"Actually, it did change women's attitudes to quite a degree in this country," said Honor Blackman. "Inasmuch as what had been depicted in television and movies before, the woman wasn't in the firing line, so to speak, and wasn't competent to be in the firing line, and suddenly it was proven that she was. And possibly more capable. And certainly more capable in the physical line, as well. Women had always taken a back seat. Let's face it, we didn't have women executives and so on and so forth [at the time]. Everything was male. They suddenly thought, 'Oh, well, I know it's just television, but it is possible.' They smelt liberty, I think, and freedom, and confidence from it."[3]

Added Macnee: "[In *The Avengers*,] one's attitude to women is not chauvinistic. It's always been sharing. Women, to me, are not women, but persons, and, consequently, we're all persons. The fact that we're the opposite sex just enables the race to continue and causes, hopefully, a lot of pleasure between both parties. But, basically, we all talk the same language and we all hopefully have the same aims in life. So we showed that in *The Avengers*."[4]

For men, too, the series made a difference. "Either men who were fairly confident were very attracted to it because they thought this is someone they'd really like to overpower, [or else there were men] who Cathy Gale made nervous," Blackman said. "I was called out to fights on occasion. I only got [involved in one] once, when I was drunk; I called a taxi driver out to fight. It was astonishing how some men felt so threatened. It was quite extraordinary. That rather proves the attitude that was alive in the country before that."[5]

Blackman dropped her own bombshell in 1964, when she announced that she was leaving the series to take on the part of Pussy Galore in the third James Bond film, *Goldfinger*. As he had when Hendry left, Macnee thought that it would mean the end of the series. Although many felt that Steed was the backbone of the show, Mrs. Gale seemed to be its main draw.

After a much-ballyhooed search, Blackman's initial replacement was Elizabeth Shepherd, a fragile beauty who ultimately did not fit into the series' format. One episode was actually completed using Shepherd ("The Town of No Return") and another begun ("The Murder Market") before the actress was dismissed and replaced by Diana Rigg, whom the producers had seen in an episode of *Armchair Theatre*.

Rigg was a relative novice to television but a veteran of the British stage. She had been born in Doncaster in July 1938. When her parents moved to India, Rigg went with them, living in Jodhpur near Bombay until she was seven. On returning to England, she took an interest in drama. At seventeen, she entered the Royal Academy of Dramatic Art in London and after a short period of modeling landed her first acting

Sean Connery and Honor Blackman in *Goldfinger,* the third James Bond film. Blackman traded on her fame as Cathy Gale in *The Avengers* to star as Pussy Galore, the most capable Bond heroine of all.

job in radio (she played a dentist's nurse and said, "The doctor will see you now"). She then appeared in the repertory production, *The Passing of the Third Floor* at the Civic Theater in Chesterfield, and joined the Royal Shakespeare Company at Stratford. Her first TV work was a comedy, "The Hothouse," on *Armchair Theater*.

She recalled that she tried out for *The Avengers* "simply as a joke really. I did a test, and two weeks later, I was suddenly making the filmed television series and I'd never done a film before, let alone a television series, or karate, or judo. So one's philosophy and attitude was, 'Let's get on with it — I'll learn as I go along.' So I did just that, more or less. The minute you stopped and thought, 'God, I can't do it,' that was fatal — absolutely fatal."[6]

Her new character was originally called Samantha, but later renamed Emma Peel (a play on the words man appeal: "m-appeal"). Like Mrs. Gale, the character was a widow. She was also of independent means and, initially, had an affinity for leather outfits (she eventually switched to cloth jumpsuits, dubbed her "Emmapeelers").

Some of the upper echelon at the production company worried about Rigg at first — she would be replacing the popular Blackman, after all — but Macnee was confident and later recalled that he hit it off with the younger thespian immediately: "... the two of us not only enjoyed an instant rapport, but shared a similar mischievous sense of humor."[7]

Rigg's approach to the character was different from that of her predecessor. Whereas Blackman was a moralistic know-it-all, slightly suspicious of Steed and certainly disapproving of his methods, Rigg's Emma Peel was equally opportunistic (she breaks into cars and safes with the devil-may-care abandon of Steed), and displayed her superior knowledge without ostentation.

Rigg also brought a different kind of sexual energy: a playful quality that was lacking in Blackman. The characters may or may not have slept (or been sleeping) together, but with Rigg's character, it was not an impossibility. "We took the sex relationship for granted," Macnee admitted. "By the mid-sixties, the pill was part of life, so it was accepted that Emma and Steed slept together, but we simply didn't dwell on it. Because we didn't have to bother about sex, we could get on with the plot."[8] Certainly, she enjoyed Steed — and saw him in off-hours, at parties and dinner dates, on her birthday — in a way that Mrs. Gale never seemed to.

Macnee explained the chemistry once, in phrases that echoed what

Diana Rigg as Emma Peel in the leather outfit she wore in her first year on *The Avengers*. The character's name came from the phrase "man appeal" (m-appeal).

Myrna Loy had said about her working relationship with William Powell: "When Diana came in she was only 28, but she had this total, complete technical comedic style and sparkle, surety, and assurance. In fact, she was so good that it sharpened, in a sense, my own comedy style which was there, but dormant.... We, and I say we advisedly, took perfectly straight situations and made them slightly ludicrous. You had to be slightly mad, but you also had to be basically cool. We tilted everything slightly, made it humorous, and it worked. Our teamwork was extraordinary — a working marriage in fact; it was that close."[9]

In truth, Rigg's entry brought the series to its peak. Macnee, and many critics, as well, felt that the black-and-white Macnee-Rigg season of 1965-66 was *The Avengers* at its best. The series took on an even more outrageous tone and was more tongue-in-cheek than ever. It also became more sophisticated and stylized, which was now possible because of a switch from videotape (and the slightly stilted, live-on-tape presentation) to film. (The conversion was made as a way to sell the series to the important American market.) Film allowed for higher production values, more outrageous plotting, and higher caliber directors. The program was also enhanced by the pop jazz scoring of Laurie Johnson, a composer who had most recently completed *Dr. Strangelove:*

Or How I Learned to Stop Worrying and Love the Bomb (1964), for director Stanley Kubrick.

Strangelove is a significant connection for other reasons, as well. It features black humor, is satirical, and depicts archetypes rather than real people. It is a dark comedy about the nuclear arms race, taking material that is played straight in *Fail Safe* (1964) and twisting it outrageously out of shape. The eccentric characters in Kubrick's movie—the wheelchair-bound mad scientist Strangelove, the crazy general Jack D. Ripper, the bomb-riding bombardier, "King" Kong—would be right at home in some later *Avengers* episodes.

The Avengers, which had started out as a fairly straight thriller with a few comic touches, became, with Rigg, even more absurd and surreal. Nonetheless, the change was gradual. In the first Emma Peel episode, "The Town of No Return" (shot with Shepherd and then reshot with Rigg), Steed comes across as playful, but as ruthless and deceitful as he had been in the Ian Hendry–Honor Blackman years. The pair investigate a puzzler straight out of Hitchcock or thriller writer John Le Carre: what's happened to the three agents who went to Little Bazzeley, a town by the sea? Once they arrive, they face a situation that could have come out of *Bad Day at Black Rock* (1954): hostile townspeople with a horrible secret.

The relationship depicted here between Steed and Mrs. Peel is more aggressive, more like the one Steed had with Mrs. Gale, and it is obvious that the writers are still defining the characters' relationship: she literally fences with him at the beginning (he cheats) and then tells him to get his own cream for his tea. But it is also more suggestive—when they are nose-to-nose in her room he says, "Isn't it time you were in bed? You have to be up early at school tomorrow?" Fade out.

By the time "You Have Just Been Murdered" was shot, nearly two years later, everything has changed. The story is absurdist to the hilt: it's all about a protection racket that targets millionaires. In one extended series of scenes, a frightened millionaire is cornered by a silent assassin, who then proceeds to "kill" him—using a retractable knife, an empty gun, etc.—showing how easy it would be to murder him. The story is simple, but nothing is treated very seriously. The villain talks to his victims over a TV monitor (welcoming them like a good talk show host); meanwhile, his name, which is Nathaniel Needle, points the way to the inevitable hideout inside—what else?—a haystack.

Similarly, in "A Funny Thing Happened On the Way to the Station," the killer whistles a wedding march before he shoots people ("Till death do us part"), parodying the whistling child murderer in *M* (1931) and his superior is a megalomaniac train ticket collector, of all things. (He: "I'm going to blow up your prime minister." Steed: "How do you know I voted for him?") There are clever plays on words ("Pop goes the diesel," says Steed when he learns of the plan to blow up the train), and some Bond-like puns ("Why are you hanging around?" asks Mrs. Peel when she sees Steed handcuffed to a steam pipe above his head). Everything is a romp, a far cry from the drug-dealing, gangland days of Ian Hendry as Dr. Keel.

Brian Clemens, who had written for the series since 1961 and became its associate producer in 1965, once talked about the series' format. "One of the supreme virtues of *The Avengers* is that no two episodes are alike, but in this concept there is a hidden vice. The average viewer, rightly or wrongly, has been conditioned to anticipate the unexpected; to expect the unfamiliar. So, in view of the versatility of our stories, we have to offer the viewer a certain rigidity of form, a story 'shape' that may be relied upon."[10]

What that usually involved was a "teaser" before the first commercial in which something odd happens: a man wakes up in his pajamas in a huge empty stadium, but hears the roar of a crowd ("The Fear Merchants"). Or, just as bizarrely, two men are seen sitting on a stoop in an idyllic-looking English village; they talk about the weather and don't seem to notice when two other men appear and one shoots the other. The villagers seem oblivious, and continue their talk: "Nice day, but it looks look rain" ("Murdersville").

After the teaser, the first scene brings in Steed and Mrs. Peel and sets up the plot with the first clues. Then, the pair — either individually or together — interview a series of bizarre suspects and or witnesses, who eventually end up dead, either moments before or moments after The Avengers arrive.

Steed or Mrs. Peel will infiltrate or encounter various oddball organizations along the way. In "What the Butler Saw," Steed joins a school for butlers (with motto, "Brighter, Better, More Beautiful Butling"); in "The Living Dead," Mrs. Peel meets members of two eccentric organizations (FOG — Friends of Ghosts, and SMOG — Scientific Measurement of Ghosts); in "Honey for the Prince," Steed signs up with QQF (Quite Quite Fantastic), an organization which allows people to live out their fantasies (shades of *Fantasy Island*!).

During the investigation, there are clues, eccentrics (an old soldier who insists on restaging the war in his garden, a man who simulates train travel in his home), and plenty of balletic fights. Finally, Mrs. Peel (often, but not always) is endangered, and Steed comes to the rescue. Clemens called this structure, the "shape" of a typical episode and noted: "Like a well-constructed building, to remove one part is to endanger the whole."[11]

He added: "I also required at least three high spots per story — action or an intriguing scene — an upfront teaser ... and then I'm ready to put the jigsaw together. In *The Avengers*, the story always comes first. I have written about half of all *The Avengers* stories. We start with a very basic idea, one that can be capsulated in a paragraph...."[12]

"For the [*New Avengers*] episode 'Target,' we started out with the writer Dennis Spooner saying to me that he would like to do a story where the episode begins with an agent phoning Steed saying, 'I am dead,' then falls dead in a phone box. The story about the agents' field-training ground with targets that were sabotaged to fire back deadly poison was expanded from that basic idea."[13]

Explained series writer Richard Bates: "Clemens and [Roger] Marshall were extremely adept and capable of writing a script — an excellent script — in a matter of days.... We tried to keep the basic story with its feet firmly on the ground, so that there was reality behind the exotica of the story. Once we had worked this out, we allowed it to flourish and nothing ordinary was allowed to be in the script. This gave all sorts of opportunities in design — whatever the story was about, it had to be something that would challenge the designer."[14]

The philosophy at play could be clearly seen in "The Danger Makers." In it, the team examines the strange death of a military officer, decorated for bravery, who dies while playing "chicken" on a motorcycle. The story involves another series device: the "club" or strange organization, and eccentric characters. This club, The Danger Makers, consists of military officers who feel that life has become too soft, and that there are too many "safety valves" in life. It is a precursor, of sorts, to a type of *X-Files* episode which will feature people addicted to something unusual — in this case, danger.

In addition, the episode showcases a classic *Avengers* gimmick, also a staple of the spy/thriller genre: a person has some crucial information but can't tell it to Steed over the phone; so he arranges to meet at a secluded spot after dark. Naturally, the informant is killed for his troubles moments before Steed arrives.

The episode also tests Mrs. Peel's mettle — another typical device — by putting her in a situation where, in order to join the club, she must walk a seesaw that could end up electrocuting her. It is a tribute to Rigg's acting abilities that she seems both cool and nervous in the sequence, and that, although we know her character is not in any real danger (it is a TV series, after all), she makes the viewer anxious.

The Macnee-Rigg series had even more followers, one of whom noted that "the most conventional things might suddenly reveal themselves to be miraculous ... [the program] shows us a world where the astonishing and the commonplace are indistinguishable."[15]

"Quick-Quick-Slow Death" is typical, following the pattern of what would become a formula later: a bizarre opening (in this case, a man in evening dress is found murdered in a baby's pram); a clue on the clothing leads the duo to a tuxedo store, and then the villains are one step ahead of the team for a good part of the story, murdering witnesses moments before they are about to reveal information to Steed and or Mrs. Peel. Most of the murders are extremely bizarre (a shoemaker has his face pushed into a plaster cast which is normally used for shoes), others are brutal: a tattoo designer is shot in the head after the murderer, face unseen, shows him the tattoo on his wrist (amazingly, even though he is shot — bloodlessly — in the head, the victim is still able to scrawl a message as to the killer's identity on a roll of salami, itself a parody of the standard mystery movie gimmick).

The trail leads to a dance studio, where Emma takes on a job as a dancing instructor. Although the plot doesn't amount to much — it's inane, actually, with a foreign power substituting its agents for lonely bachelors who sign up at the dance studio — it is all carried over by the pace and style of the direction and script, and the wit and grace of the characters.

This sort of structure was beginning to be established in the Blackman years, but it took the Rigg series to perfect it. Nowhere can this be more clearly seen than in the Rigg episodes that reused plots from the Blackman seasons. The differences between the two are telling.

In "Death of a Great Dane," for instance, Steed and Mrs. Gale investigate a magician who pulled off a grand trick: eating a 50,000 pound (as in money) breakfast. The conjurer was in a road accident and x-rays reveal a stomach full of diamonds. The smuggler's trail leads to the Litoff Organization, an international corporation based in London, and the mysterious financier Gregor Litoff— never seen but whose presence is felt throughout the world.

This episode was remade as the much better "50,000 Pound Breakfast" in the last Rigg season. In the remake, the casting is superior and so are the murders, which are more stylishly done. In addition, Steed and Mrs. Peel have a more sophisticated line of banter than Steed and Mrs. Gale, and where things are only talked about in "Death" (such as Mrs. Gale's breaking into a suspect's car to examine some documents) in "Breakfast," it is actually shown.

The plot is the same, of course, although the narrative is handled with more panache in "Breakfast" (a butler's confessional speech to Steed is more twisted in the remake as he admits that his real motive for the crime is to be rude to "handsome women"). The chief villain is greatly improved, as well, transformed from a mustachioed smoothie with slicked-back hair into a sophisticated female executive. That's a clever move since it gives her character a greater raison d'être for her actions — sexual discrimination — and also adds a layer of sexual tension to her dialogue sparring matches with Steed.

Another Blackman episode, "The Charmers," finds Steed and Mrs. Gale investigating an organization that is killing secret agents from both East and West. During the inquiry, Steed encounters an organization set up on the surface to change "mere man into gentleman" (not always successful, although worth trying for, as Steed notes, "Half a loaf is better than low bred"). In reality, it is a murderous organization set on destroying both East and West (its motto is "Seek, Hate, Kill").

The plot was reused in the final Rigg season and retitled "The Correct Way to Kill." There is a clear difference in emphasis between the two. The Blackman version certainly has absurd elements—the snob school exists in both—but it treats them gingerly, painting with a much less colorful hue. For instance, after Steed says she and a Russian spy will be working "cheek to jowl," Mrs. Peel, with a twinkle in her eye, responds that "his cheek will come nowhere near my jowl." Mrs. Gale, however, is morally indignant that Steed would suggest such an idea and the exact same line of dialogue ("His cheek will come nowhere near my jowl") is said angrily rather than mockingly. And, unlike her moralistic predecessor, Mrs. Peel is here shown to be just as devious as Steed; she breaks into a Russian's safe, even though they had just promised to work together.

Writer Brian Clemens has also improved on his original idea: in "The Charmers" Steed is partnered with an actress whom he thinks is a Russian agent; in "Kill," it is an actual agent, a Russian "Mrs. Peel," offering more room for heavy-handed parody of East-West relations. To paraphrase Hitchcock, the first version seems to be the work of a talented amateur, while the remake is by a top professional; the comedy is brought more to the forefront in the Rigg version.

By the Rigg seasons, the style of *The Avengers* had evolved on all levels, and "inversion" was a central concept. "We have always been fond of inverting the cliché," Clemens explained once. "Mother is a man, Father is a woman, the Sherlock Holmes character doesn't find clues, he plants them."[16]

Through inversion, the tired idea could become original, by allowing characters to comment on the conventions of which they are a part: in "The Danger Makers," for instance, the characters talk about the clichés of their genre: Mrs. Peel escapes her confinement so matter-of-factly that we don't even see it; she explains that she tied some sheets together and climbed out the window. Steed dismisses it as an old trick and she responds "originality" wasn't paramount. The cliché is made fresh by the offhand way it is discussed. Similarly, the characters comment on the absurdity of the plot they have just unraveled in the final scene, as Steed explains the complex chain of events that lead to the resolution, calling it a "simple" solution. Of course, it is anything but.

Clemens explained his strategy in creating and or supervising the scripts: "... I might start with a basic idea that has been done a million times before, only this time it's for *The Avengers*, so there has to be a new slant for it. Take the plague story, 'The Midas Touch' [in *The New Avengers*]. Every series has a plague story, but most of them, with slight variations, are identical. With that story, I conceived of a man who was a carrier of every disease known to mankind. But while he remained immune, a mere touch from 'Midas' and you expired from every disease in the medical book."[17]

Clemens added that "you could do anything as long as it had a certain style.... Emma Peel ... would climb up the outside of a building, across barbed wire, and get into this room to find that Steed was already there, because he'd used the key or found the door wasn't locked! That was the disparity between them and their approaches to the case. They solved it together, but in separate and quite diverse ways."[18]

Some have pointed out that the style comes from a long British tradition of surrealism. In the view of Grant Morrison, the series was influenced by "... the original Surrealist Movement of the 1920s [which itself had] picked up and developed a number of ideas which emerged out of the work of the prewar Futurists and Dadaists. One of the most important of these ideas involved the transformation of ordinary objects by placing them in extraordinary settings (Duchamp's urinal, Magritte's bowler-hatted men, etc.)."[19]

Morrison noted that English Surrealism contained an element of dark whimsy, going as far back as Lewis Carroll. "What was more unusual and, indeed, more radical," he asserted, "was the fact that here was surrealism taken out of the galleries and placed in the living rooms of millions of television viewers.... In the world of John Steed and his partners, country vicars nurtured secret dreams of conquering the world, stately homes were revealed to be Pandora's boxes of amok technology and children's board games could become the gigantic playgrounds of megalomaniac killers....

"It was even more appropriate that all this should occur at a time, in the 1960s, when people were beginning to use chemical means to affect their own transformation of the ordinary. In the series' heyday, the development of *The Avengers*' style ran almost parallel to ... the changes that were taking place in popular culture ... [It was] a funhouse mirror. Style was everything.... *The Avengers* offered a weekly distillation of the mood of the times."[20]

Some have also pointed out that the series' approach was influenced by what was known as the "pop culture" movement. In a 1960 letter, British artist Richard Hamilton defined pop as "popular, transient, expendable, low-cost, mass produced, young (aimed at youth), witty, sexy, gimmicky, glamorous, big business."[21]

As social historian David Buxton has noted, in pop literature, there was no attempt to depict people as three-dimensional figures to whom anyone could relate. Instead, heroes and villains were transformed into "archetypes representing various faces of 'human nature' but designed to double as fashion models.

"Pop rejects 'depth,'" Buxton observed, "the idea that the true meaning is hidden behind the surface appearance, a fundamental axiom of the television play constructed around the 'in-depth' exploration of character. For pop, 'psychological depth' (or 'deep problems') can only detract from the display of designed surfaces which are themselves rich in meaning."[22]

In his view, *The Avengers* "foregrounded the pop obsession with designed surfaces. *The Avengers* eliminates all trace of a human nature from its content. These features were an integral part of another style of series ... eschewing the 'realistic' illustration of human 'truths' in favor of 'glamour,' the image of conspicuous consumption.... This consumer orientation began to find favor with a younger, more urbanized audience, one that was more interesting to advertisers."[23]

If the heroes and villains were archetypes, so was the emphasis on the "Britishness" of the characters: critic Toby Miller is one of many who have commented on the manner in which the series plays on the American ideas of what it means to be English: "The landscape becomes literary, the class structure traditional, the city and the country heritage, and the industrial culture untouched. a purely historical engagement insists on freezing Britishness in a non-conflictual, racially unitary past."[24]

Writer Dennis Spooner noted that the producers were very conscious of this: "We showed England as the world thinks it is, and England as England would like it to be. It's true. If you go to America, they think of London either as it's described by Charles Dickens or by *The Avengers*. It's the shorthand of this world."[25]

Clemens admitted that part of the series' success was based on "its sheer Britishness.... It made no concessions to the mid–Atlantic, set out to please no particular group, and ended up pleasing all of them ... because it was created, lived in, and was true to its own world, it hardly dates at all."[26]

Clemens added: "I laid down certain ground rules—no women would be killed (although they could be bound and gagged and generally debased!). There would be no extras per se—everyone on screen would be a character. This was because our main characters, as outrageous as they were, would look ridiculous if placed alongside real, documentary-type people. Therefore, we never got involved in 'real' problems; there are no ethnics in the series, no blacks, no drug problems, no social problems. Ours was a fairy-tale world—the kind of Britain outsiders like to imagine it is, even if it is not."[27]

In "The Correct Way to Kill," for example, the Russians are seen as heavy, serious, blunt; but the British — even the villains—are stylish, polite, and exhibit a dry sense of humor and sense of fair play. The story, which was directed by Charles Crichton, who helmed many Ealing comedies and also *A Fish Called Wanda*, opens with a pair of proper Englishmen who only murder someone after they have been properly introduced. The Brits are as good at swordplay (it is, after all, the land of Robin Hood and King Arthur) as they are at wordplay (Noel Coward country, as well, you know). When, for instance, a character is bound and gagged with men's ties, the smoothly charming villain quips, "The binds of our old school tie fie well nigh impossible to break." And, in the end, Steed convinces his temporary partner, Olga, that there is something positive to be said for decadent, stylish British capitalism.

"The strange thing about the English character is that they understate everything," Macnee said. "It's considered bad form to comment on the food, money, romance, any of those things. So, you underplay it.... Whenever anyone asked me why I called the women 'Mrs.' or 'Miss,' I'd say, 'Well, one always does, doesn't one, until one gets to know them better....' Nobody ever knew if Steed and his partners were having an affair, because the English never look as though they are having an affair. They may show something by the way that they look at each other, by what they say to each other, by the way they touch each other, but not by what they're feeling, ever."[28]

Steed's interplay and acceptance of the eccentric characters and the eccentric forms of death was also very, very British. Said Macnee: "... I was brought up surrounded by a lot of strange women, and this made me the ideal man to make a series with these *women*, because nothing they did surprised me. The most important aspect of the way I played Steed was in *reaction*, not action....

"... my *reaction* to the many crazy characters in *The Avengers* set them off into more and more outrageous excitement, because I didn't impinge on their territory — I didn't stop them from pursuing their own devices. I was able to *listen* to what their madness or their eccentricity provided.... That was the trick of the way we played the show. I was the straight man to the women's role of activator. That's what made the show so entertaining, because you expected me, the man, to make the decisions and I didn't. The women did."[29]

The choices were all quite intentional, from the highly stylized look of the characters' clothing — Steed and Mrs. Peel have about six or seven different outfits each per episode — to other design elements. In "The Hidden Tiger," for example, the episode introduces an organization known as PURR, a haven for cat fanciers. Its headquarters is filled with cat images: huge sculptures, signs and small figures.

Such bizarre visual touches became synonymous with the series. Said art director Bob Jones: "*The Avengers* needed a very special mental approach. Writers would say, 'This guy's a solicitor. Let's make him a collector of top hats. Not one, hundreds of 'em.' A train enthusiast might live underground in a disused tube station. A bank manager couldn't be just an ordinary bank manager; we'd have him riding along the corridor to his office on a penny-farthing bicycle."[30]

In addition, the "pop" approach of *The Avengers* managed to elevate the thriller — long considered a form of escapist entertainment and, to some extent, a lowbrow diversion — into a form of sophisticated art. As Buxton noted: "An enormous shift has taken place. Psychological identification with characters on the basis of commonly established moral criteria is here dismissed as 'unsophisticated.' Previously, 'unrealistic' protagonists like Bulldog Drummond, Fu Manchu, and The Saint had a less than cerebral reputation, to put it mildly. The pop gaze establishes a new regime of truth for the television series, no longer based — however inadequately — on the 'outside world' but on the higher reality of design. Once dismissed as 'escapist,' this new reality was now valorized as 'sophisticated'."[31]

"The Winged Avenger," for example, shows how surreal the whole enterprise could become, stepping over the thin line between fantasy and reality. The plot has a ruthless executive murdered, in a locked room, on the top floor of a skyscraper. The only clues are his shredded clothes and the horrible claw marks that cover his (bloodless) body. Unlike normal detectives, however, Steed and Mrs. Peel conduct no scientific tests and simply wait for clues to fall into their laps. One of those is a mountain climber who leads them to a wacky scientist who has invented magnetic boots which allow people to walk up walls. The climax does not even try to disguise itself as reality: Steed sees the future in comic book sketches made by the killer, a demented cartoonist who has brought his creation, The Winged Avenger, to life as an instrument of vengeance.

This episode demonstrates the dramatic tension of much of the series. As Steve Chibnall pointed out, the danger to society "generally comes from one of two directions: on the one hand, a rearguard refusal of modern technology by diehard reactionaries (retired colonels, fin de race aristocrats); on the other hand, from lunatic scientists who want to extend machine principles to human beings. The nodal point around which the series' oppositions are organized is the very ideal of modernity: its acceptable dose — not too little, not too much — lies in the median ground between the two extremes, personified in the pure friendship between Steed and Emma Peel ... the proof that traditional and modern values can co-exist in a pure complicity."[32]

Indeed, if anything gives the series its popularity, it is the relationship between Steed and Mrs. Peel. Although he is describing Nora Charles, Myrna Loy biographer Lawrence J. Quirk could also be describing Emma Peel: "[She] liked men, especially her man, and was affectionately tolerant of male foibles. She accepted male chauvinism good-naturedly, with a gentle irony, resilience, and charm. She laughed at and with him. She was his good companion in adventure, savoring it with a zest equal to his. She tried to be helpful when required. She was more interested in loving a man than in working him for her own advantage. Nor did the sex war have any appeal for her. She could be a pal, a

7. M-Appeal 95

Patrick Macnee and Diana Rigg in a publicity still for the first color season of *The Avengers*. The characters are as stylized as their clothing.

co-conspirator, lover; she could be motherly or sexy, domestic or nightclubby. Chic, sleek, intelligent, perceptive, she matched a man's moods with complementary moods of her own."[33]

Consciously or unconsciously, the series — at least in its relationship between its heroes — took on more of the sophisticated bantering that was typical of Nick and Nora Charles in *The Thin Man*, a fact that has been infrequently noted by critics. Recalled Macnee: "We deliberately set out to contrive new and different ways of playing two-handed scenes for comedy. We put Emma and Steed in routine situations, like having a meal or playing a game of chess. Then, while serving the soup, we would casually discuss some mastermind's ploy to rule the world."[34]

Like Nora, Emma is intelligent, good-looking (and, incidentally, auburn-haired like Loy), witty, and attracted to her male partner. Also like Nora, Emma is admiring of her partner's abilities and personality. Unlike Nora, however (and Macnee's comments notwithstanding), it is unclear whether Emma has slept with Steed. Also unlike Nora, she is much more capable of taking care of herself mentally and physically: she has scientific know-how and is a whiz at throwing people over her shoulder.

Like Powell and Loy, actors Macnee and Rigg were instantly in sync: "... I drove her [Rigg] up to Norfolk, to refilm scenes for the aborted Beth Shepherd episode," Macnee recalled. "We drove there in my newly acquired Jaguar saloon. We discovered then that we had very much the same sense of humor and I quickly developed a great fondness for her. We hit it off right away, without saying anything but simply by being in each other's company. I'd reached out to her and she touched me with kindness and companionship."[35]

Toby Miller felt that the series was groundbreaking for a very basic reason: "... Just as *The Thin Man* saga stands out for its marital explorations alongside Hollywood's concentration on forming the couple, *The Avengers* is remarkable for its focus on day-to-day wisecracking of man and woman. Sexual tension suffuses a relationship that is neither fully collegial nor straightforwardly amicable. They are not quite lovers and not quite co-workers."[36]

In fact, part of the appeal of *The Avengers* then and now is in its reflection and refraction of current trends. In the sixties — in the hip, pop world — to be cool was to treat sexual encounters lightly. Buxton observed that sex, which had long been a taboo subject in popular arts — Nick and Nora Charles, though married, still had to sleep in separate beds — was now becoming legitimate.

"The threat to society," Buxton noted, "comes from those who put ambition and greed ahead of pleasure: the figure of the (impotent) scientist who is too involved in his projects to have cultivated the simplest social graces was a common trope in the 1960s, as was that of the unattractive, physically ambiguous and ambitious woman professional.... Deriving pleasure from object-commodities (which potentially includes people) is highly legitimate; manipulating objects for purposes of social climbing or doctrine highly illegitimate."[37]

Even more simply, *The Avengers* tapped into a childhood dream that, in the words of one fan, "you and your best friend (of whichever sex) [can solve] fun mysteries without a chance of getting hurt, physically or emotionally. Nobody gives them orders, they don't seem to need wages, and they are the wittiest, most beautiful people in the world."[38]

8

Trust No One

"When man entered the atomic age, he opened a door to a new world. What we'll eventually find in that new world, nobody can predict."

Dr. Medford (Edmund Gwenn) in Them!

A pair of New Mexico state troopers (James Whitmore and Chris Drake) finds a four- or five-year-old girl (Sandy Descher), wandering alone in the desert in her pajamas. She doesn't speak, but simply stares ahead, glassy-eyed. Further investigation uncovers a wrecked trailer, torn apart as though made of paper. The clues don't add up: no money was taken, but the sugar cupboard has been smashed and the contents stolen. And then there is that strange footprint in the sand—neither man nor animal. The troopers investigate further and find more signs of havoc a few miles away—amidst the rubble that was a grocery store, they discover the corpse of the owner, who apparently shot off four rounds of his shotgun before it was bent out of shape. One more oddity turns up at an autopsy: the corpse is filled with formic acid.

The FBI is soon on the case: a trained investigator and a female doctor—but this pair isn't FBI agents Fox Mulder and Dana Scully, heroes of *The X-Files*. It is FBI agent Bob Graham (James Arness) and Dr. Patricia Medford (Joan Weldon). That's because this may sound like a case on *The X-Files*, but is actually the scenario to *Them!* (1954), the first of the nuclear radiation/"big bug" movies of the 1950s.

When *The X-Files* first appeared in 1993, its "aliens are here" scenarios, pervasive paranoia about the government, and weekly dose of monsters, mystery, and mayhem seemed fresh and unusual. Like *The*

An FBI agent (James Arness) and a scientist (Joan Weldon) face a fearsome threat in *Them!* It's not *The X-Files*, but a precursor to the series.

Thin Man and *The Avengers* before it, however, the series only seemed new because it mixed and matched genres, styles, and ideas of the past and then reformulated them into a unique identity of its own.

The two most memorable catchphrases of *The X-Files* are "The Truth Is Out There" and "Trust No One" and the series itself is an exercise in an almost religious disbelief of much that is scientific and rational. In that, the series is following a long tradition going back to the ancient Greeks and their mercurial gods and goddesses, who had been devised as a way of explaining the whimsies of nature. In more modern times, legends of werewolves and vampires were employed for similar reasons. As Walter Kendrick noted in his book, *The Thrill of Fear*, the concept of vampirism makes "the horror of death and dying ... safe; it is turned into a celebration of being permanently alive, forever immune to decay."[1]

Vampires themselves are part of a long literary tradition (*The Vampyre*, 1819; *Varney the Vampire*, 1847) in which eroticism is closely associated with horror. In choosing vampirism, Dracula's creator, Bram

Stoker, was also tapping into myths that had held power for centuries as explanations for plagues and other illnesses. In the Victorian era, when Stoker was writing, the idea of vampires took on other meanings, as well.

"To enter the castle of Dracula is to enter the Victorian mind, upstairs and downstairs, with all its sexual contradictions and complexities, hidden rooms, and closeted skeletons," noted David J. Skal in *Hollywood Gothic*. "... *Dracula* read today is first and foremost the sexual fever-dream of a middle-class Victorian man, a frightened-dialogue between demonism and desire."[2]

Indeed, a movie such as *Horror of Dracula* (1957) explicitly lays out what was implicit in Stoker's Victorian novel: the danger of giving in to sexual desires. It also offers blood-drenched chases, a wild fist-fight, and spectacular effects, including an ending in which the vampire, forced into the rising sun, explodes into dust. Critics may have been appalled ("This film disgusts the mind and repels the senses," said one[3]), but the movie made a mint by tapping into a wellspring of deeply unconscious fears and fantasies.

By the sixties and seventies, however, horror was transforming itself. The vampire, for instance, was now shown as an angst-ridden character cursed by a compulsive disease, like alcoholism. Television soap opera *Dark Shadows* (1966–71) transformed the undead sinner into near-saint, depicting its popular vampire star Barnabas Collins (Jonathan Frid) as a heroic figure, separated by his disease from the woman he loved.

Others followed suit. In *Blacula* (1973), a centuries-old black vampire (William Marshall) is a noble figure, searching for love and carrying an incurable disease that forces him to kill or die. Such problems took on new meaning in the age of AIDS, and also in movies like *The Hunger* (1983), in which vampires are seen as seductive but lonely outcasts, frightening but frightened of being alone.

Even Christopher Lee felt that Dracula had changed with the times. "I think he's a very sad person," observed the actor. "He's not a hero, but an anti-hero in many ways. He has a tremendous ferocity and power, but he doesn't always have it under control."[4]

By the time of *Bram Stoker's Dracula* (1992), the vampire had become almost a Byronic hero, a kind of fanged Romeo searching for his Juliet among the bloodless corpses he leaves in his wake. "Blood is ... the symbol of human passion, the source of all passion. I think this is the main subtext in our story," claimed director Francis Ford Coppola at the time. "We've tried to depict feelings so strong they can survive across the centuries, like Dracula's love of Mina/Elizabeth. The idea that love can conquer death, or worse than death — that she can actually give back to the vampire his lost soul."[5]

Devil or angel, Dracula and his horror film cousins hold an ambivalent, deep-rooted fascination for audiences. Indeed, who can ever forget the thrill and the fear at seeing Bela Lugosi's voluminous cape engulfing one sleeping woman after another in *Dracula* (1931)? Or feel the disgust and the excitement as Christopher Lee's bloody mouth rises from his willing victim in *Horror of Dracula*? Was there ever a nightmare more haunting than an attractive monster that attacks while you sleep? "Most monsters take and trample. Dracula alone seduces, courting before he kills," Skal noted.[6]

"Dracula is attractive precisely because he represents the dark side of our own natures," explained Leonard Wolf in *Bram Stoker's Dracula: The Film and The Legend*. "We live in an age that admires energy and power, and we know more about erotic fantasies than may be good for us."[7]

Horror movies hold other fascinations, as well. The terror of a Dracula or a Frankenstein monster is the terror of things unknown and unknowable, of the fears of dark corners of a closet that the child inside us never outgrows. But the monsters are palpably real in such movies as *Dracula* and *The Wolf Man* (1941). It is the more subtle monsters of the unconscious that hold an even deeper grip, and they started to appear with the movies produced by Val Lewton for RKO in the forties. In Lewton's films, the horror lies under the surface, in the dark, waiting to spring out. Although the truth is out there, often it is not a scientific truth but one that depends on a belief in the magical, the mystical, and the mysterious. Women may or may not turn into panthers, as posited in *Cat People* (1942), but something or someone has been out stalking young women and seems capable of killing.

"To show that, unconsciously, we all live in fear — that is genuine horror," said *Cat People* director Jacques Tourneur. "Many people today are constantly prey to a kind of fear they don't wish to analyze. When the audience, sitting in a darkened room, recognizes its own insecurity in that of the characters in the film, then you can show unbelievable situations in the certain knowledge that the audience will follow you."[8]

The Lewton-produced horror "films hark back to the emotions of evil and sexuality common in German silent films, but [examine] them from a psychological, rather than a mythic, perspective," observed film historian Phil Hardy. "Tourneur opted for a camera style in which all his scenes have visible light sources, all the shadows have *real* origins, whether just out of the frame or in the minds of the characters."[9]

Cat People set the standard. It is a low-key thriller with Simone Simon as Irena, a woman who comes to believe she has the ability to change into a deadly panther. The movie is a personification of the terrors of the unconscious, as jealousy and hate eventually turn the sweet Irena into an obsessed killer who destroys her enemies. As is the case in the vampire or werewolf genre, the real horror is that she is driven to kill by powers beyond her control, by a curse for which there is no cure.

"Well understanding the power of suggestion, Lewton insisted on precedence being given to imagined rather than real horrors throughout the series. In a sense the whole film is predicated on suggestion," Hardy said. "... The audience's sense of apprehension is given an agonizing turn of the screw by Lewton's knack of fleshing out his own phobias (in this case his fear of cats) with the traumas of others."[10]

In many cases, the mood was more important than the story itself. In the Lewton-produced *The Seventh Victim* (1943), directed by Mark Robson, a young woman (Kim Hunter) searches for her sister and comes across a cult of New York City devil worshipers. That's it. No earth-shaking plot; no horrifying, blood-sucking demons, just a great deal of eerie lighting, mysterious goings-on, and a sense of dread, foreboding, and paranoia. "There is a psychic need to unleash evil on the world," observes Dr. Judd (Tom Conway), a character in both *Cat People* and *The Seventh Victim*, in a statement that could just as easily have been made by Fox Mulder.

The Lewton movies are clear inspirations for key elements of *The X-Files*: there are the legends (in almost every one of the films, a haunting myth is related as a background explanation for events); there is the belief in the supernatural over the rational; and, finally and technically, there is a subtle sense of horror created through editing, lighting effects, sound (or lack thereof), and music.

Such techniques are also employed in Peter Weir's *Picnic at Hanging Rock* (1975), an intriguing tale and precursor to many of the issues and stylistic mannerisms of *The X-Files*. The movie, disturbing in its simplicity, is about a St. Valentine's Day picnic in which three school girls and their teacher disappear under mysterious circumstances. It is purportedly based on a true story about an outing in the Australian outback in 1900 and is a mystery without a solution. As one character puts it, "There are some questions which got answers, and some which haven't."

Picnic often plays like an *X-File* investigation without Mulder and Scully. The girls disappear at the rock, and there are signs, as Mulder might say, of an alien abduction (all the watches stop at noon; one of the girls is eventually returned, unharmed, except that her corset is missing and her fingernails and hands are badly bruised). Other evidence is equally bizarre: the teacher who disappeared was seen moments before the girls vanished, walking rapidly up the hill in her pantaloons (without her skirt).

What does it all mean? We are never told, although there are intriguing hints: one of the girls is compared to an angel and even makes an ambiguous comment to her friend on the day she disappears, "I won't be with you much longer" (is that because term is ending or because she has a premonition of her own disappearance?).

The tale is told in a spare, deliberately paced style, and, like Lewton's movies before and *The X-Files* after, horror is suggested by subtle touches: music (a haunting flute solo), silence, and subtle signs of nature disturbed (birds taking flight). Nothing is actually seen, yet the viewer is made to feel dread, even terror. We see the girls go off, in a zombie-like state, after removing their stockings and shoes. We see a young man struggle against some power that won't allow him to go where the girls went. And questions keep cropping up. Why does the headmistress say that a student went away with her guardian when she hadn't? (She turns up, in the penultimate image, dead, an apparent suicide.)

In the end, we see the effect of this "abduction" on everyone involved with the "abductees," as the lack of knowledge destroys those who are guided by the rational. The truth may be out there, but no concrete answers are clearly offered (another technique that *The X-Files* appropriated).

Running hand-in-hand with such horror is a sense of paranoia, which began with the big bug/alien invasion genre of the 1950s. The scenarios of these horror/sci-fi thrillers generally follow a formula: something strange occurs—a person disappears, is killed (in a bizarre manner), or is somehow traumatized. The authorities can't (or won't) explain it. Enter the hero, who offers an alternative explanation that somehow fits the facts but which is scientifically implausible (but not improbable).

Created in a period of widespread paranoia about Communist infiltration of government, such movies are thrillers with double meanings. Giant ants represent the atom bomb. Body snatchers represent communist spies, and so on. As film historians Chris Steinbrunner and Burt Goldblatt put it: "The late forties were a period of American paranoia, and many had difficulty adjusting to the first years of what was called the post-atomic age. The growing hysteria of 'the flying saucer menace' was symptomatic of a countrywide unrest over the achievements of science and the point to which it had brought us. The destruction of the world and the extraterrestrial invasion — two of the dominant motifs of the period — clearly demonstrated our anxiety over the increasing complexities of the times."[11]

For example, *Them!* is about giant ants, but it is really about the fear of nuclear annihilation. As Dr. Harold Medford (Edmund Gwenn) says in the climax, "When man entered the atomic age, he opened a door to a new world. What we'll eventually find in that new world, nobody can predict." The story is well-done and, initially, at least, low-key in its horror, taking a leaf from the Lewton scrapbook. Mysterious deaths in the desert seem to be the work of giant ants, mutants created from lingering radiation left over from a-bomb tests. But, until the end, the ants are rarely seen, and are much scarier because of that.

Atomic radiation is at the heart of *Gojira* (1954), or *Godzilla: King of Monsters* (1956) as it was known in the U.S. What makes the movie resonate, however, is its message: the atomic bomb can destroy us. After visiting Hiroshima in 1946, director Ishiro Honda had became fascinated by the threat of nuclear holocaust. "When I directed that film," he said once, "... there was a heavy atmosphere — a fear the Earth was already coming to an end. That became my basis."[12]

The idea was simple: a prehistoric monster from the deep has been mutated and awakened by hydrogen bomb tests. The name for the creature was "Gojira" (pronounced GO-dzee-la), which was a combination of the English word gorilla and the Japanese word for whale (kujira). The behemoth would stand 400 feet tall with incendiary, radioactive breath which could melt objects up to 500 feet away.

The special effects were well-done for the time, especially the charcoal gray two-piece rubber monster suit that was stuffed with bamboo and urethane foam. The actor inside could open and close the mouth, while the tail was manipulated by wires. Composer Akira Ifukube created Godzilla's distinctive roar by rubbing a leather glove across a contrabass and applying an echo to the recording.

As David Kalat pointed out in his critical history of the *Godzilla* series, "Honda saw an opportunity to make radiation visible ... [he] saw his monster as a narrative device to discuss the terror of the nuclear age. This intelligent, sensitive approach gave Toho's *Gojira* a depth few monster-on-the-loose films have."[13]

Set in Tokyo a mere eight years after the atomic bomb was dropped on Japanese cities, the movie has a sense of doom and foreboding—not unlike the tone of the Lewton pictures—that continues until the closing shot. Even the first sign of Godzilla in the opening sequence is like a bomb blast: a mysterious blinding light is followed by a firestorm of destruction.

The film takes a somber, documentary-like approach, focusing on characters and moral issues. The central figures are a paleontologist who believes Godzilla should be studied, not hunted; a bitter, war-scarred scientist who holds a terrible invention that could destroy the monster; and a young couple in love but torn apart by the horrors they are witnessing.

The reclusive scientist becomes the pivotal figure: a man of principle whose discovery could save humanity, but at a terrible cost. Using his invention could lead to a new and very deadly arms race, one of the issues of the story. The last speech in the movie is a grim warning. "I cannot believe we have destroyed the last of the Godzillas," laments a paleontologist. "If we continue H-bomb testing, other creatures like Godzilla will doubtless appear again somewhere in the world."

Science also runs amok in *The Quatermass Xperiment* (1956). Based on a BBC television drama and the first of a quartet of sci-fi films featuring the maverick scientist Quatermass, the movie (released in the U.S. as *The Creeping Unknown*) is a literate alien invasion/possession movie that, again, could be a blueprint for an *X-Files* episode. It is the story of the strange aftermath of a space flight that has gone awry. Impatient with government delays, Dr. Quatermass (Brian Donlevy) sends a rocketship with three astronauts into outer space. While out there, radio contact is broken and the ship returns to earth. But only one of the three astronauts remains on board, and he is hollow-eyed and stiff, able to repeat only two words, "Help me." No one can.

The astronaut is taken to the laboratory of Dr. Quatermass, who with his obsession for the truth and knowledge above all else might be a great-uncle of *The X-Files*' Fox Mulder. It turns out the astronaut brought back an alien life form that slowly consumes its host and then reproduces, becoming larger and larger as it transforms the former astronaut into a giant, fungus-like monstrosity that absorbs the life essence of all living things. If it is not stopped, it will eventually absorb the world.

As a hero, Quatermass is an unusual figure. Unlike the kindly and knowing Dr. Medford of *Them!*, he is a blunt and no-nonsense fanatic, almost impervious to human feelings and human suffering. He does have an instinct for self-preservation — he destroys the alien creature when it threatens to obliterate the world — but also does not hesitate to continue his experiments in space exploration once the monster is defeated.

Quatermass and the Pit (1967) finds Quatermass (this time played by Andrew Keir) as almost the lone voice of (mystical) reasoning in a world about to go bad. The plot involves the discovery of a mysterious cylinder in a London subway station. It may be a space vehicle from five million years ago, but it soon becomes very, very dangerous. The late inhabitants of the ship, in silhouette, look like man's pictures of the devil. Quatermass, as Mulder might, postulates that the image of Satan originated with these creatures. Things get bizarre when any human being who comes within range of the ship is overcome by an uncontrollable telekinetic power. Done with intelligence, this low-key horror film has a bang-up — if slightly implausible — finish.

The horror and science fiction movies of these eras are odd recipes, mixing horror elements with science fiction concepts, and then tossing in techniques from the detective/film noir genre: the heroes assemble extraordinary clues, trying to make sense of the nonsensical. In all of them, it is knowledge that is key to conquering the unknown. Whether it is the mystical knowledge of the vampire-hunter (he knows the right ways to ward off or kill vampires) or the empirical know-how of the ant expert (he knows how to stop the mutant bugs from breeding), to understand is to have power.

Increasingly, though, as times changed, knowledge itself became suspect, as the paranoia of such films became unhinged from its subtextual moorings, setting an entirely new genre adrift. *Quatermass II: Enemy from Space* (1957) had touched on anti-government paranoia in which aliens conspire with government officials to take over the world, but the paranoia thriller in its purest form flowered in the sixties and seventies.

Beginning with *The Manchurian Candidate* (1962) and carrying on in *The Ipcress File* (1965), *Mickey One* (1965), and *Seconds* (1966), the very question of identity became suspect. In these movies, it is impossible to trust anyone; even the idea of "self" is suspect.

Mickey One, directed by Arthur Penn, is perhaps the most unusual of this genre. Warren Beatty plays a nightclub comedian on the lam from a faceless syndicate. He assumes a new identity (using a Polish man's social security card he comes across; the last name — "Won ..." is unpronounceable, so he is christened "One"). The movie questions the concepts of trust, identity, fear, love, hate, power, and fame by using skewed camera angles, disorienting time frames, stylized performances, and a nameless, unseen villain. Mickey is the ultimate non-conformist; a man without an identity, frantic and formless, in a movie that crosses sixties counterculture hipness with elements of the French New Wave.

These ideas are also utilized in *The Prisoner* (1967), a British TV series, and *The Invaders* (1967-68), an American program about alien invaders taking over human bodies as a prelude to invasion. In both shows, paranoia is the norm: even your best friend may not be who he says he is.

The Prisoner finds a former secret agent (Patrick McGoohan) kidnapped and imprisoned in a seaside resort town known only as "The Village." Everyone has numbers instead of names, and the agent is rechristened Number Six. "The information in your head is valuable," The Village leader, Number Two (Guy Doleman), tells the new captive, and The Village authorities believe Number Six is a security risk. Number Six insists that his life is his own. "I will not be pushed, filed, stamped,

Number Six (Patrick McGoohan) runs for election in **The Prisoner**, one of the "paranoia TV series" that served as an indirect influence on **The X-Files**.

indexed, briefed, debriefed, or numbered," he asserts. It is the cry of the defiant individual in a dehumanized society.

The Prisoner, like *Picnic at Hanging Rock* and *The X-Files*, often leaves its meanings ambiguous. "Each person would look at it and I hope have a different interpretation of what it is supposed to be about," said McGoohan, who co-created the show. "That is the intention — to be left hanging somewhat and to lead people to say, 'Well, maybe this was intended.' But as long as they looked at it and thought about it and argued about it, that was the whole concept."[14]

In other words, the truth is out there — and to understand it, one has to question not only others, but oneself. And with the corruption of government in the Richard Nixon–Watergate scandals of the seventies, a new notion cropped up which would be pivotal in *The X-Files*: the idea of a shadow government of conspirators who secretly pulled the strings.

The Parallax View (1974), for instance, uses the John and Robert Kennedy and Martin Luther King assassinations as a starting off point for a theory about a shadowy organization, The Parallax Corporation, that traffics in political killings. The story focuses on an iconoclastic reporter, a guy called Joe (Warren Beatty) — an "ordinary Joe," get it? — who becomes suspicious when an old friend (Paula Prentiss) turns up dead. Although the coroner rules suicide — she was depressed and the cause of death is a mixture of barbiturates and alcohol — Joe thinks otherwise. Only weeks before, she had come to him in fear of her life. She, like Joe, was one of a dozen or so witnesses at the assassination three years before of a popular senator running for higher office. She had told Joe that six of the witnesses had died from "natural causes," including one 40-year-old man in good health who had a heart attack.

Although Joe had been skeptical, he now begins a relentless search for the truth. He discovers the Parallax Corporation, which uses a survey to recruit malcontents and psychopaths as assassins. Although it is never precisely explained how the company operates, it is enough that it is there, pulling the strings behind-the-scenes, controlling while letting people think that they are in control. At one point, Joe observes that it uses the government, corrupts the government, but is not *the* government, thus holding out some chance of change if people wake up. But it is a slim hope. Those who stand in opposition to it — Joe and his boss (Hume Cronyn), for instance — turn up dead, through "natural" causes or as patsies for an assassination. The movie feeds into the public perception of conspiracy theories and is ultimately pessimistic about anyone's chances to combat such a cabal.

The Parallax View's close cousin is *Three Days of the Condor* (1975), another paranoia thriller (also, coincidentally, co-scripted by *Parallax*'s author, Lorenzo Semple Jr.) Unlike *The Parallax View*, *Condor* says that it is not a rogue government operation operating outside the law; it is the government itself. The story opens with a branch of the CIA: a group of male and female file clerks are ruthlessly gunned down at their office. The only survivor is "Condor" (Robert Redford), whom we know is an iconoclast because he rides a bicycle to work, arrives 18 minutes late, and likes to read Dick Tracy comic books (he's also a tech head, knowing how to repair the hardware in his computer). When he goes out to lunch, his entire section — seven people — is murdered by Joubert (Max Von Sydow), a professional hit man whose loyalty is only to the highest bidder.

Like most of the movies in this genre, the story becomes a game of "trust you, trust you not" as Condor avoids hit men apparently sent from within the CIA and searches for an explanation. The movie cleverly trades on the uncertainties of everyday life. When Condor abducts a girl (Faye Dunaway) so he can use her car and hide out at her house (his own home not being safe), it soon evolves into a "relationship"; they make love and soon demonstrate all the trust and mistrust one encounters in the early stages of dating.

The twisty plot is complicated but always engrossing, with Joubert as the most philosophical of hit men (he could easily be a prototype for the villainous, cynical Cigarette-Smoking Man on *The X-Files*). He finds it simpler, he says about his job, to have no politics and no ideology. To him, it is not about whom you kill or whom you are loyal to but about when you get paid and how much. He is the politician as assassin, tailoring his beliefs to the needs of the moment. Redford's Condor is a resourceful innocent, seeking truth — and someone to trust — in a world spinning out of control.

Many of these paranoia thrillers share common elements besides the paranoia. Each involves a rebel figure who challenges the accepted order of things. Condor, Joe, Number Six — all are initially introduced as iconoclasts who do things their own way. That characteristic was grafted onto Fox Mulder in *The X-Files*, also a non-conformist within the ranks of the FBI.

Other staples include the shadow government operating outside the law; the friends who may be enemies (it is often unclear whose side Mulder's boss, Walter Skinner, is on); and the pervasive quest for the truth wherever it may lead, regardless of the consequences. The paranoia thrillers also have no ready answers. By their very nature, they are open-ended and sometimes inexplicable — *The Prisoner*'s concluding episodes are dense metaphorical exercises in the loss of individual freedoms — which add to their appeal, since they mirror the mysteries of life.

"The fifties was the decade in which anxiety, paranoia, and complacency marched hand in hand," noted Hardy. "On the threshold of space, man had discovered and used a force so frightening that it could mean the extinction of the species."[15]

Dracula, Lewton, Godzilla, big bugs, paranoia — put them all together and you have a recipe for *The X-Files*.

9

The Truth Is Out There

"There's no question that the key to *The X-Files* is not only that we have two terrific actors, but also terrific stories and scripts. Without those scripts, there wouldn't be a show. But on the other hand, if it's not properly executed, it could be a very cheesy-looking show. It could have fallen flat on its face. It could have been a joke."
— Bob Goodwin, co-executive producer, The X-Files[1]

Science fiction has been a hard sell on television. For many years, it was an industry axiom that the genre of the fantastic was not worth the money needed for the special effects and costumes. It was low-rated kid stuff. Early TV sci-fi seemed to bear that out, featuring Rod Brown of the Rocket Rangers and Captain Video in silly adventures on cheap sets. Such later entries as *Voyage to the Bottom of the Sea* and *Lost in Space* found their heroes battling gun-toting clowns and talking carrots. Serious work was to be found on *Playhouse 90* or *The Defenders*, not *Space Patrol*.

Things began changing in 1959, however, when Rod Serling, a veteran writer of such serious TV dramas as *Requiem for a Heavyweight*, turned to science fiction and fantasy writing for adults with the anthology series *The Twilight Zone*. *The Twilight Zone* was, more or less, sci-fi for grown-ups, or at least 18-year-olds of all ages. In 25 minutes, Serling or his writers (including Richard Matheson and Charles Beaumont) would tell a bizarre story, usually with an O. Henry-ish twist ending. Typical is "To Serve Man," in which seemingly friendly aliens come to earth, bringing a large book with them; its title is the first thing the humans translate: *To Serve Man*. After a number of earth people are taken to the alien's planet, though, someone translates the rest of the volume and discovers that *To Serve Man* is a cookbook!

The Twilight Zone featured a variety of plots, ranging from fantastic tales of the end of the world to whimsical stories about deals with the devil—and the series itself was influential. There were other fantasy-oriented anthologies like *Alfred Hitchcock Presents* (again, featuring the clever twist ending), *One Step Beyond* (supernatural stories that were supposedly fact-based), *Boris Karloff Presents Thriller* (horror stories, some quite terrifying like "Pigeons from Hell"), and *The Outer Limits* (science fiction). *The Outer Limits*, although hardly as successful as *The Twilight Zone* (it ran a year and a half to *Zone*'s five), was in some ways the better show, less rooted in fantasy and less dependent on surprise endings.

All of these series had two things in common: none were roaring successes and none featured continuing characters. In the late fifties and early sixties, westerns, cop shows, spy dramas, and comedies were the rage. Science fiction was still marginal.

The turning point came with *Star Trek*. Although it was never a Top 25 hit in its brief, three-year run on NBC (from 1966 to 1969), the series had a great influence. Created by ex-cop Gene Roddenberry, the show told the story of a spaceship crew in the 23rd century and was the first sci-fi series to feature regular characters facing adult dilemmas. The people were believable, the issues, thinly disguised parables about the times that were a-changing. It was both literate and thought-provoking, dealing with a wide range of issues that were often not addressed in prime time entertainment programming (Vietnam, race relations, state-sanctioned murder, sexism). *Star Trek*, like *The Twilight Zone* and *The Outer Limits*, used its sci-fi format to disguise controversial, thought-provoking morality plays. And in doing so, the series set the tone for many future programs by proving that fantastic television wasn't just for kids.

The series also blended a number of different genre elements—soap opera, western, action, and horror—in a concoction that was appealing to teenagers and adults alike. As such, the series reached a key demographic that advertisers would later want: the 18 to 35 year olds. Judged by later standards when networks valued a program not on its overall audience but on how well it played to this key group, *Star Trek* was a success.

Still, at the time its low ratings were considered another sign that sci-fi didn't play. Subsequent genre attempts only seemed to confirm that idea: a number of successful s.f. movies flopped as weekly TV series

(*Planet of the Apes*, *Logan's Run*), and others were only marginally sci-fi (*The Six Million Dollar Man* and *The Incredible Hulk* used fantastic premises for mundane melodramas).

But one other failed sci-fi show had a significant influence beyond its brief run: *Kolchak: The Night Stalker*. The 1974 series was based on a pair of highly rated horror/sci-fi TV-movies: *The Night Stalker* (1972) and *The Night Strangler* (1973). Both had starred Darren McGavin as an intrepid reporter who encountered supernatural and or paranormal goings-on. No one believed him, but he knew that the truth was out there — and was being suppressed by the authorities.

The Night Stalker, penned by *Twilight Zone* alum Richard Matheson, is about a vampire wandering the streets of Las Vegas. Although something allegorical could be made about a bloodsucker running wild in a city of sin, the movie is a straight-ahead thriller, with intrepid (some might say obnoxious) reporter Carl Kolchak (McGavin) hoping to turn the vampire story into his ticket back to big-time reporting in New York. Although the movie was well-received at the time, it is actually just a typical TV-movie of the era, with inept action sequences, poor pacing, and inane plotting.

Nonetheless, it and its sequel were huge ratings successes, proving that the mixture of horror and anti-government paranoia were a new and potent mixture on television. Naturally, a series soon followed. The series found Kolchak working in Chicago, still dreaming of the big time, but now a little less obnoxious. In "The Vampire," a typical episode, a bloodsucker from Las Vegas is loose in Los Angeles and Kolchak tricks his editor into sending him there. The action sequences are more adeptly handled than they are in the pilot movie, and the finale, with a burning cross on a hilltop, is vivid. There is a sense of "been there, done that," however: the closer Kolchak gets to the truth, the more the authorities want to shut him down. They simply do not believe, or else do not want the public to know.

"The Werewolf" finds Kolchak on a cruise ship where he accidentally runs into a werewolf. The episode highlights the main problem with the program's concept: the reporter doesn't seek out the monster, he just happens on it, which ultimately starts stretching the bounds of coincidence. It also follows the same formula as its predecessor: Kolchak is the only one who suspects the truth, the authorities threaten to shut him down, the evidence of the monster disappears (government conspiracy?), etc., etc., etc.

The Night Stalker died after only 20 episodes, but the series made a lasting impression on a young man named Chris Carter. "*The Night Stalker* ... scared the hell out of me when I was a kid. I loved that," said Carter, who was a teenager at the time Kolchak was running down bloodsuckers and other beasts.²

Born on October 13, 1957, and raised in Bellflower, California, at age 12 he took up surfing. But his primary interest was reporting and writing. He attended journalism school at Cal State University at Long Beach and then spent thirteen years working for *Surfer* magazine, five of them as editor. Carter began writing fiction at the urging of his girlfriend (later wife) Dori Pierson, a screenwriter who encouraged him to write for movies. The Walt Disney Studio's Jeffrey Katzenberg hired him in 1985 for a three-feature deal, but Carter instead started writing for television instead.

"I think the first eight or nine things I wrote for television got made," he recalled. "The result was that I started moving farther and farther away from the feature world, which is glacial in its speed compared to television.... Television was a chance to see my work up on the screen, see what worked, see what didn't. Most of the early stuff I did, the way it was approached, didn't work, and so I realized I would have to become a producer if I wanted to be happy with what I saw."³

By the time Carter had turned to screenwriting, science fiction on television — and in films — was on an upswing, thanks primarily to *Star Wars* (1977), which had broken box office records and studio expectations to become the highest-grossing picture of all time. Its story about a conflict a long time ago in a galaxy far, far away combined myth, fantasy, Flash Gordon–style thrills, and flashy effects to revive the genre.

Copycat films and TV entries followed, as did more adult-themed sci-fi entries. *Star Trek* was revived as a series of highly profitable big-screen adventures with the original cast and in 1987 it returned to broadcast TV as *Star Trek: The Next Generation*, which featured a new crew but even greater popularity than its predecessor (it ran for seven years).

The Next Generation's arrival was fortuitous for sci-fi/fantasy on TV in general, and Carter in particular. It was among the first series to bypass the old guard broadcast networks (CBS, NBC, and ABC) and be marketed directly to stations not affiliated with a network. Until then, these independents had typically not been offered high-quality original programming. The success of *Star Trek: The Next Generation* changed the playing field.

That series' success also gave Rupert Murdoch the confidence to launch a fourth network, consisting of some of those same stations. Murdoch, an Australian media baron, owned the Twentieth Century–Fox film and television studios and was itching to become a national player on the broadcast scene (he already owned a string of TV stations, newspapers, and magazines). With much fanfare, Murdoch began the Fox network in 1987. Its appeal initially was scattershot and lowbrow, its biggest hits being the foul-humored sitcom *Married ... with Children* and the reality series *Cops*.

Fox, unlike the established networks, was willing to take a chance on an unusual series. With less to lose and much to gain, it experimented with different formats. The timing could not have been better for Carter. He had been writing and producing TV series for a few years now and had gained a reputation as a creative writer and effective producer. In 1992, he signed a deal to develop a series for Fox. His first pitch was *The X-Files*.

"I was interested in doing something scary, like *The Night Stalker*," he recalled, noting that there was an absence of horror programming on television. "... I set out to develop my own show that was scary and smart and had what I felt were remedies to what I felt were the shortcomings of *The Night Stalker*. I remembered it had became a sort of monster-of-the-week series, and it was best when it was chasing vampires and no one would believe the main character, Carl Kolchak."[4]

Carter had also read a book called *Abduction: Human Encounters with Aliens*, by a Harvard University psychiatrist named John Mack. Mack concluded that there was some truth in alien abduction stories. "I found it fascinating to hear this," Carter recalled. "This man in the highest levels of academia and a scientist using rigorous scientific methods had come up with something quite astounding. So I thought it was a wonderful entry into an exploration of the paranormal."[5]

On the big screen, *The Silence of the Lambs* had just been both a commercial and critical hit, with Jodie Foster as a female FBI agent investigating horrific crimes. Carter had also recently seen a real FBI agent on TV's *Larry King Live* talking about a unit of the bureau that investigated ritual abuse and murder. Things began falling into place. "I came up with the characters of Mulder and Scully, the FBI, and this fictitious investigative unit called the X-Files," he noted.[6]

The show featured a man and a woman, two FBI agents named Fox Mulder and Dana Scully, who were assigned to a special division of the agency called "The X-Files" which looked into unexplained happenings. (Mulder was the maiden name of Carter's mother and Fox was the first name of someone Carter had known growing up; Scully was taken from L.A. Dodgers broadcaster Vin Scully).

The series, like *The Avengers* and *The Thin Man*, would be a genre-bending exercise in attracting as many people as possible by stretching the boundaries of what television could do. It would cannily mix the police procedural, as perfected in *Dragnet* and *Law and Order*, with horror and sci-fi elements and a strong mixture of film noirish visual effects. Its semi-documentary look (there were superimposed titles at the beginning of scenes, announcing locations, times, and dates) were a nod to the reality programming that was so popular at the time (*Unsolved Mysteries*, *Cops*), but also a clever dramatic move by Carter.

"To make it convincing, you make it believable," said the producer. "I felt that the characters and the investigative process had to be really believable, so I set out to do just that. Credible, believable characters and credible, believable situations dealing with incredible and unexplainable phenomena. I did as much research as I could through the FBI, and they were rather reluctant then. But I did research on all the things that I was writing about, aliens, UFOs, and the FBI just by reading about it."[7]

The X-Files would have two continuing characters but would be more like an anthology series in many ways, since the characters roamed the country, investigating strange crimes and other odd occurrences. "In a way, Mulder and Scully are tour guides to the postwar chaos that we're having to navigate," said executive producer/writer Howard Gordon. "The show is really about the power of the individual and the necessity of the individual in that context. It's a testament."[8]

To play Mulder, Carter cast David Duchovny, 32, a former teacher and up-and-coming actor who had appeared in *Twin Peaks* as a transvestite FBI agent and in the feature *Kalifornia* (1992). The latter was an intense psychological thriller about a writer (Duchovny) and his girlfriend (Michelle Forbes), who go on a cross-country car trip with a serial killer (Brad Pitt). They initially don't know that, of course: the idea is to get material for a book about serial killers by going to the sites of their serial killings to photograph/write about them. They pick up Early Grayce and his girlfriend Adele (Juliette Lewis) as a way to save on gas costs. After seeing the movie, it's clear why Carter chose Duchovny: his dry yet impassioned performance offers a prototype of his Mulder persona: questioning, slightly offbeat, attracted to the unusual, and intense. Carter recalled that he saw Mulder as "a romantic hero and the X-Files are the object of his romantic quest." His "wise-cracking" attitude, and character are "exactly like David."[9]

For Scully, the producer selected (over some objections from Fox),

9. *The Truth Is Out There*   117

Fox Mulder (David Duchovny) and Dana Scully (Gillian Anderson), the no-nonsense descendants of Nick and Nora Charles and John Steed and Emma Peel.

Gillian Anderson, a 24-year-old actress whose most significant credit up until that point was a Theater World Award for an off–Broadway play, *Absent Friends*. He was enthusiastic: "Gillian comes out with that intensity. That's why I hired her in the first place, because she brought a tremendous amount of intensity and seriousness to the role."[10]

In the pilot episode, agent Fox Mulder is introduced as an odd, obsessive outcast, known as "spooky" because of his strange obsessions. He's a brilliant psychologist great at turning out criminal profiles but he also believes in extraterrestrials. Dana Scully is presented as a skeptic who feels that science can explain everything. She is initially sent to spy on Mulder, but soon comes to trust him simply because she is also a searcher for truth.

In the pilot, the series' obsessions are seen in nascent form: Mulder's search for his missing, abducted sister is revealed, while the government conspiracy is hinted at by a strange figure who stands in the shadows and is seen hiding evidence in a secret pentagon vault (known throughout the program only as the "Cigarette-Smoking Man," or "Cancerman," because of his constant smoking).

The series proper begins with "Deep Throat." Scully is skeptical, Mulder eager to believe. He has evidence that there are strange goings-on at a military base that was one of the repositories—or so UFO lore goes—of pieces from a downed UFO at Roswell in 1947. Mulder suspects that the military is testing a jet that was made from study of the alien craft and that the effects of flying the planes is seen in the strange behavior of pilots on the base. The episode doesn't amount to much, story-wise, but is crucial for its tone and approach. In what would become typical for the show, nothing is resolved, nothing is proven except that the government is very good at mind control and in keeping secrets very secret (they practice a neat trick whereby they selectively erase portions of a person's memory).

The episode introduces a character called Deep Throat (named for the Watergate source, not the porn star), a shadowy government employee (played by Jerry Hardin) who will guide the team to new adventures in their first year (he is killed at the end of the season, and replaced by the mysterious "X" who also eventually gets bumped off). The government is depicted as capable of doing anything to protect its secrets.

Through it all, the appearance of reality was the key. "You can lay on the bullshit really thick if you lay on a good scientific foundation," Carter noted once. "The show's only as scary as it is believable. Everything has to take place within the realm of extreme possibility."[11]

The writers constantly based their scenarios on incidents they had read about in the newspapers, newsmagazines, or scientific journals. "The Erlenmeyer Flask," for example, took one idea (poisonous fumes from a hospital-bound injured man) from news headlines about a real-life incident that sickened an entire roomful of hospital personnel.

"If there's anything current or topical, I try to use it as an element inside of a bigger story," explained Carter. "You can make the connections, but they weren't the perfect connections. It wasn't like you might see in another show, where they exactly recreate the woman who's brought in and when they open her up, these fumes come out. I wanted this to be a little bit different, obviously. This guy's got alien blood in him. I wanted to speculate a little about what this might be."[12]

The time travel episode "Synchrony" was suggested by an article in the March 1994 *Scientific American*, "The Quantum Physics of Time Travel," while the main plot devices for "Demons" were lifted from *An*

Anthropologist on Mars, a book of short essays by writer-neurologist Oliver Sacks. The two-part story, "Tunguska" and "Terma," took its inspiration from an announcement by NASA that the space agency had found evidence of primitive life on Mars more than 3.6 billion years ago because they had discovered fossils of bacteria-like organisms inside ancient Martian rock that had fallen to earth. "After the news broke, I came in the next morning and said, 'Well, *X-Files!*'" said Frank Spotniz, a writer and producer on the series.[13]

Carter did not want the series to fall into the trap of having the agents chasing aliens every week, so he began varying the format with the third — and first really terrific — episode, "Squeeze." This one has a nifty plot: someone is killing people in locked rooms and removing livers with his bare hands. The only clue: a weird, elongated fingerprint that was found at a series of murders going back 90 years. The episode is, in many ways, a cross between *The Outer Limits* and *The Avengers*, with a little Dashiell Hammett detective work tossed in on the side.

The series eventually developed a pattern of alternating between the so-called "mythology" episodes and the stand-alone horror, mystery, suspense one-shots. The mythology installments, more popular with the fans, told the story of the grand government conspiracy that sought to cover up the existence of extraterrestrials. Over the first seven years of the series, various story arcs reveal more of the characters' histories, usually in (sometimes contradictory) dribs and drabs. There is a consortium of shadowy, international conspirators (who say things like, "We predict the future, and the best way to predict the future is to invent it"), whose chief agent and force for evil is the Cigarette-Smoking Man (William B. Davis). This group is apparently in a partnership with shape-shifting aliens to either block or ensure an invasion. This group of men seem to have links to the government, the CIA, and the military.

Along the way, Mulder's father — a former member of the consortium — is killed and it is hinted that the agent's real dad may be the Cigarette-Smoking Man. Scully's sister, too, is murdered; her father dies and comes to her in a dream; and she is abducted by aliens, the government, or both. She develops cancer and is cured. She becomes pregnant. Mulder disappears, kidnapped by aliens himself. And on and on and on ...

The mythology shows would generally follow a formula, of sorts: Mulder is given a hint or clue that some crime or incident was not what it seemed. He and Scully investigate and find an anomaly of some sort. They disagree about what it means; then Mulder or Scully find some

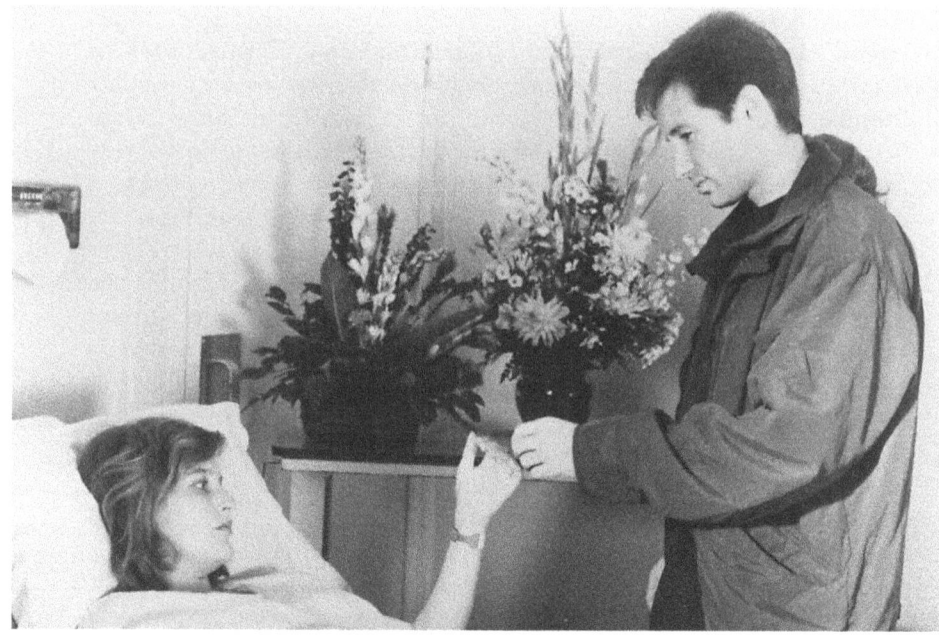

Mulder (David Duchovny) visits Scully (Gillian Anderson) after her bout with cancer: the characters have an emotional bond that goes beyond their professional relationship.

new evidence that confirms suspicious goings-on. Mulder will make an imaginative leap (he does this in the non-mythology shows, too), as in "Folie a Deux" where he hypothesizes: "Just bear with me for a moment. I mean, what if such a creature existed that could camouflage itself by clouding the minds of its victims. There are antecedents for it in nature, right? In the insect world. Mantids, for instance. They're said to be able to hypnotize their prey.... What if it could induce a visual hallucination? A sort of temporary conversion disorder?"

Then someone is threatened. An informant will appear out of the shadows and either egg them on or warn them off. More strange goings-on, usually involving eerie lighting and flashlight beams piercing through the darkness. Mulder and or Scully will see something unbelievable and get evidence — only to lose it by episode's end, with Mulder saying to Scully, "We were so close." The government conspiracy is seen destroying the evidence.

Formula or not, the series hit a nerve. "The show's original spirit has become kind of the spirit of the country — if not the world," Carter said. "There is a growing paranoia. With the Berlin Wall down, with the global nuclear threat gone, with Russia trying to be a market economy, there is a growing paranoia, because as somebody once said, there are no easy villains anymore. On their own, people are starting to say things like 'Trust No One,' 'The Truth Is Out There.' That the world is run by selfish people whose motives are selfish — and as we all buy into the money culture, it is only going to get worse. The truth is that this has been my philosophy from the beginning."[14]

The non-mythology-shows, while also being infused with paranoia, were less convoluted, usually with a clear-cut dilemma — catching a killer of some sort — and involved Mulder and Scully's attempts to track him/her/it down. "Ice," a semi-remake of Howard Hawks's *The Thing* (1951), is a good example of the best of those, taking paranoia to new levels, and through adversity, tightening the bonds between Scully and Mulder.

The installment opens with a terrifically bizarre opening: two men stalking each other, end up in a face-off, pistols pointing at each other's heads. Then, the two of them, almost simultaneously put the guns to their own heads and perform an act of double suicide. We learn later that the pair are research scientists in an arctic way station, drilling far beneath the earth's surface (the cliché of sci-fi thrillers, going where no one has gone before). Mulder and Scully are part of a team sent to investigate the loss of radio contact with the station. What they find there is something out of "Who Goes There?" the John Campbell short story which inspired *The Thing*: death, destruction, and a scenario in which the scientists all apparently killed each other and or themselves.

It soon becomes apparent why when a dog attacks Mulder and bites the pilot. It is infected with an alien organism, a worm that stimulates the violent centers of the brain. From then on, the series takes the paranoia built into the series' format to brilliant extremes: "Trust No One" becomes the watchword, as the rescue party members each suspect the other of being infected. Scary, moodily lit, and well-acted, the first season episode is the most perfectly realized up until this point, even working in some of Mulder's philosophical concerns about studying and preserving the alien life form rather than destroying it (also a concern of scientists in B-films of the fifties, who were generally overruled by their more practical military colleagues).

Both the mythology and stand-alone episodes share common elements besides Mulder, Scully, and the FBI: all are atmospherically lit and ingeniously executed (with excellent special effects); and all have, to some extent, open-ended stories. "The more you give away, the more light you shine on something, the less mysterious it becomes, and therefore the more you reveal the more you're sort of chipping away at what makes *The X-Files* great," explained series writer/producer Vince Gilligan, echoing the Val Lewton philosophy. "The less you show, the better. People's imaginations are better than anything you can completely give them."[15]

Indeed, from the beginning, Carter felt it was important to offer the possibility that there were dual explanations for the phenomena that the team encountered. He also believed, as Lewton did in his RKO horror films of the forties, that showing less was often more horrific because more was left to the audience's imagination.

The series eventually developed two different tones, as well, ranging from the darkly ominous and or heartfelt speeches of "Grotesque" and "One Breath" to the blackly humorous visuals, situations, and dialogue of "Humbug" and "Clyde Bruckman's Final Repose."

"We work in the dark. We do what we can to battle the monsters that would otherwise destroy us," says Mulder in "Grotesque." "Yet sometimes the weight of this burden causes us to bend and falter, allowing evil to breach the fragile fortress of our mind. Allowing the monsters without to turn within. And we are left alone, staring into the abyss ... into the laughing face of madness."

Nonetheless, the same character would have this exchange in "Clyde Bruckman":

Detective Cline: "Yeah, this is more like it. No more psychics and their vague visions and predictions. Hell, we don't even need our own hunches. This case is now just about good old-fashioned forensic police work."

Scully: "Mulder! It's the bellhop! He's the killer. The bellhop at the hotel."

Cline: "How the hell does she know that?"

Mulder: "Woman's intuition."

What is the appeal of the series? "*The X-Files* plays it straight — its tone is without irony — and in doing so, it has created a world where the creatures and conspirators are truly to be feared. Everything has consequences, and no more so than for its two protagonists," wrote one critic in *Cinefantastique*. "*The X-Files* taps into a wellspring of post–Vietnam concerns — government intransigence and duplicity, a sense that things are spinning out of control — and ... into examinations of such issues as family dysfunction and the truth of repressed memories."[16]

The show also deals with the darkest beliefs viewers have in the government. In "Nisei," paranoia runs rampant in the first of a very exciting, intriguing two-part episode which has echoes of Nazi war crimes. The mythology gets darker and darker as black-suited death squads keep swarming onto the scene, and soldiers execute prisoners whose bodies drop into a mass grave. It's all dark and getting darker, with a grim, Watergate-era view of a government out of control. More importantly, it is a government that knows what we are doing almost as soon as we have done it. No sooner does Mulder show up at the scene of a possible crime than black-suited commandos arrive, running about in a menacing way, and obviously searching for him.

"Mythology" is an appropriate term for these paranoid *X-Files* episodes: for what the series proposes is a belief even more comforting than the belief in a benign God: it is a belief that *someone* is *responsible* for all the bad things that happen. Assassinations, mysterious deaths, even cancer, we find out, have their origin with a malevolent force, perhaps a combination of aliens and humans working together, experimenting for reasons only they know. This paranoid "religion" ends up, ironically, being about reassuring us that things are okay because someone — even if that person is evil — is in charge, which makes the world a much less scary place. Life is a knowable mystery if someone, anyone, is behind all the horrible things that happen in the world. There is a God out there, after all (so what if he's really the Devil?).

"To me, the idea of faith is really the backbone of the entire series — faith in your own beliefs, ideas about the truth, and so it has religious overtones always," admitted Carter, who said that he adopted the phrase "I believe" as a catchphrase for the series because "the truth is that we all want to believe. To say 'I believe' is to accept things faithfully and ignorantly, in so many cases. I think faith is a complete giving over, so if you're a person of any doubt or skepticism, or in many cases, intellect, I believe that faith comes with difficulty. I describe myself as a non-religious person looking for a religious experience and in that way, I want to believe."[17]

Nonetheless, the creators of the show cleverly and constantly keep viewers off-balance. "Believing is the easy part," says Scully at one point. "I need proof." It is science versus a belief in the supernatural, and even though the answers are weighted towards the latter, there is enough science to keep a dramatic tension going between the doubters and the believers. "Let it go," warns Scully about the train that Mulder is following in "Nisei." She might just as well have been talking about his beliefs. "I can't!" he replies.

In "Nisei," the agents investigate a video of an alien autopsy that Mulder gets through a mail order house. He believes it's the real thing; an investigation finds the man who made it has been murdered, and there is a kickboxing Japanese national on the scene. The trail leads the two to a rail car containing what looks like an alien and a conspiracy that seems to involve the governments of the U.S. and Japan and a group of war criminal scientists. That war crimes can be linked to Americans on an American TV series is remarkable and shows how far TV science fiction has evolved since *Rod Brown of the Rocket Rangers*.

"One of the most disturbing things in my life as an American is apathy towards the government and by the government," Carter said once. "And I think one way to jolt people out of their complacency is to show them that in the absence of political or public mindedness, the people who wield the power will wield it in dangerous ways."[18]

10

A Man and a Woman

"What made *The Thin Man* series work, what made it fun, was that we didn't attempt to hide the fact that sex is part of marriage. But it was deft, done with delicacy, and humor."

Myrna Loy[1]

"I'll tell you why *Moonlighting* failed. The two people were so possessed with themselves. They thought they were the cat's whiskers. We didn't."

Patrick Macnee[2]

"I never will write a 'woman in distress,' unable to take care of herself [story]. I'm not interested in that kind of character. First of all, I wanted Scully to be Mulder's equal in every way in terms of her grit and her ability to take care of herself. I never wanted her to need his help. It was important to me."

Chris Carter[3]

The Thin Man. The Avengers. The X-Files. Three very different series, crafted in three very different eras. Yet how different are they? Consider this scenario: someone or something is killing prominent businessmen. The corpses' clothes have been torn to shreds, as though the victim had been clawed to death by a lion. Yet the victims have been found in locked rooms. A case for Nick Charles? Or for Fox Mulder and Dana Scully? Neither. It is a mystery for John Steed and Emma Peel ("The Hidden Tiger"). Consider another scenario: a series of murders have occurred in a small town. The clues point to a conspiracy involving mind control through television signals. *The Avengers*? No, "Wetwired" on *The X-Files*.

From left to right, The mysterious Cigarette-Smoking Man (William B. Davis), the traitorous agent Alex Krycek (Nicholas Lea), and FBI Assistant Director Walter Skinner (Mitch Pileggi), three characters who play central roles in *The X-Files'* complex "mythology" episodes, which have no parallel in *The Thin Man* or *The Avengers*.

Certainly there are great stylistic and content differences between the three series. *The Thin Man* is very much of its era, fitting primarily in the detective genre. Its stories rarely exhibit the darkness of *The X-Files*, nor does it ever feature science fiction or supernatural elements (although 1939's *Another Thin Man* does include a man who says he has dreams of another man's death). And while many of the stand-alone episodes of *The X-Files* often bear remarkable similarities in structure to *The Avengers*, the tone is markedly different: generally darker, more nihilistic about the world and its ways. And there is nothing in either *The Thin Man* or *The Avengers* to match the convoluted and engrossing "mythology" episodes, which, over a seven-year period, lay out a grand conspiracy, with mysterious figures known only as the Cigarette-Smoking Man, the Well-Manicured Man, and the Alien Bounty Hunter.

Still, there are also an amazing number of similarities among the three series—the times in which they were made; the genre-bending nature of each; the dark and offbeat humor which offsets the grisly goings-on; the fantasy/wish fulfillment nature of each; the distinct yet frequently comparable formulae; and, above all, the relationship between the male and female protagonists.

THE TIMES

Each series was created as a reflection of and a reaction to its times. When *The Thin Man* bubbled forth, the Depression was in full swing, and the movie's effervescent mixture of comedy, crime, and romance was a heady tonic to bread lines and bad times. Similarly, *The Avengers* appeared in the midst of the swinging sixties and the youthful rebellion against tradition. By flattening out the traditional differences between men and women, the series also staged its own rebellion of sorts, while its pop iconography and light, stylized approach to crime-solving and murder made a welcome antidote to campus riots, anti–Vietnam war protests, and other upheavals. Finally, *The X-Files*, coming on the heels of real-life government lies and cover-ups in the Watergate and Iran-Contra scandals, both validated growing paranoia and offered two ready answers for those looking for meaning: "The Truth Is Out There" and "Trust No One."

GENRE-BENDERS

Although they are all primarily detective series, *The Thin Man*, *The

Steed (Patrick Macnee) and Mrs. Peel (Diana Rigg) face misguided feminists in "How to Succeed ... at Murder." The series took contemporary issues and reinterpreted them for a pop idiom.

Avengers, and *The X-Files* each appropriated elements from a host of different genres that had come before, molding them into unique shapes. *The Thin Man* took the roguishness of the gangster movie, cleverly appropriating its iconoclastic, smart-mouth tough guys who operated outside the bounds of traditional structures. Just as significantly, it took comedy elements—from the Howard Hawks–style screwball films and the sentimental Frank Capra movies—and blended them with offbeat detectives and the conventions that went with those: Charlie Chan, Philo

Vance, and, of course, Sherlock Holmes. Nick Charles discovers what others cannot and operates outside the normal structures of law enforcement.

The Avengers built on all these elements, downplaying the romance but adding sex — although discreet and very British in the Alfred Hitchcock style. It also ratcheted up the offbeat, black comedy elements — present in the Charleses' laidback approach to death — and then drew from the long English tradition of absurdism and also from the more recent Ealing Studios comedies of the forties and fifties. In addition, it included elements that had not been part of *The Thin Man*: with "The Cybernauts" and other episodes, it drew on the science fiction and horror film genres that had become prominent in the forties and fifties and the spy genre which was extraordinarily popular in the sixties. It also played up an element only touched on subtextually in *The Thin Man* series: the idea that the individual is more efficient and trustworthy than government bureaucracies. Although ostensibly agents of "the Ministry" (the ministry of *what* never being clear), The Avengers, for most of the run of the series, seem to work outside normal government channels, almost as free agents.

Reflecting the times — when the women's liberation movement was first getting started — the series also pushed the idea of equality of the sexes more forcefully than *The Thin Man* did. "[*The Thin Man*'s] use of Myrna Loy is — 'Oh, my God, the woman's come up with the clue that solves the case! A little woman!'" observed Patrick Macnee. "And William Powell deigns to take his hat off! (He plays it mostly with his hat on.) And then he looks with a sort of raised eyebrow as if the little woman did it, 'What's she doing? My God, she should be at her desk!' We took it way ahead of that, I thought. Not that I'm knocking *The Thin Man* because Dashiell Hammett and all the writing was terrific anyway and the playing was marvelous; but it was completely of the twenties and the thirties."[4]

In "Mandrake," to take just one instance of *The Avengers*' different approach, Steed is traditionally tough and suave, yet it is Mrs. Gale who utilizes her knowledge of photography and chemistry to find the solution. Her practical rather than intuitive skills foreshadow those of Dana Scully in *The X-Files*.

By the time of *The X-Files*, the ideas concerning equality had become so standard that a man partnered with a woman was not even worth comment. As with Steed and Mrs. Peel, FBI agents Mulder and Scully are equal partners and also seem to work more as private investigators

Emma Peel (Diana Rigg) throws an opponent. Although the character has many similarities to Nora Charles, she is very different — and very 1960s — in her ability to get physical with bad guys.

than employees of a government organization. Until the seventh season — when Mulder is humorously called to task by an agency accountant for his expenses— the two often go where they want when they want, regardless of cost.

Additionally, the horror and science fiction elements in *The X-Files* are even more prominent than in *The Avengers*, and the series is heavily influenced by the Val Lewton horror movies of the forties, the "big bug" films of the fifties, and the paranoia thrillers of the sixties and seventies. "The thing I love about *The X-Files* is that it's genuinely spooky," Macnee noted. "My daughter says [the same] about *The Avengers*—that they were real spooky, sort of 'frightening-what's-round-the-next-corner horror type' things in *The Avengers*, which a lot of people overlooked [at the time] and which is abundant in *The X-Files*."[5]

In contrast to the previous two series, however, sex in *The X-Files* is downplayed. In fact, there has been a curious progression: from the happily married couple of *The Thin Man* to the happily unmarried couple (but, maybe, in the case of Steed and Mrs. Peel, one that is sleeping together) of *The Avengers* to the happily unmarried working couple (just good friends) of *The X-Files*.

Dark Humor

Each series uses dark humor as a way to make the grimmer and scarier aspects more palatable, a technique pioneered by Alfred Hitchcock in the 1920s and 1930s. In "The Bird Who Knew Too Much," Steed and Mrs. Peel investigate the deaths of two operatives and their only clue is a bag of bird seed that one of the agents was carrying at the time of his death. This episode features the kind of tongue-in-cheek humor for which Hitchcock is known, including two ruthless killers with bird-like names (Robin and Ferret) who enjoy their work ("You get all the fun," cries one after the other has committed a murder), and an eccentric bird-custodian called Twitter (John Wood). Although investigating a series of murders and theft of top-secret documents, Steed and Mrs. Peel are constantly wry (for example, each offers the same pun when introduced to Twitter. "Mrs. Peel," says Steed, "Twitter." Her reply: "I don't do bird impressions").

The Thin Man films offer even more comedy than *The Avengers*, with dry comments (Nick: "You wouldn't be a widow for long." Nora: "You bet I wouldn't." Nick: "Not with your money."), raised eyebrows, and a bit of not-so-subtle slapstick in the final installments (*The Thin Man Goes Home*, 1945, even has Nick falling off a hammock).

The X-Files, however, is more varied in its comic approach: the mythology episodes rarely employ any type of humor, dark or otherwise, while the stand-alone investigations range from Mulder and Scully's ironic or self-mocking comments ("Can anyone tell me how I can get this off my finger without betraying my cool exterior?" Mulder says in "Squeeze" when he gets a gooey substance on his hand) to entire episodes that are played for (dark) laughs. This latter trend starts with "Humbug," which features Mulder and Scully's investigation of murder in a freak show, and continues into the seventh season's "Hollywood A.D." in which a screenwriter writes a movie about Mulder and Scully and tells them: "You're both crazy. You're crazy for believing what you believe, and you're crazy for not believing him." (The Mulder-Scully image is parodied in that episode with the casting of the sarcastic and slightly beefy Gary Shandling as the fictional movie's "Mulder" and the sexy bimbo Tea Leoni as "Scully.")

WISH-FULFILLMENT FANTASY

Each series offers a fantasy view of criminal investigation. Nick and Nora are well-off and well-dressed, investigating crime as a lark. Scully and Mulder are also well-dressed and rarely seem to be concerned about balancing a checkbook or the drudgery of desk work. Steed is always the perfect gentleman, even when fighting (he uses an umbrella, not a gun) while Mrs. Peel is everyone's ideal: with no visible means of support, she is always well-dressed and superbly multi-talented, able to either fence, flirt, or discuss scientific studies with equal ease. All three series offer the fantasy of the wealthy crime-solvers who do it for fun not profit.

FORMULA

The Thin Man, *The Avengers*, and *The X-Files* all developed their own formulae, each of which shows some overlap. Every adventure generally starts with an intriguing teaser involving the victim of the unusual crime. Each next introduces the protagonists and their personal quirks. The suspects are then paraded out, along with more potential victims.

By the climax, one of the two protagonists is frequently placed in danger and the other rescues him or her. Finally, the solution is offered.

The formula in The Thin Man series follows this general outline, but less closely than *The Avengers* or *The X-Files*. *After the Thin Man* (1936) sees The Thin Man format taking shape. The movie finds Nick Charles once again the reluctant gumshoe egged into a case by Nora. This time, the case involves Nora's snobbish San Francisco family. Her cousin Selma's (Elissa Landi) ne'er-do-well husband Robert (Alan Marshal) has disappeared. Nick finds the missing man in Chinatown, and runs across a sharp-tongued songstress (Penny Singleton), three murders, and seven suspects. Typically, the movie squeezes comedy out of the contrast between Nick's lowbrow but decent friends and Nora's highbrow but dull family. The plot and the suspects become more tangled following the murder, but Nick is never frazzled, unraveling it all in his patented "I'm drinking and can't be bothered now" style. As in the first movie, Nora is flip and knowing, while Nick defers to her in everything except letting her become overly involved in the case. The murderer is the biggest surprise, although he is the only one upon whom no suspicion is cast.

This formula solidifies in *Another Thin Man*. As is now typical, the personal aspect of the sleuthing is brought into the foreground. The first movie showed us a couple in love; the second demonstrated the problems with in-laws; and now, in the third, we see Nick and Nora — back in New York — as parents of eight-month-old Nick Jr. facing parenting problems. This personal element goes hand-in-hand with complex murder mystery plotting, starting with a visit to the estate of Colonel Mac-Fay (C. Aubrey Smith), another relative of Nora's who is in trouble. MacFay, an explosives manufacturer, believes his life is being threatened by an ex-partner, Phil Church (Sheldon Leonard), whom he had sent to prison. Church says he has "dreams" of MacFay's death. The formula is followed to a "t": unwilling participation by Nick, various red herrings, plot twists, lots of drinking, affectionate comedy, antics by Asta, and a gathering of the suspects who listen to Nick deliver a monologue, during which the murderer makes a slip. As in *The Thin Man*, the least suspected figure turns out to be the murderer.

Shadow of the Thin Man (1941) shows the formula firmly in place. Once again, Nick is the reluctant gumshoe, with Nora urging him on. Once again, he gathers all the suspects together, tying all the loose ends up until someone makes a slip. As usual, it is the person who is least suspected and he makes a rather obvious slip-up. The personal and professional aspects are easily intertwined.

William Powell, Myrna Loy, and baby in *Another Thin Man*, the beginning of the domestication of the series.

The formula in *The Avengers* eventually became just as solid and almost as predictable as that of *The Thin Man*. It also more closely blueprints many episodes of *The X-Files*. "The Positive-Negative Man" finds Steed and Mrs. Peel looking into a series of highly unusual deaths: scientists who had been working on a hush-hush, discontinued government project are found dead, as though they had been walloped with a tremendous electrical force. What follows then is a typical pattern for the series: the team is brought in, it finds a connection to another similar death, and then is one step behind the killer for most of the story (he shows up in a blue van before the two sleuths arrive and leaves just as Steed or Mrs. Peel pulls up in his or her car). Mrs. Peel uncovers the scientific

William Powell, Myrna Loy, Asta, and baby in *Another Thin Man*: Powell objected to the addition of the child to the series, feeling it would age them and take away much of the spirit of free-wheeling fun. He was right.

basis for the killings, but then, she is put in danger and needs Steed to rescue her. There is black humor about the deaths—which are not treated very somberly—and also dialogue which pokes fun at bureaucracies (Bureaucrat: "All the confidential war records are kept here." Steed: "Have there been many confidential wars?").

The *X-Files* has two types of formula episodes: the "mythology" installments, which are dark and depict the soap opera-esque grand conspiracy that Mulder and Scully fight against and have little similarity to either *The Thin Man* or *The Avengers* (and more closely resemble TV's *Twin Peaks*); and the stand-alone installments in which similarities to *The Avengers*' formula can be most clearly seen.

In "Squeeze," for instance, the opening pre-credits teaser is directly out of *The Avengers*' playbook. The sequence, which has some similarities to the openers of *The Avengers*' "The Positive-Negative Man" and "The Hidden Tiger," begins with a title, "Baltimore, Maryland," on the left-hand side of the screen over a shot of the city. A car drives by, and a man in a business suit is seen walking down the street. There is a shot of a sidewalk drain. Then a shot of the man walking. Then the drain; the man; the drain — and now a suggestion of eyes glowing in the drain's darkness. Cut to a security monitor that shows an elevator door opening in an office building. The businessman comes out, accompanied by atonal, ominous music. He walks out and we go back to the elevator door that has just closed. Something, unseen by us, is climbing up the cable. The man is in his office on the phone, leaving a message for his wife that he will be working late. He goes for coffee. Cut to a tiny grate on the wall; a screw is turning from the inside and the grate is coming off. We go back to the man getting coffee; he returns to the office, shuts the door, and we hear sudden screams, followed by the sounds of a struggle on the other side. Then, silence, and we are shown the executive, dead, blood and destruction everywhere. The camera pans up to the tiny grate being replaced. Fade out.

Compare that with "The Positive-Negative Man," in which an executive is also shown working late at night and, through similar editing techniques, is menaced by a nighttime visitor who ends up killing him. Also, compare it with "The Hidden Tiger," which also keeps the menacing and murderous creature out of the camera's view.

The subsequent structure of "Squeeze" then follows what could be called classic *Thin Man* and *Avengers* patterns: there are clues, more murders, with the agents always one step behind the killer, whose motive — also like "The Positive-Negative Man" and other *Avengers* episodes — is maddeningly unclear. Finally, Scully (read: Mrs. Peel) is herself placed in danger, with Mulder (Steed) on the way to the rescue.

In these non-mythology episodes, Mulder also displays a Nick Charles/John Steed-like sense of humor: dark, puckish, and offbeat. While "Squeeze" — unlike *The Thin Man* and *The Avengers* — is generally somber and serious, it is much less intensely paranoid than the mythology episodes. It is also similar to Dashiell Hammett's *The Thin Man* and the Continental Op series in its use of the detective genre techniques: the duo engage in stakeouts, research old files, and perform the sort of legwork which is standard in the police procedural.

Formula influences can be subtle or they can be broad. Some episodes of *The Avengers* seem as though they were based on the tone of *The Thin Man*, if not the formula: "Dead Man's Treasure" is a lighthearted romp, with a mysterious murderer and dozens of suspects; "The Superlative Seven," on the other hand, is darker, more *Thin Man* crossed with Agatha Christie, as Steed plays out *And Then There Were None* with a group of seven adventurers, one of whom could be a killer. Still other *Avengers* might be blueprints, structurally if not tonally, for scenarios of *The X-Files*. "From Venus with Love" involves a claim that extraterrestrials are murdering astronomers from a Venusian society; "The Winged Avenger," as mentioned before, finds a ruthless executive murdered in a locked room on the top floor of a skyscraper, the only clue being the horrible claw marks covering his body; and "The Living Dead" depicts Steed and Mrs. Peel's investigation of a ghost who appeared in a graveyard and rang the church bell.

CHEMISTRY AND CASTING

Similarities in the formula aside, it is the casting and the personal chemistry between the co-stars that is the crucial element in the success of each series. Before *The Avengers*, Macnee's roles had not been noteworthy. His pairing with Blackman and then Rigg changed him from a journeyman actor into a star. Similarly, Blackman's image altered significantly, leading to big-screen stardom in *Goldfinger* and beyond, usually as a karate-chopping femme fatale. "For a certain length of time I was sent play after play after play that I was supposed to hurl people about all night on stage," recalled Blackman. "Can you imagine how exhausting that would be? And the number of people I would need in a line, because I would probably damage everybody on stage. It was just ridiculous."[6] In Rigg's first roles after leaving *The Avengers*—in *The Assassination Bureau* (1968) and *On Her Majesty's Secret Service* (1969)—she faced similar typecasting.

On *The X-Files*, Duchovny and Anderson's personal chemistry lightened the often dark material, making it succeed where Carter's other spooky series, *Millennium*, had failed. Significantly, neither actor has been successful in roles outside of their pairing (both have attempted big-screen vehicles and both have failed).

As for Powell and Loy, their personal chemistry is even more interesting, since each had appeared in dozens of movies before being paired, and unlike Duchovny, Anderson, Macnee, Blackman, and Rigg, had clearly established personae in the eyes of producers. "I remember Bill Powell when he started out as a melodramatic actor," recalled director George Cukor in 1983. "Then, by some alchemy, he suddenly became comic."[7] That "alchemy" was Loy.

Indeed, one only has to look at the pair apart to see how much one enhanced the other. Pre-Loy, William Powell had primarily portrayed villains. Although he essayed the heroic figure of sleuth Philo Vance in a series of four pictures, he was still not seen as a leading man by studio executives. The answer becomes apparent when viewing the best of the Vances, *The Kennel Murder Case* (1933), directed by Michael Curtiz. While *The Thin Man* is unusual in its sensibility, mixing genres and showcasing Powell's comic gifts, *The Kennel Murder Case* is antique, lacking humor, romance, and many of the special genre-bending attributes that made the series unusual. Most significantly, it lacks Loy.

The format of that movie is conventional. Whereas Nick Charles is, comically, always reluctant to give up his "drinking time" to solve a crime, Vance is the opposite: a wealthy dilettante detective eager to sacrifice his vacation to Paris when he stumbles on a puzzling case. Certainly, the one he faces in *Kennel* is a whopper, markedly better than many found in *The Thin Man* series: a locked room conundrum in which an apparent suicide has been knifed, shot, and hit over the head by an assailant who left by means unknown. The movie is a drawing room mystery of the best sort, in which Vance works out the intricacies of the killing with an impressively methodical approach. The direction and camera work are unusual for the period, employing wipes and other gimmicks to keep the story moving, while the talky explanation of the crime is made interesting by a visual reenactment. But there is little of interest in the Vance character, and, although Powell makes stabs at dry wit, the actor's talents are wasted.

It is Myrna Loy's sly humor that would bring out the best performances in Powell, as demonstrated by a pallid *Thin Man* imitation called *Star of Midnight* (1935). In this routine whodunit, Powell attempts another version of Nick Charles, with Ginger Rogers as an inferior substitute for Loy. Powell plays an amateur sleuth who drinks prodigiously while Rogers is the woman who wants to marry him and who assists him in a murder investigation. Seeing Powell trading quips with Rogers illustrates what Loy brought to the partnership. Whereas Loy's bantering with the actor is always wry, coy, and sophisticated even in subpar scripts, Rogers comes across as brash and heavy-handed, and the "light" comedy sinks under its own obviousness. Without the Powell-Loy chemistry, all that is left is a complex plot and a murderer in a rubber mask.

Pre–Powell, Myrna Loy was also hard-pressed to get it right, and her roles were also frequently off-the-mark. Her most famous appearance before *The Thin Man* was as the villain's daughter, Fah Lo See in *Mask of Fu Manchu*, directed by Charles Brabin. The movie may be camp fun but Loy seems stiff and awkward in her role. The plot: Fu Manchu (Boris Karloff) wants to obtain the mask of Genghis Khan, so that his Oriental followers will see him as the descendant of the great Khan and help overthrow the Western world (why he needs a mask for this, when they already follow his orders, is never explained). Standing in his way is Sir Nayland Smith (Lewis Stone) of the British secret service.

As a character who enjoys torturing prisoners, Loy is both beautiful and exotic but also much too intelligent an actress to deliver the melodramatic speeches she is given: "I have seen a vision. The prophecy is about to be fulfilled. Genghis Khan's mask of gold, bearing the scimitar that none but he could ever wield, comes back to us. I have seen a vision of countless hordes swarming to recapture the world. I have seen them victorious. I have seen and heard the shouts of the dead and the dying drowned by the victorious cries of our peoples. Ghengis Kahn comes back! Genghis Kahn leads the east against the world!"

It is one of Loy's gifts that she cannot read such camp material with any kind of conviction because she seems too intelligent. "She always struck me as being on a higher level of understanding and intelligence," MGM producer Sam Marx once said about the actress. "She read and appreciated good writing. She once said in an interview: 'How can you fail when you've got such a great collection of writers?' We didn't hear that very often."[8]

It took *Thin Man* director W.S. Van Dyke to see the true Loy persona: a woman of integrity and wit. Van Dyke's *The Prizefighter and the Lady* (1933) cast Loy in one of her best early parts. The movie is the story of a boxer, Steve Morgan (Max Baer), who heads to the top of the fighting world. The "lady" of the title is Belle (Loy), a gangster's moll. The boxer aggressively courts her — despite threats from the gangster — and ends up marrying her. The road gets rocky, however, when Steve "cats around" with other women. Belle leaves him but comes back in time to save him from his own self-destructiveness. Even though the movie is a conventional melodrama about the rise and fall of an innocent rube who becomes overconfident (Belle to Steve: "You need those shoulders to carry that head of yours"), Loy's intelligent performance makes the picture succeed, even to the point of overcoming its biggest flaw: she seems much too smart to be attracted to or fooled by Baer's character.

Penthouse (1933), another Van Dyke effort, is much better, however, and can be seen almost as a dry run for *The Thin Man* (and also *The Avengers*). It is a comedy-mystery featuring some of the elements that would make the *Thin Man* series so popular: a bizarre murder mystery, a crusading investigator with a fondness for alcohol (Warner Baxter); a smart, sexy, and clear-headed woman whom he loves (Loy), and a collection of gangster-types with whom the hero pals around, despite the objections of his hoity-toity friends.

The story is fast-paced and economical: the hero, attorney Jackson Durant, is jilted by his girlfriend because he won't give up his criminal element clients (his reason: "There's a kick in fighting for a man's life"); but she soon has need of his services herself: the man she has decided to marry is accused of the murder of a young woman. Later, the lawyer's gangster friend, Tony Gazotti (Nat Pendleton) introduces him to a woman who can help him on the case, the victim's roommate, Gertie Waxted (Loy).

Loy, in one of her finest early performances, is charming, intelligent, and wryly direct (Jackson: "I'm afraid you think I'm taking advantage of you." Gertie: "I'm afraid you won't"), with the sort of comebacks that would become a trademark of *The Thin Man* series. "I've been stupid, very stupid," moans Jackson after realizing he has falsely accused Gertie. "Of course," she replies with a matter-of-fact smile. "You're a man."

Penthouse was the actress's first encounter with the screenwriting team of Francis Goodrich and Albert Hackett, who penned the three best *Thin Man* movies, and also her first role for Van Dyke, who knew how to utilize Loy's unique gifts. The actress is marvelously modern, with poise, grace, and a knowing humor in her eyes. Baxter is fine as her partner, a sort of road-show Clark Gable; but he is a little more lowbrow than William Powell, still not quite the perfect match for Loy's special skills. "You're the strangest girl I've ever met," he says to her. "You're a new one on me, too," she replies.

In this movie, even more than in *The Thin Man*, Loy serves as a prototype for Diana Rigg on *The Avengers*. Here, Loy takes on a dangerous job to help out the man she loves; she's as smart as (or perhaps smarter than) the more forceful male. There is also an emphasis on the glamour and glitter of high-society life that would be a staple of *The Thin Man*, and, to some extent, *The Avengers*. And the one-liners are lovely (Jackson: "Gertie, you're the grandest girl in the world." Gertie: "I'd rather be the cutest.").

Powell and Loy were finally teamed up in *Manhattan Melodrama*, and the team's first pairing is as electric as the movie is hokey, the story of two boyhood pals who grow up to be prosecutor (Powell) and a hoodlum (Clark Gable). Gable's girl is Loy, but she soon leaves him for the upright Powell, who must prosecute his old buddy for murder. Powell is droll and amusing, even when the lines are supposed to be but aren't, while Loy is beautiful, sophisticated, and witty, even when the dialogue is supposed to be but isn't. Whenever the two interact, the screen crackles.

Powell once reflected on Loy: "Even my best friends never fail to tell me that the smartest thing I ever did was to marry Myrna Loy on the screen. And it was the pleasantest, I might add. We were married in 13 pictures ... and I never saw Myrna go into a temperamental tantrum, rave and rant, or walk off the set in a huff. She never lets her emotions come too near the surface and remains calm and poised in the most difficult situations."[9]

In her autobiography, Loy analyzed her chemistry with Powell: "He was so naturally witty and outrageous that I stayed somewhat detached, always a little incredulous. From the very first scene, a curious thing passed between us, a feeling of rhythm, complete understanding, an instinct of how one could bring out the best in the other. In all our work together you can see this strange — I don't know what ... a kind of rapport. It wasn't conscious. If you heard us talking in a room, you'd hear the same thing. He'd tease me a little and a kind of blending emerged that seemed to please people. Whatever caused it, though, it was magical."[10]

That chemistry was easily transferred to other roles, as well, such as *Libeled Lady* (1936), perhaps the best of the non–*Thin Man*s to feature Powell and Loy. Directed by Jack Conway and co-starring Spencer Tracy and Jean Harlow, it is a terrifically entertaining farce, with Powell and Loy in what could almost be the story of how Nick and Nora met. He plays Bill Chandler, an ace reporter who is tops at breaking up libel suits, and is called in to do the same in one initiated by Connie Allenbury (Loy) against Chandler's employer. In the course of the job, the pair fall in love, but not without a number of bumps along the way. One of them is Gladys Benton (Harlow), whom Powell has married as part of the plan. He has to do some fancy footwork to keep the two women apart and that's where a great deal of the comedy comes in. *Libeled Lady* is breezy, sophisticated, and entertaining, showing the Powell-Loy chemistry working at full throttle. Powell is adept at the sophisticated banter but also equally adroit at falling on his face (both literally and figuratively), a smoothie but not a sharpy, a man with smarts but also decency, a "good egg." What's nice about the Powell-Loy relationship (in this and other pictures) is the characters' intelligence and obvious delight in each other's company.

Loy discussed her most famous screen character in her autobiography: "Nora was hardly the perfect wife in the sense of being the chaste, virginal creature that seemed to be so much admired.... I prefer Gore Vidal's description of my image, 'the eternal good-sex-woman-wife,' which removes the puritanical connotation of perfect. What man would want a perfect wife, anyway? What made *The Thin Man* series work, what made it fun, was that we didn't attempt to hide the fact that sex is part of marriage. But it was deft, done with delicacy, and humor. Then, too, the Charleses had enormous tolerance for each other's imperfections. It wasn't any sticky, idealistic perfection that made their marriage fun to watch—quite the contrary. Ye gods! *The Thin Man* virtually introduced modern marriage to the screen. Previously people married and lived happily ever after, but you never saw the undercurrents."[11]

UNIQUE ELEMENTS

Above all else, *The Thin Man*, *The Avengers*, and *The X-Files* have each proved hard to copy successfully. Not that there haven't been attempts. There were a string of *Thin Man* wannabes in the 1930s, including *Star of Midnight* and *The Ex–Mrs. Bradford* (1936), both with Powell. On television, *McMillan and Wife*, *Hart to Hart*, *Remington Steele*, and *Moonlighting* were all clear attempts to ape *The Thin Man*.

Although it was said to be based primarily on the Howard Hawks picture, *The Front Page* (1940), *Moonlighting*, the 1985–89 detective series, certainly has surface similarities to both *The Thin Man* and *The Avengers*: Bruce Willis and Cybill Shepherd play a male-female sleuthing team, David Addison and Maddie Hayes, who become involved in complicated mysteries laced with comedy, just as Powell and Loy and Macnee and Rigg did. Maddie's the amateur and David's the professional. Unlike their predecessors, however, they initially can't stand each other (this is similar to other screwball comedies such as *Bringing Up Baby*). But *Moonlighting* is generally overcooked, with stars and scripts that keep winking at the audience and saying, "Aren't we clever?" It is not helped by Willis's smirky charm or the tendency for the leads to cutely break the fourth wall by commenting on the plot devices and or guest stars ("Are you sure you're supposed to be in this episode?").

"I'll tell you why *Moonlighting* failed," Macnee observed. "The two people were so possessed with themselves. They thought they were the cat's whiskers; we didn't. Whenever Diana Rigg threw someone over her shoulder, she would push her hair back, [as if to say,] 'My God, I did that?' On *Moonlighting*, because of their own egos, [the stars] ruined the thing. They thought they were so clever. They thought that was all that was needed. It wasn't. A little humility would have helped. They were both so bad-tempered and unlikable. You've got to be likable."[12]

"*The X-Files* is the anti–*Moonlighting*," wrote critic Ken Tucker. "Where the Bruce Willis–Cybill Shepherd show featured ceaseless amounts of mock-hostile flirting and finally succumbed to s-e-x, *The X-Files* presents intensely focused work roles as a form of chaste courtship. Existing in a prime time full of mostly boorish sitcom unions or drama shows in which a couple's emotional life is conveyed through earnest arguments or the ever-present option of divorce, Mulder and Scully's ongoing plunges into the unexpected have resulted in something more inexplicable than the knottiest X-File: TV's most successful, progressive marriage."[13]

But *Moonlighting* looks like high art compared to other imitations, such as *Scarecrow and Mrs. King*, a 1984–87 adventure series about a spy, Lee "Scarecrow" Stetson (Bruce Boxleitner) and the divorcée/mother, Mrs. Amanda King (Kate Jackson), whom he recruits for assignments. A bad cross between *The Thin Man* and *The Avengers*, the series demonstrates how dreadfully boring the male-female pairing can be in mediocre creative hands. The series is banal to the nth degree, an *Avengers* without class, wit, or style. The pair, who start as colleagues, eventually become lovers, as in *The Thin Man*, but all similarities end there. The show is dumb. In "Photo Finish," for instance, Mrs. King investigates the security at a top-secret government installation as part of a spy school assignment. Surprisingly, even though there had been a suspicious death two months before she started her assignment, no one had apparently questioned it until the naive, midwest-accented Mrs. King gets involved. Hampered by hackneyed writing ("That takes us back to square zero"; "If Amanda King winds up in our hair, I'll make sure she never bothers us again") and inane plotting, the series is woefully conventional. The only thing noteworthy about it at all is that the male-female partnering has become so common, even in a mundane series such as this, that it does not even merit comment.

Another reason the original series are difficult to imitate are the keen personal visions of those overseeing them. Chris Carter has guided *The X-Files* for eight years, insisting on a distinct feeling and mood, and has been intimately involved in every decision concerning the scripting, casting, and production, and has written or co-written the bulk of the episodes himself.

Similarly, W.S. Van Dyke knew what he wanted when he crafted *The Thin Man* with his screenwriters: it was the romance and the characters that appealed to him, not the mystery. Clearly, what *The Thin Man Goes Home* and *Song of the Thin Man* (1947) lack most of all is Van Dyke's sure hand. Without that, Nora is no longer a naive sophisticate but a more conventional character, while Nick is no longer a reluctant gumshoe but starts investigating almost as soon as the first body hits the floor.

"We missed Woody Van Dyke's certain inspiration on the fifth *Thin Man* picture," admitted Loy in her autobiography, where she also observed: "*Song of the Thin Man* was a lackluster finish to a great series. I hated it. The characters had lost their sparkle for Bill and me, and the people who knew what it was all about were no longer involved. Woody Van Dyke was dead. Dashiell Hammett and Hunt Stromberg had gone elsewhere. The Hacketts were writing other things."[14]

The Avengers, too, was guided firmly by writer/producer Brian Clemens, who began writing for the series with its second episode in 1961, became its associate producer/script editor in 1965, and finally its full-time producer in 1967 (he also produced the 1976-77 follow-up series, *The New Avengers*). "Brian Clemens was our creative strength," Macnee said. "Oh God, yes, there was no comparison. Howard Rosenberg gave a lovely contrast between the film and television [versions of] *The Avengers*. There's a sword fight [in both]—Uma Thurman and [Ralph] Fiennes have a sword fight—and I and Diana Rigg had a sword fight [in "The Town of No Return"]. At the end of the one with Uma Thurman, Uma Thurman wins. Now, in the other one, I win, and then she, Diana Rigg, comes out from behind the curtain, and says, 'You cheated.' And I say, 'Well, I never said I'd fight fair.' Now, that's *The Avengers*."[15]

William Powell and Myrna Loy in *Song of the Thin Man*, the last and least entry in the series.

Indeed, *The Avengers* film clearly shows what happens when the original visionary is absent from the picture. Ralph Fiennes and Uma Thurman play a John Steed and Emma Peel who have little in common with the original pairing outside of their outfits and names. Without Clemens's unique vision, the movie is left to ape the forms of the TV series but cannot capture its soul. Fiennes lacks Macnee's panache while Thurman can only imitate Rigg's mannerisms, without registering as either brainy or very beautiful. The plot (never the strongest point in the TV series anyway) is downright nonsensical, as though someone took all the elements he remembered from the show and mashed them together in a blender. There is a roving ministry headquarters on a double-decker bus; James Bondian double-entendres; a male boss called Mother who is crippled and a female superior named Father who is blind; silly acronyms (BROLLY for a weather organization); dry understatement following violence; and a mad genius (Sean Connery) with a plan for ruling the world. The movie is ultimately an exercise in imitation (even the premise is primarily lifted from the episode "A Surfeit of H_2O").

FBI agents Dana Scully (Gillian Anderson) and Fox Mulder (David Duchovny) in action. In *The X-Files*, the equality of the sexes is a given in a way it never is in *The Thin Man*.

A MAN AND A WOMAN

What *The Avengers* movie does touch on, however, is the appeal of all three series: the reaffirmation of the bond between a man and a woman, and the absolute trust one can have in the other. "I'm interested in male and female relationships generally. I think they're the most interesting relationships in life," admitted Chris Carter. "They're non-competitive and can be, beyond anything romantic, more interesting and honest. It's a very natural relationship, and one where people can do their best for reasons that go beyond sex or romance, but for the complementary elements of the relationship."[16]

Although the partnership is significantly different in each series, the fact that it exists at all is both remarkable and telling. Unlike other film and television series of the times, the man respects and admires the woman *as a person not just as a woman*. She is his partner, his bulwark against an uncaring world. He helps her and saves her; but she also helps him and saves him. Their feelings are revealed through their playful banter and through their anxiety about the other person when he or she is facing danger.

"I think their relationship is defined not by what's said but by what's being withheld," observed Carter about Fox Mulder and Dana Scully, although he could also be discussing Nick and Nora Charles or John Steed and Emma Peel. "But it's absolutely plain that they love each other — in their own way. And it's the best kind of love. It's unconditional. It's not based on a physical attraction, but on a shared passion for life and for their quest. These are romantic heroes, romantic heroes in the literary tradition."[17]

"... it is *The X-Files*' most interesting achievement that it has managed to build a slam-bang scarefest around a quietly nuanced relationship between a man and a woman," wrote Ken Tucker in *Entertainment Weekly* during the series' third season. "By now, the original dichotomy between the two — he's a believer; she's a skeptic — has been dissolved.... What's left is something more interesting; mutual respect mingled with subtextual love. When, during this season's premiere, Mulder told his partner, 'I need you to know I'm okay, Scully,' it was, in X context, tantamount to a declaration of devotion and an acknowledgment of his awareness of her feelings for him as well."[18]

The choice to downplay sex and play up the personal relationship in *The X-Files* reflected the times and was a conscious reaction against other genre series, such as *Moonlighting*, which overdid the romance and sexual tension to the detriment of the stories. "I was really the lone voice saying we cannot have these people romantically involved," explained Carter. "There cannot be real TV sexual tension or else the show won't work. As soon as you have them looking googly-eyed at each other, they're not going to want to go out and chase those aliens. The relationship will supplant or subvert what's going to make the show great, which is the pursuit of these cases."[19]

Still, as Tucker correctly noted, the relationship eventually became as important in a non-sexual and adult way as the stories: "Carter ... had the foresight to avoid the lone-male-hero setup that characterizes so much science fiction–derived television. In having the man-woman thing to play around with, Carter and his producer-writers possess a built-in advantage: even when the main plot is weak, an exciting mini-drama about the Mulder-Scully magilla ... can light up the hour. Conversely, a good series entry can seem terribly slight when there's no meaningful S&M action."[20] The same is true of both *The Thin Man* and *The Avengers*.

So, in the end, what does all this say about connections found in *The Thin Man*, *The Avengers*, and *The X-Files*? No grand conspiracies or grand coincidences are involved; the truth out there is actually far simpler. Despite all their plots and paradoxes, *The Thin Man*, *The Avengers*, and *The X-Files* are each, ultimately, about one universal belief: that true friendship can last forever and that it can be the most central and meaningful part of a person's life. Indeed, true friendship goes beyond love, beyond sex, beyond mundane daily concerns. True friendship defies expectations, enhances our existence, and makes life worth living. Whether the names are Nick and Nora, Steed and Mrs. Peel, or Mulder and Scully, the point is clear: we are not alone. In a darkly troubling world of lies and deceit, of double-dealing and death, that message is as timeless as it is simple, and it is endlessly reassuring.

APPENDIX 1

The Thin Man: *A Guide*

The Thin Man is a terrific movie, a once-in-a-lifetime blending of stars, writers, director, and material, and it would be fitting to say that it all ended there, and that everyone lived happily ever after. But Hollywood being Hollywood, and the system being what it was, MGM continued to milk Dashiell Hammett's characters with varying degrees of success for years. The series and its offshoots:

THE THIN MAN (1934)

Director: W.S. Van Dyke II. *Screenplay:* Albert Hackett and Frances Goodrich, from the novel by Dashiell Hammett. *Guest Cast:* Maureen O'Sullivan, Nat Pendleton, Cesar Romero, Edward Ellis.

Introducing Nick and Nora Charles in the first and best of the mysteries showing that marriage and murder can mix as smoothly as dry martinis. Nick reluctantly searches for a missing inventor who seems to be on a killing spree. (By the way, the "Thin Man" of the title is not William Powell, but Edward Ellis.)

AFTER THE THIN MAN (1936)

Director: W.S. Van Dyke II. *Screenplay:* Albert Hackett and Frances Goodrich, from a story by Dashiell Hammett. *Guest Cast:* James Stewart, Joseph Calleia, Alan Marshal, Dorothy McNulty (Penny Singleton).

After the Thin Man appeared in 1936, delayed by a contract dispute with Loy and script problems with Hammett. (He had been hired by MGM at $2,000 a week for ten weeks to concoct an original story the Hacketts would then adapt.) The sequel, using elements from the unpublished first *Thin Man* novel fragment, repeats the format of the initial movie and is almost as entertaining. It features a 28-year-old Jimmy Stewart in one of his first major roles.

William Powell and Myrna Loy, so perfect on-screen, were finding that such perfection had its problems offscreen. "We shot exteriors in San Francisco, so I went up on the train with Bill and Jean Harlow," recalled Loy in her autobiography. "She wasn't in the picture, but he had somehow managed to get her away from her mother. The grip she had on that girl was unbelievable. Bill and Jean were unofficially engaged, and he'd given her an enormous sapphire ring, which she proudly displayed on the train. It really was *too* big, I thought, and Bill kept making jokes about it....

"At the St. Francis in San Francisco, they had reserved the Flyshaker Suite for Bill and me. The management assumed we were married. Already they considered us a couple after only five pictures together! Well, of course, it was hysterical. Here was Jean, but we couldn't be obvious about the situation with the press on our heels ... Jean was marvelous. 'There's nothing for you to do,' she said. 'We'll just have to put Bill downstairs.' I never saw his room, so I don't know how bad it was."[1]

ANOTHER THIN MAN (1939)

Director: W.S. Van Dyke II. *Screenplay:* Albert Hackett and Frances Goodrich, from a story by Dashiell Hammett. *Guest Cast:* C. Aubrey Smith, Otto Kruger, Sheldon Leonard.

Another Thin Man, the last in the series to be written by the Hacketts from a Hammett story, was held up by tragedy in Powell's life: the unexpected death of his fiancée, Jean Harlow, followed by his own near-fatal battle with cancer. At Van Dyke's insistence, the recuperating Powell worked on a reduced schedule, only six hours a day, and was chauffeured to and from three different sound stages in a special limousine.

But Powell, who was happy to be working, was not pleased by the arrival of Nick Jr., conceived by the Hacketts to add a new character to the fun. As Loy recalled in her autobiography, the actor groaned, "Why do we want this kid? First thing you know, he'll be in kindergarten, then prep school, then college. How old will that make us?"[2]

This time, Nick and Nora — back in New York — are parents of eight-month-old Nick Jr. (Nick calls Nora "Mommy") and visit the estate of Colonel MacFay (C. Aubrey Smith), another relative of Nora's who is in trouble. MacFay, an explosives manufacturer, believes his life is being threatened by an ex-partner (Sheldon Leonard) whom he sent to prison. As in all their movies together, Powell and Loy's intelligent bantering and obvious affection for each other more than make up for any holes in the story.

SHADOW OF THE THIN MAN (1941)

Director: W.S. Van Dyke II. *Screenplay:* Irving Brecher and Harry Kurnitz, from a story by Harry Kurnitz. *Guest Cast:* Barry Nelson, Donna Reed, Sam Levene, Stella Adler.

Age is showing in the fourth installment, which could be subtitled "Murder at the Race Track." The plot could be out of a Charlie Chan picture, with family hijinks mixing with murder; once again, Nick is constantly greeted by lowlifes who always think Nora isn't the missus. The wrinkle is that Nick and Nora are parents now, with a six-year-old son. Famed acting teacher Stella Adler turns up as a suspect.

By this time, Van Dyke had lost interest, as had the Hacketts. (Years later, Albert explained to Loy why he had quit. "Finally I just threw up on my typewriter. I couldn't do it again. I couldn't write another one."[3]) Hammett was gone, too. The author had sold his interest in the characters to MGM for $40,000 and was subsequently fired by the studio after submitting a *Thin Man* idea in which Nick is threatened by a murderous transvestite. However, MGM was reportedly more upset by his pro–trade union stance. In 1957, Hammett claimed, "The Thin Man always bored me."[4]

THE THIN MAN GOES HOME (1945)

Director: Richard Thorpe. *Screenplay:* Robert Riskin and Dwight Taylor, from a story by Robert Riskin. *Guest Cast:* Lucile Watson, Gloria DeHaven.

The series continued after Van Dyke's death in 1944. Loy had retired from the screen to perform Red Cross work during World War II and Irene Dunne was announced as the new Nora for this installment; Loy ultimately returned, however. "The fans wanted Myrna," Powell told James Kotsilibas-Davis, "and they didn't want anyone else. I wanted Myrna, too."[5] It is a weak entry, however, with the formerly fun couple looking decidedly middle-aged and less than sophisticated.

In this one, Nick, Nora, and Asta return to Nick's birthplace, a small town in upstate New York. It turns out that Nick has an Andy Hardy kind of past: a knowledgeable father who disapproves of Nick's drinking and detecting and who always wanted his son to be a doctor (naturally, after he sees his son in action, his opinion changes). Nick drinks nary a drop of alcohol and there are few of the romantic interludes that the Hacketts did so well. It's tired, and even the obligatory wrap-up with the suspects all in one room can't get up much juice.

SONG OF THE THIN MAN (1947)

Director: Edward Buzzell. *Screenplay:* Steve Fisher, Nat Perrin, from a story by Stanley Roberts. *Guest Cast:* Keenan Wynn, Dean Stockwell, Gloria Grahame, Jayne Meadows.

This was the last trip to the well after which, in Powell's words, "The Thin Man, his perfect wife, and their pooch with personality"[6] retired permanently. Last and the least of the celebrated series, this episode finds Nick and Nora almost completely domesticated. They've moved from their posh San Francisco house to a New York apartment and have an eight-year-old child (Stockwell) who likes to work out solutions to murders with his dad. Nick and Nora seem a little long-in-the-tooth to be chasing criminals, although they manage some energy when needed. The plot is negligible — something about the murder of a bandleader — and it features some embarrassing moments of "hipness" when Nick and Nora get in among the "hep cats" who play in a jazz band.

Powell-Loy Films

After the success of *The Thin Man,* Powell and Loy became a busy team. Their non–*Thin Man* films showed that they shone even when the material didn't.

Manhattan Melodrama (1934)

Director: W.S. Van Dyke II. *Screenplay:* Oliver H.P. Garrett and Joseph Mankiewicz, from a story by Arthur Caesar. *Cast:* Clark Gable, Nat Pendleton.

Two boyhood chums grow up to be on the either side of the law. Gable is the gangster, Powell the crusading district attorney, and Loy the woman they both love. The movie is aptly titled, although the three leads make it worth watching.

Evelyn Prentice (1934)

Director: William K. Howard. *Screenplay:* Lenore Coffee, from the novel by W.E. Woodward. *Cast:* Una Merkel, Rosalind Russell.

Cashing in on the success of *The Thin Man*, MGM paired Powell and Loy in an inferior melodrama about a famous trial lawyer (Powell) whose wife (Loy) thinks she has murdered someone. Loy recalled that "this thing was kind of a bore" and that making it sent Powell "into occasional depressions."[7] Rosalind Russell makes her screen debut.

The Great Ziegfeld (1936)

Director: Robert Z. Leonard. *Screenplay:* William Anthony McGuire. *Cast:* Luise Rainer, Frank Morgan.

An Academy Award–winner as Best Picture of 1936, this lavish film biography tells the story of the great Broadway showman Florenz Ziegfeld (Powell). Loy plays Ziegfeld's second wife, Billie Burke (best known today as Glinda the Good Witch in 1939's *The Wizard of Oz*). Loy later said that she was uncomfortable in the part because Burke was still alive when the picture was made.

Libeled Lady (1936)

Director: Edward Buzzell. *Screenplay:* Maurine Watkins, Howard Emmett Rogers, George Oppenheimer, from a story by Wallace Sullivan. *Cast:* Jean Harlow, Spencer Tracy, Walter Connolly.

Perhaps the best of the non–*Thin Man*s to feature Powell and Loy. He plays Bill Chandler, an ace reporter who is tops at breaking up libel suits, and is called in to do the same in one initiated by Connie Allenbury (Loy) against Chandler's employer. In the course of the job, the pair fall in love, but not without a number of bumps along the way. Tracy and Harlow offer sterling support.

DOUBLE WEDDING (1937)

Director: Richard Thorpe. *Screenplay:* Jo Swerling. *Cast:* John Beal, Edgar Kennedy, Sidney Toler, Mary Gordon.

Double Wedding, with a programmer-level script by frequent Capra collaborator Jo Swerling, miscasts Powell as a free-spirited bohemian and Loy as the woman who hates him, a hoity-toity control freak who thinks Powell wants to marry her sister (he's really using that as a ploy to get hooked up with Loy). The story is predictable, with more farcical elements than the *Thin Man* series, but Powell and Loy's comic timing is as impeccable as ever. Sidney Toler appears as a bumbling detective/butler in his pre–Charlie Chan days; while Mary Gordon is a housekeeper before she became Sherlock Holmes's landlady in *The Hound of the Baskervilles* (1939).

I LOVE YOU AGAIN (1940)

Director: W.S. Van Dyke II. *Screenplay:* Charles Lederer, George Oppenheim, Harry Kurnitz. *Cast:* Frank McHugh, Edmund Lowe.

I Love You Again, a delightful screwball comedy, casts Powell as George Carey, a man coming out of a nine-year bout with amnesia to find that, under the name Larry Wilson, he has married and is about to divorce the beautiful Kay Wilson (Loy). A stuffy, penny-pinching bore in his Wilson incarnation, Carey, as himself, is a suave, man-about-town. The story finds Carey courting the skeptical, soon-to-be-married-to-someone-else Kay. Powell and Loy have rarely been better, with Powell handling both the pratfalls and the debonair romantic moments with equal aplomb.

LOVE CRAZY (1941)

Director: Jack Conway. *Screenplay:* William Ludwig, Charles Lederer, David Hertz. *Cast:* Gail Patrick, Jack Carson.

Love Crazy, a sitcom-style farce with Powell and Loy as estranged-but-still-in-love married couple. She thinks he's lied to her on their fourth wedding anniversary; he pretends he's insane as a way to postpone a final divorce hearing. It's all contrived and silly, making a mockery of the Powell-Loy "perfect marriage, perfect trust" relationship. Director Jack Conway, who handled things a lot more deftly in the pair's *Libeled Lady*, has one thing going for him: the Powell-Loy chemistry, which still shines despite the weak script. The movie ends with Powell, in drag (and sans mustache), pursued by the police as a killer. Nick Charles would have made light of the whole affair and had a highball.

THE SENATOR WAS INDISCREET (1947)

Director: George S. Kaufman. *Screenplay:* Charles MacArthur, from a story by Edwin Lanham. *Cast:* Ella Raines, Ray Collins.

Loy has a cameo appearance at the end of this satire of Washington politics, the only picture directed by Broadway legend George S. Kaufman. Powell plays a bumbling senator who runs for president. Loy appears briefly at the conclusion when the senator, after running into trouble, phones "Momma"—his wife.

The Thin Man Without Powell and Loy

The *Thin Man* series seems inconceivable without Powell and Loy, but there have been three additional couples who played the pair, two on television, the third in a Broadway musical.

THE THIN MAN (1957–59)

Director: various. *Screenplay:* various. *Cast:* Peter Lawford, Phyllis Kirk.

Running from September 20, 1957, through June 26, 1959, this 72-episode, half-hour mystery series featured Peter Lawford and Phyllis Kirk as Nick and Nora Charles. Kirk later recalled that she had never seen the original movies, but that she "adored" Loy, adding: "I didn't want to try to mimic her or be like her."[8] In *The Peter Lawford Story*, director John Newland claimed that Lawford disliked Kirk so much that he did not want her to touch him — a recollection belied, however, by hand-holding moments in the episodes themselves.

NICK AND NORA (1975)

Cast: Craig Stevens and Jo Ann Pflug.

A failed TV-movie attempt to revive the *Thin Man* series, with former *Peter Gunn* star Stevens as Nick Charles, and former *Candid Camera* co-host Pflug as Nora. Neither star lists the movie in his or her filmography.

NICK AND NORA (1991)

Director: Arthur Laurents. Book: Arthur Laurents. *Music:* Charles Strouse. Lyrics: Richard Maltby Jr. *Cast:* Barry Bostwick, Joanna Gleason, Christine Baranski.

A modern look at the Nick and Nora marriage, with Nora attempting to solve a case on her own. Set in 1937, this Broadway musical follows the format of the films — Nick is reluctant to take on a case, Nora insists — but puts a women's lib spin on it. When Nick turns the case down and mocks Nora, she investigates the case on her own. She eventually abandons Nick, saying she needs to reexamine their "perfect" marriage. The songs include "Is There Anything Better Than Dancing?" "Look Who's Alone Now" (after Nick has been deserted by Nora), and "Married Life." Needless to say, audiences did not flock to this reinvention of the classic couple. It closed after only nine performances.

APPENDIX 2

The Avengers: *A Guide*

The Avengers ran from 1961 to 1969 in Britain and co-starred Patrick Macnee as John Steed with various partners: Ian Hendry as David Keel (1961), Honor Blackman as Cathy Gale (1962–64), Diana Rigg as Emma Peel (1965–67), and Linda Thorson as Tara King (1967–69). Macnee also appeared in the short-lived revival, *The New Avengers*, from 1976 to 1977, with Joanna Lumley as Purdey and Gareth Hunt as Mike Gambit. The broadcast dates are for the British telecast; in America, some Linda Thorson episodes appeared in 1968, before their premiere in England. Until 1990, the Blackman episodes went unseen in the United States; the Hendry episodes, except for "The Frighteners," were apparently destroyed. The bulk of the series is being released on tape and DVD by A & E Home Video. (For more information, call 1-800-423-1212; or log in at www.originalavengers.com.)

PATRICK MACNEE AND IAN HENDRY (1961)

1. HOT SNOW

Director: Don Leaver. *Teleplay:* Ray Rigby. *Recorded:* 12/30/60. *Broadcast:* 1/7/61.

Introducing Dr. David Keel who enters a world of drug smugglers when his secretary is accidentally gunned down. He partners with the mysterious John Steed.

2. BROUGHT TO BOOK

Director: Peter Hammond. *Teleplay:* Brian Clemens. *Recorded:* 1/12/61. *Broadcast:* 1/14/61.

The sequel to "Hot Snow," in which Steed and Keel track down and bring the killers to justice.

3. SQUARE ROOT OF EVIL

Director: Don Leaver. *Teleplay:* Richard Harris. *Broadcast live:* 1/21/61.

Steed and Keel hunt down counterfeiters lead by a mysterious figure known only as The Cardinal.

4. NIGHTMARE

Director: Peter Hammond. *Teleplay:* Peter Hammond. *Broadcast live:* 1/28/61.

Steed and Keel become involved in a mistaken identity-assassination plot.

5. CRESCENT MOON

Director: John Knight. *Teleplay:* Geoffrey Bellman, John Whitney. *Broadcast live:* 2/4/61.

Steed and Keel investigate the purported death of a Spanish general.

6. GIRL ON THE TRAPEZE

Director: Paul Bernard. *Teleplay:* Dennis Spooner. *Broadcast live:* 2/11/61.

The Avengers look into a drowning that involves a circus.

7. DIAMOND CUT DIAMOND

Director: Peter Hammond. *Teleplay:* Max Marquis. *Broadcast live:* 2/18/61.

Steed and Keel pursue diamond smugglers.

8. THE RADIOACTIVE MAN

Director: Peter Tronson. *Teleplay:* Fred Edge. *Broadcast live:* 2/25/61.

The Avengers search for an illegal immigrant who, unknowingly, is carrying a radioactive isotope.

9. ASHES OF ROSES

Director: Don Leaver. *Teleplay:* Peter Ling, Sheilagh Ward. *Broadcast live:* 3/4/61.

Steed and Keel versus a gang of arsonists.

10. HUNT THE MAN DOWN

Director: Peter Hammond. *Teleplay:* Robert Fuest. *Recorded:* 3/12/61. *Broadcast:* 3/18/61.

Steed and Keel become involved with a vicious gang of bank robbers.

11. PLEASE DON'T FEED THE ANIMALS

Director: Dennis Vance. *Teleplay:* Dennis Spooner. *Recorded:* 3/30/61. *Broadcast:* 4/1/61.

Official secrets, blackmailers, and a zoo are the three ingredients confronting the Avengers.

12. DANCE WITH DEATH

Director: Don Leaver. *Teleplay:* Peter Ling, Sheilagh Ward. *Recorded:* 4/13/61. *Broadcast:* 4/15/61.

Keel is framed for the murder of one of his patients.

13. ONE FOR THE MORTUARY

Director: Peter Hammond. *Teleplay:* Brian Clemens. *Recorded:* 4/26/61. *Broadcast:* 4/29/61.

Steed involves Keel in a plan to smuggle a new medical formula to Geneva.

14. THE SPRINGERS

Director: Don Leaver. *Teleplay:* John Whitney, Geoffrey Bellman. *Recorded:* 5/11/61. *Broadcast:* 5/13/61.

Steed and Keel investigate a prison escape route, with Keel going undercover as a convict.

15. THE FRIGHTENERS

Director: Peter Hammond. *Teleplay:* Berkely Mather. *Recorded:* 5/25/61. *Broadcast:* 5/27/61.

Steed recruits Dr. Keel to investigate an organization that offers vicious beatings on demand. The leader of the group is a fat man called The Deacon.

16. THE YELLOW NEEDLE

Director: Don Leaver. *Teleplay:* Patrick Campbell. *Recorded:* 6/8/61. *Broadcast:* 6/10/61.

Steed and Keel examine the assassination attempt of an old friend of Keel's, Sir Wilberforce Lungi, in London to negotiate independence for his country, Tenebra.

17. DEATH ON THE SLIPWAY

Director: Peter Hammond. *Teleplay:* James Mitchell. *Recorded:* 6/22/61. *Broadcast:* 6/24/61.

When investigating a murder Steed encounters an old enemy, a spy who wants the plans for a nuclear submarine.

18. DOUBLE DANGER

Director: Roger Jenkins. *Teleplay:* Gerald Verner. *Recorded:* 7/6/61. *Broadcast:* 7/8/61.

Steed and Keel on the trail of diamond smugglers who have kidnapped the doctor's nurse.

19. TOY TRAP

Director: Don Leaver. *Teleplay:* Bill Strutton. *Recorded:* 7/20/61. *Broadcast:* 7/22/61.

Keel and Steed examine the case of department store employees who have disappeared and return as prostitutes.

20. TUNNEL OF FEAR

Director: James Goddard. *Teleplay:* John Kruse. *Recorded:* 8/3/61. *Broadcast:* 8/5/61.

A carnival offers the solution to a secret smuggling operation.

21. THE FAR-DISTANT DEAD

Director: Robert Fuest. *Teleplay:* John Lucarotti. *Recorded:* 8/14/61. *Broadcast:* 8/19/61.

Keel becomes involved in a murder plot in Mexico City.

22. KILL THE KING

Director: Roger Jenkins. *Teleplay:* James Mitchell. *Recorded:* 8/30/61. *Broadcast:* 9/2/61.

Steed attempts to prevent the assassination of a foreign leader.

23. DEAD OF WINTER

Director: Don Leaver. *Teleplay:* Eric Paice. *Recorded:* 9/7/61. *Broadcast:* 12/9/61.

Steed and Keel versus an ex–Nazi, a neo-fascist party, and a scientist who can suspend life through a deep freeze.

24. THE DEADLY AIR

Director: John Knight. *Teleplay:* Lester Powell. *Recorded:* 9/20/61. *Broadcast:* 12/16/61.

Steed and Keel become involved in a plot to discredit an important new vaccine.

25. A CHANGE OF BAIT

Director: Don Leaver. *Teleplay:* Lewis Davidson. *Recorded:* 9/27/61. *Broadcast:* 12/23/61.

Steed versus Lemuel Potts, an inept smuggler and arsonist.

26. DRAGONSFIELD

Director: Peter Hammond. *Teleplay:* Terence Feely. *Recorded:* 10/18/61. *Broadcast:* 12/30/61.

Sabotage at a radiation testing installation becomes a case for Steed.

PATRICK MACNEE AND HONOR BLACKMAN (1962–64)

Blackman did not appear in every episode of the 1962-63 season; Macnee was occasionally paired with Jon Rollason (as Dr. Martin King) and Julie Stevens (as nightclub singer Venus Smith).

27. DEAD ON COURSE

Director: Richmond Harding. *Teleplay:* Eric Paice. *Recorded:* 5/9/62. *Broadcast:* 12/29/62.

Steed and Dr. King investigate a mysterious air crash on the Irish coast.

28. MISSION TO MONTREAL

Director: Don Leaver. *Teleplay:* Lester Powell. *Recorded:* 5/15/62. *Broadcast:* 10/27/62.

Steed and Dr. King get involved with a neurotic singer and microfilm on a cruise ship traveling to Montreal.

29. THE SELL-OUT

Director: Don Leaver. *Teleplay:* Anthony Terpiloff, Brandon Brady. *Recorded:* 6/9/62. *Broadcast:* 11/24/62.

Steed and Dr. King must uncover a traitor with murderous intent when they attempt to protect a United Nations official who is attending an international conference.

30. DEATH DISPATCH

Director: Jonathan Alwyn. *Teleplay:* Leonard Fincham. *Recorded:* 6/23/62. *Broadcast:* 12/22/62.

Steed impersonates a murdered courier and Mrs. Gale follows him as the Avengers attempt to stop a revolution in Argentina.

31. WARLOCK

Director: Peter Hammond. *Teleplay:* Doreen Montgomery. *Recorded:* 7/7/62. *Broadcast:* 1/26/63.

Steed and Mrs. Gale investigate magic and the sale of state secrets.

32. PROPELLANT 23

Director: Jonathan Alwyn. *Teleplay:* Jon Manchip White. *Recorded:* 7/21/62. Broadcast 10/6/62.

Steed and Mrs. Gale search for a new rocket fuel, which may fall into enemy hands.

33. MR. TEDDY BEAR

Director: Richmond Harding. *Teleplay:* Martin Woodhouse. *Recorded:* 8/4/62. *Broadcast:* 9/29/62.

The Avengers pursue Mr. Teddy Bear, a contract killer whose next job is to kill John Steed.

34. THE DECAPOD

Director: Don Leaver. *Teleplay:* Eric Paice. *Recorded:* 8/12/62. *Broadcast:* 10/13/62.

Steed and Venus Smith hunt an assassin who hides behind the identity of a wrestler known as the Decapod.

35. BULLSEYE

Director: Peter Hammond. *Teleplay:* Eric Paice. *Recorded:* 9/30/62. *Broadcast:* 10/20/62.

Somebody is killing stockholders in Anderson's Small Arms Limited. The killer is also a gunrunner, which brings Steed and Mrs. Gale onto the scene.

36. THE REMOVAL MEN

Director: Don Leaver. *Teleplay:* Roger Marshall, Jeremy Scott. *Recorded:* 10/4/62. *Broadcast:* 11/3/62.

Jack Dragna runs a professional assassination firm, known as The Removal Men. Steed infiltrates the organization and Venus Smith finds a job at Dragna's nightclub.

37. THE MAURITIUS PENNY

Director: Richmond Harding. *Teleplay:* Malcolm Hulke, Terrance Dicks. *Recorded:* 10/18/62. *Broadcast:* 11/10/62.

Steed and Mrs. Gale find a connection between the death of a stamp dealer and a plan to stage a revolution in Europe.

38. DEATH OF A GREAT DANE

Director: Peter Hammond. *Teleplay:* Roger Marshall, Jeremy Scott. *Recorded:* 11/1/62. *Broadcast:* 11/17/62.

Steed and Mrs. Gale investigate a magician who pulled off a grand trick: eating a 50,000 pound breakfast. The conjurer was in a road accident and x-rays reveal a stomach full of diamonds. (This episode was remade as "The 50,000 Pound Breakfast" in the Rigg series.)

39. DEATH ON THE ROCKS

Director: Jonathan Alwyn. *Teleplay:* Eric Paice. *Recorded:* 11/15/62. *Broadcast:* 12/1/62.

Steed and Mrs. Gale track down a diamond-smuggling operation.

40. TRAITOR IN ZEBRA

Director: Richmond Harding. *Teleplay:* John Gilbert. *Recorded:* 11/29/62. *Broadcast:* 12/8/62.

Steed and Mrs. Gale try to plug a leak of defense secrets that seems to be emanating from HMS *Zebra*.

41. THE BIG THINKER

Director: Kim Mills. *Teleplay:* Martin Woodhouse. *Recorded:* 12/13/62. *Broadcast:* 12/15/62.

Plato, an advanced computer, is being sabotaged and the supervising scientists' lives are threatened. Enter Steed and Mrs. Gale. (The episode features a "Dr. Clemens"—an in-joke reference to *Avengers* writer Brian Clemens.)

42. INTERCRIME

Director: Jonathan Alwyn. *Teleplay:* Terrance Dicks, Malcolm Hulke. *Recorded:* 12/29/62. *Broadcast:* 1/5/63.

Steed enlists Mrs. Gale's help in infiltrating Intercrime, a criminal organization.

43. IMMORTAL CLAY

Director: Richard Harding. *Teleplay:* James Mitchell. *Recorded:* 1/10/63. *Broadcast:* 1/12/63.

Murder and blackmail involving an unbreakable ceramic cup that is broken.

44. BOX OF TRICKS

Director: Kim Mills. *Teleplay:* Peter Ling, Edward Rhodes. *Recorded:* 1/17/63. *Broadcast:* 1/19/63.

A faith healer and a magician work together to steal official secrets. Steed and Venus Smith are on the case.

45. THE GOLDEN EGGS

Director: Peter Hammond. *Teleplay:* Martin Woodhouse. *Recorded:* 1/31/63. *Broadcast:* 2/2/63.

Steed and Mrs. Gale hunt for two gold-plated eggs which contain a deadly virus.

46. SCHOOL FOR TRAITORS

Director: Jonathan Alwyn. *Teleplay:* James Mitchell. *Recorded:* 2/7/63. *Broadcast:* 2/9/63.

Steed and Venus Smith go back to school — a university near London — to probe an alleged suicide that was anything but.

47. THE WHITE DWARF

Director: Richmond Harding. *Teleplay:* Malcolm Hulke. *Recorded:* 2/14/63. *Broadcast:* 2/16/63.

A pair of shady characters attempt to defraud the stock market by offering proof that the White Dwarf, a star, is about to destroy the earth.

48. MAN IN THE MIRROR

Director: Kim Mills. *Teleplay:* Geoffrey Orme. *Teleplay:* Geoffrey Orme, Anthony Terpiloff. *Recorded:* 2/22/63. *Broadcast:* 2/23/63.

At a carnival, Venus Smith accidentally discovers proof that a dead cipher clerk isn't dead — and puts her life and Steed's in danger.

49. CONSPIRACY OF SILENCE

Director: Peter Hammond. *Teleplay:* Roger Marshall. *Recorded:* 3/1/63. *Broadcast:* 3/2/63.

A murderous clown, the Mafia, and an attempt on Steed's life all figure in this bizarre tale.

50. A CHORUS OF FROGS

Director: Raymond Menmuir. *Teleplay:* Martin Woodhouse. *Recorded:* 3/8/63. *Broadcast:* 3/9/63.

Steed and Venus Smith look into the death of a diver who was testing a new type of bathysphere.

51. SIX HANDS ACROSS A TABLE

Director: Richmond Harding. *Teleplay:* Reed R. de Rouen. *Recorded:* 3/15/63. *Broadcast:* 3/16/63.

Two businessmen get involved in a murder scheme involving a nuclear submarine. A short-lived love interest for Mrs. Gale is introduced in this episode.

52. KILLER WHALE

Director: Kim Mills. *Teleplay:* John Lucarotti. *Recorded:* 3/22/63. *Broadcast:* 3/23/63.

Mrs. Gale manages a boxer named Joey Frazer and, with the help of Steed, uncovers an illegal perfume smuggling operation.

53. CONCERTO

Director: Kim Mills. *Teleplay:* Terrance Dicks, Malcolm Hulke. *Recorded:* 4/24/63. *Broadcast:* 3/2/64.

A naive Russian pianist is blackmailed into making an assassination attempt at East-West trade talks.

54. BRIEF FOR MURDER

Director: Peter Hammond. *Teleplay:* Brian Clemens. *Recorded:* 5/1/63. *Broadcast:* 9/29/63.

Steed goes on trial for the murder of Mrs. Gale, all part of a scheme to expose crooked lawyers.

55. THE NUTSHELL

Director: Raymond Menmuir. *Teleplay:* Philip Chambers. *Recorded:* 5/10/63. *Broadcast:* 10/19/63.

Steed is the chief suspect in the theft of secret documents from The Nutshell, an underground security center.

56. THE GOLDEN FLEECE

Director: Peter Hammond. *Teleplay:* Roger Marshall, Phyllis Norman. *Recorded:* 5/25/63. *Broadcast:* 12/7/63.

Steed and Mrs. Gale investigate a gold smuggling operation involving the Chinese.

57. DEATH A LA CARTE

Director: Kim Mills. *Teleplay:* John Lucarotti. *Recorded:* 6/14/63. *Broadcast:* 12/21/63.

The Avengers protect the Emir Akaba who is in London for his annual medical checkup.

58. MAN WITH TWO SHADOWS

Director: Don Leaver. *Teleplay:* James Mitchell. *Recorded:* 6/21/63. *Broadcast:* 10/12/63.

An important scientist and then Steed himself are replaced by doubles, giving new meaning to the term "double agent."

59. DON'T LOOK BEHIND YOU

Director: Peter Hammond. *Teleplay:* Brian Clemens. *Recorded:* 7/5/63. *Broadcast:* 12/14/63.

Mrs. Gale accepts an invitation to a remote country house for a weekend party—only to find it all but abandoned and her life threatened by a madman. (This episode was remade as the Rigg episode "The Joker.")

60. THE GRANDEUR THAT WAS ROME

Director: Kim Mills. *Teleplay:* Rex Edwards. *Recorded:* 7/19/63. *Broadcast:* 11/30/63.

The Avengers versus a madman who dreams of recreating the Roman Empire after releasing bubonic plague on the world.

61. THE UNDERTAKERS

Director: Bill Bain. *Teleplay:* Malcolm Hulke. *Recorded:* 8/2/63. *Broadcast:* 10/5/63.

The Avengers investigate a scam involving a rest home for millionaires.

62. DEATH OF A BATMAN

Director: Kim Mills. *Teleplay:* Roger Marshall. *Recorded:* 8/14/63. *Broadcast:* 10/26/63.

Steed investigates fraud and forgery on the stock exchange.

63. BUILD A BETTER MOUSETRAP

Director: Peter Hammond. *Teleplay:* Brian Clemens. *Recorded:* 8/28/63. *Broadcast:* 2/15/64.

Mrs. Gale joins a motorcycle gang to uncover why mechanical devices in a certain area are not working. The ending features a tongue-in-cheek *Avengers* twist.

64. NOVEMBER FIVE

Director: Bill Bain. *Teleplay:* Eric Paice. *Recorded:* 9/27/63. *Broadcast:* 11/2/63.

Steed has Mrs. Gale run for election to parliament as part of an investigation into the theft of a nuclear warhead.

65. SECOND SIGHT

Director: Peter Hammond. *Teleplay:* Martin Woodhouse. *Recorded:* 10/11/63. *Broadcast:* 11/16/63.

Steed suspects that an eye operation, involving a live donor and a cornea container, is not what it seems.

66. THE SECRETS BROKER

Director: Jonathan Alwyn. *Teleplay:* Ludovic Peters. *Recorded:* 10/19/63. *Broadcast:* 2/1/64.

Steed and Mrs. Gale investigate a group that uses blackmail to get official secrets. A standard plot features a few typically bizarre touches, such as a séance that is employed as the contact point to give a killer a gun.

67. THE GILDED CAGE

Director: Bill Bain. *Teleplay:* Roger Marshall. *Recorded:* 10/25/63. *Broadcast:* 11/9/63.

Steed and Mrs. Gale on the trail of a crooked millionaire. The lure: a million pounds worth of gold.

68. THE MEDICINE MEN

Director: Kim Mills. *Teleplay:* Malcolm Hulke. *Recorded:* 11/8/63. *Broadcast:* 11/23/63.

Murder at a pharmaceutical company brings The Avengers on the scene.

69. THE WHITE ELEPHANT

Director: Laurence Bourne. *Teleplay:* John Lucarotti. *Recorded:* 11/22/63. *Broadcast:* 1/4/64.

Steed and Mrs. Gale investigate the disappearance of a white elephant from a zoo called Noah's Ark, which eventually leads to ivory smuggling. Mrs. Gale tricks one of her opponents by saying, "Do you really need a gun to deal with a woman?" and then, after he puts the weapon down, promptly flips him with a judo move. Behind the scenes, Macnee badly sprained his ankle during the climax, a bird died from shock when a gun was fired during the taping, and the cast was shooting when news came that President John F. Kennedy had been killed.

70. DRESSED TO KILL

Director: Bill Bain. *Teleplay:* Brian Clemens. *Recorded:* 12/6/63. *Broadcast:* 12/28/63.

A New Year's Eve costume party aboard a speeding train turns deadly when one of the passengers begins killing his fellow revelers. The motive involves a defense department early warning station.

71. THE WRINGER

Director: Don Leaver. *Teleplay*: Martin Woodhouse. *Recorded:* 12/20/63. *Broadcast:* 1/18/64.

A conventional spy thriller, similar to a 1965 film, *The Ipcress File.* Steed investigates the disappearance of seven agents—one of them a close friend. When he finds the man, however, he accuses Steed of murdering the other six agents, and has photos to prove it.

72. THE LITTLE WONDERS

Director: Laurence Bourne. *Teleplay:* Eric Paice. *Recorded:* 1/3/64. *Broadcast:* 1/11/64.

The Avengers cope with gun-wielding priests. The episode inverts clichés: the priests are all tough-talking, lower-class toughs, who drink, smoke, and gamble yet all address the Bishop as "your lordship" or "your grace." They are members of Bibliotek, a 300-year-old criminal organization with agents all over the world, involved in murder and smuggling operations. Steed infiltrates the organization as Johnny the Horse, a notorious gambler.

73. MANDRAKE

Director: Bill Bain. *Teleplay:* Roger Marshall. *Recorded:* 1/16/64. *Broadcast:* 1/25/64.

Steed and Mrs. Gale investigate the strange deaths of elderly millionaires who die in England but end up in a Cornish cemetery.

74. TROJAN HORSE

Director: Laurence Bourne. *Teleplay:* Malcolm Hulke. *Recorded:* 1/30/64. *Broadcast:* 2/8/64.

Skullduggery at the racetrack. The Avengers look into a Murder Inc.-style organization that blackmails heavy debtors into killing people.

75. THE OUTSIDE-IN MAN

Director: Jonathan Alwyn. *Teleplay:* Philip Chambers. *Recorded:* 2/12/64. *Broadcast:* 2/22/64.

Steed protects a defector from an assassination attempt by one of his own agents. This episode presents Steed's superior operating out of a freezer in a butcher's shop! The plot is similar to the *Secret Agent* episode "Fair Exchange," also from 1964, in which a spy who had been imprisoned by the other side seeks revenge on the man who tortured him — and almost causes an international incident in the process. (It also includes the same twist: his own people want to kill the torturer.)

76. THE CHARMERS

Director: Bill Bain. *Teleplay:* Brian Clemens. *Recorded:* 2/27/64. *Broadcast:* 2/29/64.

Steed and Mrs. Gale investigate an organization that is killing agents from both the East and the West. (The plot was reused in the Rigg series and retitled "The Correct Way to Kill.")

77. ESPRIT DE CORPS

Director: Don Leaver. *Teleplay:* Eric Paice. *Recorded:* 3/11/64. *Broadcast:* 3/14/64.

Brigadier General Sir Ian Stuart-Bollinger plans to use his regiment to overthrow the monarchy, and wants to make Mrs. Gale his queen.

78. LOBSTER QUADRILLE

Director: Kim Mills. *Teleplay:* Richard Lucas (pseudonym for Brian Clemens and Richard Bates). *Recorded:* 3/20/64. *Broadcast:* 3/21/64.

A dope-smuggling operation becomes the focus of The Avengers' investigation when a man's charred body is tied to a lobster-fishing business. In the last scene, there is a veiled reference to Blackman's next role as Pussy Galore in the James Bond adventure *Goldfinger* (Steed talks about her "pussyfooting around").

Patrick Macnee and Diana Rigg (1965–67)

79. THE MURDER MARKET

Director: Peter Graham Scott. *Teleplay:* Tony Williamson. *Filmed:* December 1964/January 1965. *Broadcast:* 11/13/65.

Someone is murdering eligible bachelors—and the clues lead the Togetherness Marriage Bureau, and the "death" of Mrs. Peel.

80. THE MASTER MINDS

Director: Peter Graham Scott. *Teleplay:* Robert Banks Stewart. *Filmed:* December 1964/January 1965: *Broadcast:* 11/6/65.

The Ransack Club, a haven for those with high IQs, becomes the focal point of Steed and Mrs. Peel's investigation into acts of treason performed by high government officials.

81. DIAL A DEADLY NUMBER

Director: Don Leaver. *Teleplay:* Roger Marshall. *Filmed:* January 1965. *Broadcast:* 12/4/65.

Murder by telephone, as Steed and Mrs. Peel investigate a stock market investor who profits by his competitor's deaths.

82. DEATH AT BARGAIN PRICES

Director: Charles Crichton. *Teleplay:* Brian Clemens. *Filmed:* January/February 1965: *Broadcast:* 10/23/65.

This excellent installment involves strange goings-on at a department store: a top agent is murdered there, and Steed and Mrs. Peel find that a mad millionaire is planning to blow up London with an atom bomb. Steed uses a ping-pong gun; Mrs. Peel wears a Cathy Gale-esque leather outfit.

83. TOO MANY CHRISTMAS TREES

Director: Roy Baker. *Teleplay:* Tony Williamson. *Filmed:* February/March 1965. *Broadcast:* 12/25/65.

Steed is plagued by recurring nightmares that involve a satanic Santa Claus and official secrets.

84. THE CYBERNAUTS

Director: Sidney Hayers. *Teleplay:* Brian Clemens. *Filmed:* March 1965. *Broadcast:* 10/16/65.

The first of three stories involving *The Avengers'* most popular foes: the robotic assassins who break down doors and kill their victims with mechanical karate chops.

85. THE GRAVEDIGGERS

Director: Quentin Lawrence. *Teleplay:* Malcolm Hulke. *Filmed:* March/April 1965. *Broadcast:* 10/9/65.

Britain's early warning defense system is menaced by dead men who won't stay dead.

86. ROOM WITHOUT A VIEW

Director: Roy Baker. *Teleplay:* Roger Marshall. *Filmed:* April 1965. *Broadcast:* 1/8/66.

Steed and Mrs. Peel investigate the Chessman Hotel, where eminent scientists check in but don't check out — disappearing and returning months later as brainwashed shells of their former selves.

87. A SURFEIT OF H_2O

Director: Sidney Hayers. *Teleplay:* Colin Finbow. *Filmed:* April/May 1965. *Broadcast:* 10/23/65.

Freak rainstorms are used as a means of murder. (This was the uncredited basis for *The Avengers* feature film.)

88. TWO'S A CROWD

Director: Roy Baker. *Teleplay:* Philip Levene. *Filmed:* April/May 1965. *Broadcast:* 12/18/65.

Double trouble when an impostor of Steed seems to have replaced the real McCoy and stolen important documents.

89. MAN-EATER OF SURREY GREEN

Director: Sidney Hayers. *Teleplay:* Philip Levene. *Filmed:* May/June 1965. *Broadcast:* 12/11/65.

A spaceship brings mind-controlling plants from outer space.

90. SILENT DUST

Director: Roy Baker. *Teleplay:* Roger Marshall. *Filmed:* June 1965. *Broadcast:* 1/1/66.

A life-destroying fertilizer, Silent Dust, figures in a blackmail scheme.

Appendix 2: The Avengers   173

91. THE HOUR THAT NEVER WAS

Director: Gerry O'Hara. *Teleplay:* Roger Marshall. *Filmed:* June 1965. *Broadcast:* 11/27/65.

On a visit to his old RAF base, Steed loses an hour — and Mrs. Peel — before stumbling on a brainwashing plan involving an evil dentist.

92. THE TOWN OF NO RETURN

Director: Roy Baker. *Teleplay:* Brian Clemens. *Filmed:* July 1965. *Broadcast:* 10/2/65.

Steed and Mrs. Peel investigate the disappearance of three agents who vanished at Little Bazzeley, a town by the sea, in a dark, film noirish installment. This was the first Emma Peel episode filmed, with Elizabeth Shepherd as Emma; it was almost completely reshot when Diana Rigg was cast.

93. CASTLE DE'ATH

Director: James Hill. *Teleplay:* John Lucarotti. *Filmed:* July/August 1965. *Broadcast:* 10/30/65.

Steed and Mrs. Peel encounter ghostly goings-on when they investigate the death of a diver found in a castle moat.

94. THE THIRTEENTH HOLE

Director: Roy Baker. *Teleplay:* Tony Williamson. *Filmed:* September 1965. *Broadcast:* 1/29/66.

The Avengers on the golf course, looking into death by golf ball at the Thirteenth Hole.

95. SMALL GAME FOR BIG HUNTERS

Director: Gerry O'Hara. *Teleplay:* Philip Levene. *Filmed:* September 1965. *Broadcast:* 1/15/66.

Sleeping sickness, voodoo, and murder — all 25 miles from London.

96. THE GIRL FROM AUNTIE

Director: Roy Baker. *Teleplay:* Roger Marshall. *Filmed:* September/October 1965. *Broadcast:* 1/21/66.

The kidnapping of Mrs. Peel leads Steed to an organization that auctions off artwork, monuments, and state secrets. (The episode is full of in-jokes: "Lady Bracknell, don't forget your handbag"; John, Paul, George, and Fred; Barrett, Barrett & Wimpole; and the title, poking fun at competing spy show, *The Man from U.N.C.L.E.*) Victims are killed by an old woman with knitting needle.

97. QUICK-QUICK-SLOW DEATH

Director: James Hill. *Teleplay:* Robert Banks Stewart. *Filmed:* October/November 1965. *Broadcast:* 2/5/66.

A trail of murder leads to a dance studio, where Emma takes on a job as a dancing instructor.

98. THE DANGER MAKERS

Director: Charles Crichton. *Teleplay:* Roger Marshall. *Filmed:* November/December 1965. *Broadcast:* 2/12/66.

The team examines the strange death of a military officer, decorated for bravery, who dies while playing "chicken" on a motorcycle.

99. A TOUCH OF BRIMSTONE

Director: James Hill. *Teleplay:* Brian Clemens. *Filmed:* December 1965. *Broadcast:* 2/19/66.

Comic situations turn deadly: diplomats are humiliated in public and the trail leads to a wealthy hedonist, John Cartney, the founder of the Hell Fire Club. Mrs. Peel turns up as Lady Sin (in a costume that got the episode banned from American television), and she kicks some characters around, including the whip-snapping Cartney.

100. WHAT THE BUTLER SAW

Director: Bill Bain. *Teleplay:* Brian Clemens. *Filmed:* December 1965/January 1966. *Broadcast:* 2/26/66.

Tired episode that is meant to be funny but is merely strained. Steed and Mrs. Peel try to find out which of three officers is a traitor. Their one clue: each has a suspicious butler. The story is thin — even by *Avengers* standards — and the acting is arch. Steed infiltrates a school for butlers (with the motto, "Brighter, Better, More Beautiful Butling"); he also encounters an eccentric old soldier who insists on restaging the last war in his garden.

101. THE HOUSE THAT JACK BUILT

Director: Don Leaver. *Teleplay:* Brian Clemens. *Filmed:* January 1966. *Broadcast:* 3/5/66.

Mrs. Peel, visiting an inherited house from an uncle she never knew, encounters an electronic death trap.

102. A SENSE OF HISTORY

Director: Peter Graham Scott. *Teleplay:* Martin Woodhouse. *Filmed:* January/February 1966. *Broadcast:* 3/12/66.

The Avengers go back to college, in particular, in a bona fide mystery that has the team trying to figure out who, from a group of obvious red herrings, killed the economics professor with an arrow! Seems the professor had a radical theory that could bring world peace, so he had to go.

103. HOW TO SUCCEED ... AT MURDER

Director: Don Leaver. *Teleplay:* Brian Clemens. *Filmed:* February 1966. *Broadcast:* 3/19/66.

A twist on ideas of feminism, this episode finds women knocking off men and taking over their businesses. The villain is Sylvia, a ventriloquist's dummy! Steed actually does some sleuthing in this one and makes an ingenious deduction in the climax; also, atypically, he uses a gun to dispose of the villain.

104. HONEY FOR THE PRINCE

Director: James Hill. *Teleplay:* Brian Clemens. *Filmed:* February/March 1966. *Broadcast:* 3/23/66.

The Avengers in a mystery involving honey and assassination, with a gallery of eccentrics and an organization which allows people to live out their fantasies, pre–*Fantasy Island* (Steed is offered a fantasy life as an agent with a license to kill. "That would be a change," he notes dryly). Two odd villains are on hand: one who spends most of the episode giving orders from a sauna and another who appears at the puff of a lamp. There is also the Arabian prince who has 320 wives but is more interested in cricket.

105. THE FEAR MERCHANTS

Director: Gordon Flemyng. *Teleplay:* Philip Levene. *Filmed:* September 1966. *Broadcast:* 1/21/67.

Steed and Mrs. Peel examine an organization that uses fear to destroy its enemies.

106. ESCAPE IN TIME

Director: John Krish. *Teleplay:* Philip Levene. *Filmed:* September/October 1966. *Broadcast:* 1/28/67.

Steed and Mrs. Peel are on the trail of criminals who seem to have found a perfect hiding place: the past. The escape route sequence, in which the Avengers follow the first escapee, is shot with tongue firmly placed in cheek, and makes fun of the entire spy genre. At one point, Steed comments on the clichés of the genre by summing up his predicament — "Mrs. Peel in the hands of the enemy, my associate lying unconscious, a loaded gun pointing at my head" — and then easily disarms his assailant. Mrs. Peel faces torture and laughs it off, presumably expecting — and receiving — rescue from Steed, her knight in shining armor.

107. THE BIRD WHO KNEW TOO MUCH

Director: Roy Rossotti. *Teleplay:* Brian Clemens, from a story by Alan Pattillo. *Filmed:* October 1966. *Broadcast:* 2/11/67.

Steed and Mrs. Peel investigate the deaths of two operatives and their only clue is a bag of bird seed that one of the agents was carrying at the time of his death.

108. FROM VENUS WITH LOVE

Director: Robert Day. *Teleplay:* Philip Levene. *Filmed:* October/November 1966. *Broadcast:* 1/14/67.

Are visitors from Venus murdering the members of the Venusian society?

109. THE SEE-THROUGH MAN

Director: Robert Asher. *Teleplay:* Philip Levene. *Filmed:* November 1966. *Broadcast:* 2/4/67.

Weak episode, another Cold War comedy (like the equally poor "Two's a Crowd"). The thin story has the Russians apparently employing an invisible agent.

110. THE WINGED AVENGER

Director: Gordon Flemyng and Peter Duffell. *Teleplay:* Richard Harris. *Filmed:* November/December 1966. *Broadcast:* 2/18/67.

A ruthless executive is murdered, in a locked room, on the top floor of a skyscraper. The only clue is the horrible claw marks that cover his (bloodless) body.

111. THE LIVING DEAD

Director: John Krish. *Teleplay:* Brian Clemens. *Filmed:* December 1966/January 1967. *Broadcast:* 2/25/67.

Steed and Mrs. Peel investigate the apparent appearance of a ghost who appeared in a graveyard, rang the church bell, and then disappeared.

112. THE HIDDEN TIGER

Director: Sidney Hayers. *Teleplay:* Philip Levene. *Filmed:* January 1967. *Broadcast:* 3/4/67.

Someone or something is clawing to death prominent businessmen. The corpses' clothes are in tatters and they look as though they were clawed to death by a lion. Yet the victims are usually in locked rooms.

113. THE CORRECT WAY TO KILL

Director: Charles Crichton. *Teleplay:* Brian Clemens. *Filmed:* January/February 1967. *Broadcast:* 3/11/67.

Someone is killing off Russian agents and Steed and Mrs. Peel form a truce with their Russian counterparts to investigate. (This is a remake of the Blackman episode, "The Charmers.")

114. NEVER, NEVER SAY DIE

Director: Robert Day. *Teleplay:* Philip Levene. *Filmed:* February 1967. *Broadcast:* 3/18/67.

Steed and Mrs. Peel wonder why a dead man won't stay dead — and what role Dr. Frank N. Stone has in the affair.

115. EPIC

Director: James Hill. *Teleplay:* Brian Clemens. *Filmed:* February 1967. *Broadcast:* 4/1/67.

Mrs. Peel is kidnapped and forced to star in a snuff film called *The Destruction of Emma Peel*.

116. THE SUPERLATIVE SEVEN

Director: Sidney Hayers. *Teleplay:* Brian Clemens. *Filmed:* March 1967. *Broadcast:* 4/8/67.

Trapped on a desert island with six other men and women, Steed has to find out which among them is a killer — or be killed himself.

117. A FUNNY THING HAPPENED ON THE WAY TO THE STATION

Director: John Krish. *Teleplay:* Bryan Sheriff (pseudonym for Brian Clemens and Roger Marshall). *Filming completed:* 3/22/67. Broadcast: 4/15/67.

Steed and Mrs. Peel investigate a missing agent and a station that seems to exist in two places. The assassin whistles a wedding march before his murders and the chief villain is a megalomaniac ticket collector (He: "I'm going to blow up your prime minister." Steed: "How do you know I voted for him?"). Good puns ("Pop goes the diesel," says Steed when he learns of the plan).

118. SOMETHING NASTY IN THE NURSERY

Director: James Hill. *Teleplay:* Philip Levene. *Filming completed:* 4/2/67. Broadcast: 4/22/67.

The Avengers investigate high-level leaks that involve a machine-gun-wielding nanny in a wheelchair, a box containing a hand holding a gun which springs up and shoots people, and a ball which "regresses" anyone who touches it into a child-like state. There's also an "Avengersland" organization called the Guild Of Noble Nannies (GONN). Mrs. Peel notes that key witnesses are always killed moments before Steed and or Mrs. Peel arrive on the scene.

119. THE JOKER

Director: Sidney Hayers. *Teleplay:* Brian Clemens. *Filmed:* March 1967. Broadcast: 4/29/67.

Mrs. Peel accepts an invitation to a remote country house for a weekend with a chess master — only to find her life threatened by a madman. (This episode is a remake of Blackman episode, "Don't Look Behind You.")

120. WHO'S WHO???

Director: John Moxey. *Teleplay:* Philip Levene. *Filmed:* April 1967. Broadcast: 5/6/67.

A mind-swapping device turns Steed and Mrs. Peel into enemy agents.

121. DEATH'S DOOR

Director: Sidney Hayers. *Teleplay:* Philip Levene. *Filming completed:* 6/7/67. *Broadcast:* 10/7/67.

Steed and Mrs. Peel try and discover why important government ministers, on the eve of a major peace conference, are having nightmares foretelling their deaths. The dreams seem to be based on the Salvador Dalí sequence in Alfred Hitchcock's *Spellbound* (1945).

122. RETURN OF THE CYBERNAUTS

Director: Robert Day. *Teleplay:* Philip Levene. *Filming completed:* 6/15/67. *Broadcast:* 9/30/67.

Well-crafted revenge story in which the Avengers deal with the brother of the man who invented the cybernauts two years before. The pacing is superb and there appears to be something more substantial in the Steed-Peel relationship than has been hinted at before. Peter Cushing plays a villain who is both charming and ruthless, an evil Steed. Best line: after being told that the wristwatch will control his mind, Steed retorts: "Yes, but does it keep good time?"

123. DEAD MAN'S TREASURE

Director: Sidney Hayers. *Teleplay:* Michael Winder. *Filming completed:* 7/5/67. *Broadcast:* 10/21/67.

Steed, Mrs. Peel, two of the opposition, and a mysterious third party all join in a wild search for secret documents.

124. THE 50,000 POUND BREAKFAST

Director: Robert Day. *Teleplay:* Roger Marshall. *Filmed:* July 1967. *Broadcast:* 10/14/67.

Steed and Mrs. Peel investigate the mysterious never-seen-but-often-heard financier Litoff, who seems to be involved in high-level smuggling and murder. (This episode is a remake of the Blackman episode, "Death of a Great Dane.")

125. YOU HAVE JUST BEEN MURDERED

Director: Robert Asher. *Teleplay:* Philip Levene. *Filming completed:* 8/2/67. *Broadcast:* 10/28/67.

The Avengers encounter a protection racket that targets millionaires. Steed and Mrs. Peel are very much in the amateur sleuth mode, with a nod to *Goldfinger* and the 007 Aston Martin electronic tracking device.

126. THE POSITIVE-NEGATIVE MAN

Director: Robert Day. *Teleplay:* Tony Williamson. *Filming completed:* 8/31/67. Broadcast: 11/4/67.

Steed and Mrs. Peel investigate a series of highly unusual deaths: scientists who had been working on a hush-hush, discontinued government project are found dead from a powerful electrical force.

127. MURDERSVILLE

Director: Robert Asher. *Teleplay:* Brian Clemens. *Filmed:* August 1967. Broadcast: 11/11/67.

Mrs. Peel encounters a town where murder is a way of life.

128. MISSION ... HIGHLY IMPROBABLE

Director: Robert Day. *Teleplay:* Philip Levene. *Filmed:* September 1967. Broadcast: 11/18/67.

Steed gets cut down to size when enemy agents try to steal a new miniaturizing ray.

PATRICK MACNEE AND LINDA THORSON (1967–69)

129. INVASION OF THE EARTHMEN

Director: Don Sharp. *Teleplay:* Terry Nation. *Filmed:* November 1967. Broadcast: 4/27/69.

Steed and Tara stumble across a madman planning to invade outer space.

130. THE CURIOUS CASE OF THE COUNTLESS CLUES

Director: Don Sharp. *Teleplay:* Philip Levene. *Filmed:* January 1968. Broadcast: 5/18/69.

Steed and Tara investigate a murder case with too many clues.

131. THE FORGET-ME-KNOT

Director: James Hill. *Teleplay:* Brian Clemens. *Filmed:* January 1968. Broadcast: 1/12/69.

Mrs. Peel hands off to Tara King in an episode involving a weapon that produces amnesia in its victims. (This was the only installment in the series in which Steed's partners actually met.)

132. SPLIT

Director: Roy Baker. *Teleplay:* Brian Clemens. *Filmed:* February 1968. *Broadcast:* 2/2/69.

A dead Soviet agent seems to be reincarnated in top government officials, who are killing each other.

133. GET-A-WAY!

Director: Don Sharp. *Teleplay:* Philip Levene. *Filmed:* February 1968. *Broadcast:* 7/27/69.

Russian agents have gained the power to disappear at will.

134. HAVE GUNS, WILL HAGGLE

Director: Ray Austin. *Teleplay:* Donald James. *Filmed:* February 1968. *Broadcast:* 3/30/69.

Steed becomes a participant in an illegal auction of 3,000 rifles.

135. LOOK (STOP ME IF YOU'VE HEARD THIS ONE) BUT THERE WERE THESE TWO FELLERS ...

Director: James Hill. *Teleplay:* Dennis Spooner. *Filmed:* March 1968. *Broadcast:* 3/23/69.

Monty Python's John Cleese guest stars in a story about two vaudeville-style killers.

136. MY WILDEST DREAM

Director: Robert Fuest. *Teleplay:* Philip Levene. *Filmed:* March-April 1968. *Broadcast:* 9/7/69.

Murderous dreams are becoming reality for frustrated executives.

137. WHOEVER SHOT POOR GEORGE OBLIQUE STROKE XR40?

Director: Cyril Frankel. *Teleplay:* Tony Williamson. *Filmed:* April 1968. *Broadcast:* 2/16/69.

Steed and Tara look into the shooting of a computer.

138. YOU'LL CATCH YOUR DEATH

Director: Paul Dickson. *Teleplay:* Jeremy Burnham. *Filmed:* May 1968. *Broadcast:* 2/2/69.

A killer virus is on the loose, with symptoms like a common cold.

139. ALL DONE WITH MIRRORS

Director: Ray Austin. *Teleplay:* Leigh Vance. *Filmed:* June 1968. *Broadcast:* 3/2/69.

Secrets are being stolen by impostors.

140. SUPER-SECRET CYPHER SNATCH

Director: John Hough. *Teleplay:* Tony Williamson. *Filmed:* June 1968. *Broadcast:* 1/26/69.

A glass-cleaning company is a cover for an organization that steals secrets.

141. GAME

Director: Robert Fuest. *Teleplay:* Richard Harris. *Filmed:* June 1968. *Broadcast:* 1/19/69.

A vengeful ex-colleague of Steed's sets up a bizarre game of death, with Tara and Steed's lives in the balance.

142. FALSE WITNESS

Director: Charles Crichton. *Teleplay:* Jeremy Burnham. *Filmed:* July 1968. *Broadcast:* 2/23/69.

Steed and Tara investigate why a key government witness has changed his testimony.

143. NOON DOOMSDAY

Director: Peter Sykes. *Teleplay:* Terry Nation. *Filmed:* July 1968. *Broadcast:* 3/16/69.

Steed, laid up in a rest home, becomes the target of an old foe.

144. LEGACY OF DEATH

Director: Don Chaffey. *Teleplay:* Terry Nation. *Filmed:* August 1968. *Broadcast:* 3/9/69.

A parody of *The Maltese Falcon* (1941) finds Steed and Tara dealing with an ornate dagger and the various odd characters who want it.

Appendix 2: The Avengers

145. THEY KEEP KILLING STEED

Director: Robert Fuest. *Teleplay:* Brian Clemens. *Filmed:* August 1968. *Broadcast:* 4/6/69.

A double of Steed could cause havoc at a top-level peace conference.

146. WISH YOU WERE HERE

Director: Don Chaffey. *Teleplay:* Tony Williamson. *Filmed:* September 1968. *Broadcast:* 5/25/69.

A parody of *The Prisoner* TV series finds Tara held prisoner at a seaside hotel. (Don Chaffey directed a number of episodes of *The Prisoner*.)

147. KILLER

Director: Cliff Owen. *Teleplay:* Tony Williamson. *Filmed:* September 1968. *Broadcast:* 5/4/69.

A computer begins killing Steed's colleagues.

148. THE ROTTERS

Director: Robert Fuest. *Teleplay:* Dave Freeman. *Filmed:* October 1968. *Broadcast:* 4/20/69.

Two killers employ a fungus that turns wood into sawdust.

149. THE INTERROGATORS

Director: Charles Crichton. *Teleplay:* Richard Harris and Brian Clemens. *Filmed:* October 1968. *Broadcast:* 4/13/69.

When Steed and Tara investigate a school for spies, Steed becomes a target.

150. THE MORNING AFTER

Director: John Hough. *Teleplay:* Brian Clemens. *Filmed:* October–November 1968. *Broadcast:* 5/11/69.

Steed and an enemy agent, Merlin, handcuffed together and unconscious for 24 hours, wake to find a state of martial law in place — and their lives in danger.

151. LOVE ALL

Director: Peter Sykes. *Teleplay:* Jeremy Burnham. *Filmed:* November 1968. *Broadcast:* 7/13/69.

Public officials seem to be falling in love with enemy agents.

152. TAKE ME TO YOUR LEADER

Director: Robert Fuest. *Teleplay:* Terry Nation. *Filmed:* November 1968. *Broadcast:* 6/15/69.

Steed and Tara follow a briefcase loaded with secrets and money.

153. STAY TUNED

Director: Don Chaffey. *Teleplay:* Tony Williamson. *Filmed:* December 1968. *Broadcast:* 6/8/69.

Steed is brainwashed into attempting to assassinate his superior, Mother.

154. FOG

Director: John Hough. *Teleplay:* Jeremy Burnham. *Filmed:* December 1968. *Broadcast:* 6/23/69.

Two foreign delegates to a disarmament conference seem to have been killed by a modern-day Jack the Ripper.

155. WHO WAS THAT MAN I SAW YOU WITH?

Director: Don Chaffey. *Teleplay:* Jeremy Burnham. *Filmed:* January 1968. *Broadcast:* 8/31/69.

Evidence points to Tara as a double-agent.

156. PANDORA

Director: Robert Fuest. *Teleplay:* Brian Clemens. *Filmed:* January 1969. *Broadcast:* 8/10/69.

Tara is kidnapped and brainwashed into thinking she is Pandora, a woman living in 1918.

157. THINGUMAJIG

Director: Leslie Norman. *Teleplay:* Terry Nation. *Filmed:* January 1969. *Broadcast:* 8/1/69.

Two electrical boxes begin killing an archaeological team.

158. HOMICIDE AND OLD LACE

Director: John Hough. *Teleplay:* Malcolm Hulke and Terrance Dicks. *Filmed:* January 1969. *Broadcast:* 7/6/69.

Mother tells his two aunts the tale of the Great Britain crime that was thwarted by Steed and Tara.

159. REQUIEM

Director: Don Chaffey. *Teleplay:* Brian Clemens. *Filmed:* February 1969. *Broadcast:* 8/17/69.

Trouble, in threes: Steed is in hiding with a top government witness; Mother is apparently dead, murdered in a bomb blast; and Tara is badly injured.

160. TAKE-OVER

Director: Robert Fuest. *Teleplay:* Terry Nation. *Filmed:* February 1969. *Broadcast:* 8/24/69.

In a take-off of *The Desperate Hours* (1955), Steed visits an old friend who is being held prisoner by a gang of criminals.

161. BIZARRE

Director: Leslie Norman. *Teleplay:* Brian Clemens. *Filmed:* March 1969. *Broadcast:* 9/14/69.

Steed and Tara look into the undead at the Happy Meadows cemetery.

Patrick Macnee, Joanna Lumley, and Gareth Hunt (1976-77)

162. THE EAGLE'S NEST

Director: Desmond Davis. *Teleplay:* Brian Clemens. *Broadcast:* 10/22/76.

The New Avengers versus Nazi monks who want to revive Hitler.

163. THE MIDAS TOUCH

Director: Robert Fuest. *Teleplay:* Brian Clemens. *Broadcast:* 11/12/76.
Steed, Purdey, and Gambit search for a plague carrier.

164. HOUSE OF CARDS

Director: Ray Austin. *Teleplay:* Brian Clemens. *Broadcast:* 10/29/76.
Brainwashed agents are brought into play against a Russian defector.

165. THE LAST OF THE CYBERNAUTS...?

Director: Sidney Hayers. *Teleplay:* Brian Clemens. *Broadcast:* 11/5/76.

The Cybernauts are reborn, this time with a half-human/half-cybernaut leader.

166. TO CATCH A RAT

Director: James Hill. *Teleplay:* Terence Feely. *Broadcast:* 12/3/76.

Former *Avengers* star Ian Hendry returns as Irwin Gunner, an agent who has been missing for 17 years but is determined to complete his mission: catch a double agent known as The White Rat.

167. CAT AMONGST THE PIGEONS

Director: John Hough. *Teleplay:* Dennis Spooner. *Broadcast:* 11/19/76.

The New Avengers face killer birds.

168. TARGET!

Director: Ray Austin. *Teleplay:* Dennis Spooner. *Broadcast:* 11/26/76.

Five agents die mysteriously after completing their training session.

169. FACES

Director: James Hill. *Teleplay:* Brian Clemens and Dennis Spooner. *Broadcast:* 12/17/76.

A plastic surgeon creates doubles to infiltrate the government.

170. THE TALE OF THE BIG WHY

Director: Robert Fuest. *Teleplay:* Brian Clemens. *Broadcast:* 12/10/76.

Gambit and Purdey pursue secret documents.

171. THREE-HANDED GAME

Director: Ray Austin. *Teleplay:* Dennis Spooner and Brian Clemens. *Broadcast:* 1/21/77.

Master spy Juventor uses a thought-transference machine to steal a secret code.

172. SLEEPER

Director: Grahame Clifford. *Teleplay:* Brian Clemens. *Broadcast:* 1/14/77.

Steed, Purdey, and Gambit are the only ones up against a gang of criminals who use a sleeping gas to execute a theft.

173. GNAWS

Director: Ray Austin. *Teleplay:* Dennis Spooner. *Broadcast:* 12/21/76.
A radioactive monster is lurking in the sewers of London.

174. DIRTIER BY THE DOZEN

Director: Sidney Hayers. *Teleplay:* Brian Clemens. *Broadcast:* 1/7/77.
The New Avengers versus a group of mercenary soldiers.

175. HOSTAGE

Director: Sidney Hayers. *Teleplay:* Brian Clemens. *Broadcast:* 10/21/77.
A double agent kidnaps Purdey and blackmails Steed into stealing secret defense documents.

176. TRAP

Director: Ray Austin. *Teleplay:* Brian Clemens. *Broadcast:* 10/14/77.
The New Avengers team up with the CIA to battle Chinese spies.

177. DEAD MEN ARE DANGEROUS

Director: Sidney Hayers. *Teleplay:* Brian Clemens. *Broadcast:* 9/9/77.
A traitor with a bullet lodged near his heart is out to kill Steed.

178. MEDIUM RARE

Director: Ray Austin. *Teleplay:* Dennis Spooner. *Broadcast:* 9/23/77.
A team of informers is exposed with the help of a medium.

179. ANGELS OF DEATH

Director: Ernest Day. *Teleplay:* Terence Feely and Brian Clemens. *Broadcast:* 9/16/77.
Steed investigates a clinic at which 47 people have died, apparently from natural causes.

180. OBSESSION

Director: Ernest Day. *Teleplay:* Brian Clemens. *Broadcast:* 10/7/77.
Purdey encounters a former flame who plans to destroy the Houses of Parliament.

181. THE LION AND THE UNICORN

Director: Ray Austin. *Teleplay:* John Goldsmith. *Broadcast:* 9/30/77.

The New Avengers go to France to arrest the Unicorn, a renowned killer.

182. K IS FOR KILL — PART I: THE TIGER AWAKES

Director: Yvon Marie Coulais. *Teleplay:* Brian Clemens. *Broadcast:* 10/28/77.

Steed calls on Mrs. Peel (via old footage) while investigating Russian soldiers who had disappeared and have apparently been revived from World War II.

183. K IS FOR KILL — PART II: TIGER BY THE TAIL

Director: Yvon Marie Coulais. *Teleplay:* Brian Clemens. *Broadcast:* 11/4/77.

The president of France is targeted for death — and only The New Avengers can save him.

184. COMPLEX

Director: Richard Gilbert. *Teleplay:* Dennis Spooner. *Broadcast:* 11/11/77.

The New Avengers travel to Canada, searching for X41, a deadly agent.

185. THE GLADIATORS

Director: Claude Fournier. *Teleplay:* Brian Clemens. *Broadcast:* 11/25/77.

In Canada, Steed, Purdey, and Gambit investigate a modern-day gladiator training camp.

186. FORWARD BASE

Director: Don Thompson. *Teleplay:* Dennis Spooner. *Broadcast:* 11/18/77.

Steed fishes in Lake Ontario for a Russian secret weapon.

187. EMILY

Director: Don Thompson. *Teleplay:* Dennis Spooner. *Broadcast:* 12/17/77.

Steed pursues The Fox, a mysterious spy whose identity is a mystery.

THE AVENGERS WITHOUT PATRICK MACNEE

The Avengers seems inconceivable without Patrick Macnee as John Steed, but there have been two versions done without him. In 1971, Simon Oates played Steed in a London stage production, co-starring Sue Lloyd as Hannah Wild. Although the play was written by long-time series writers Brian Clemens and Terence Feely, it only ran a few weeks in London. Clemens felt that the play was too ambitious for its time and was unsuccessful because it didn't have the budget to match its elaborate plotting. Macnee, however, claimed the series should never have been moved from television.

"It was dreadful. It was perfectly dreadful," he said. "I couldn't have done it anyway. But I wouldn't have been seen dead in it. *The Avengers* is a little television show and that's what it is. And a very good television show.... The stage version was excremental."[1]

Macnee offered similar comments about *The Avengers*, a 1998 big-screen version directed by Jeremiah Chechik, starring Ralph Fiennes and Uma Thurman as a new Steed and Mrs. Peel. "It never should be a movie," Macnee said. "The movie's proved it.... [Brian Clemens] was furious [that they didn't involve him]. The movie was completely [awful]—I felt so sorry for Ralph Fiennes because I read that script and it was rather good. And, do you know, the producer, [Sy] Weintraub, he insisted that the woman be dominant. Of course, that ruins that show altogether. So consequently all the scenes that they had done together, they cut all of Ralph Fiennes' stuff out."[2] Sean Connery was cast as the villain and the plot was a retread of "A Surfeit of H_2O." Macnee had a cameo role as an invisible spy.

APPENDIX 3

The X-Files: *A Guide*

The X-Files aired its first episode on September 10, 1993. The program began its eighth season in the winter of 2000 with its most significant cast addition: Robert Patrick (best-known as the villain in *Terminator 2: Judgment Day*) joined the cast as FBI agent John Doggett, a skeptical former New York City cop. He filled the gap created by the reduced workload of David Duchovny, who signed on for only 11 of the season's 24 episodes. The bulk of the series is being released on tape and DVD by Fox Home Video.

1. THE X-FILES: PILOT

Director: Robert Mandel. *Teleplay:* Chris Carter. *Broadcast:* 9/10/93.

Meet Mulder and Scully. He's known as "spooky" because of his strange obsessions (he's a brilliant psychologist great at turning out criminal profiles but he also believes in extraterrestrials). She's a skeptic who feels that science can explain everything. Their first case involves the mysterious deaths among a particular high school graduating class.

2. DEEP THROAT

Director: Daniel Sackheim. *Teleplay:* Chris Carter. *Broadcast:* 9/17/93.

Mulder has evidence that there are strange goings-on at a military base that was one of the repositories—or so UFO lore goes—of pieces from a downed spaceship at Roswell in 1947. Mulder suspects the military of testing a jet made with extraterrestrial know-how. Introducing the mysterious "Deep Throat," a figure who gives Mulder vital information that helps (and or hinders) him.

3. SQUEEZE

Director: Harry Longstreet. *Teleplay:* Glen Morgan and James Wong. *Broadcast:* 9/24/93.

Someone is killing people in locked rooms and removing their livers. The only clue: a weird elongated fingerprint that was found at various murders going back 90 years.

4. CONDUIT

Director: Daniel Sackheim. *Teleplay:* Alex Gansa and Howard Gordon. *Broadcast:* 10/1/93.

A teenager disappears under mysterious circumstances — she seems to have been abducted — and her young brother is apparently picking up binary signals from the static of the television set.

5. THE JERSEY DEVIL

Director: Joe Napolitano. *Teleplay:* Chris Carter. *Broadcast:* 10/8/93.

Something is killing people and eating parts of them outside of Atlantic City, New Jersey.

6. SHADOWS

Director: Michael Katleman. *Teleplay:* Glen Morgan and James Wong. *Broadcast:* 10/22/93.

A ghost story. Mulder and Scully investigate strange happenings occurring around Lauren Kyte: three people who have come into contact with her have died.

7. GHOST IN THE MACHINE

Director: Jerrold Freeman. *Teleplay:* Alex Gansa and Howard Gordon. *Broadcast:* 10/29/93.

A computer is the prime suspect in a murder.

8. ICE

Director: David Nutter. *Teleplay:* Glen Morgan and James Wong. *Broadcast:* 11/5/93.

Mulder, Scully, and four other people are stranded at an Arctic research lab with an alien virus on the loose which could turn one of them into a killer. Scary, well-lit, and well-acted, the episode is the most perfectly realized to this point.

9. SPACE

Director: William Graham. *Teleplay:* Chris Carter. *Broadcast:* 11/12/93.

Mulder and Scully find clues that a ghost from outer space is interfering with NASA shuttle flights.

10. FALLEN ANGEL

Director: Larry Shaw. *Teleplay:* Alex Gansa and Howard Gordon. *Broadcast:* 11/19/93.

An unidentified flying object crash lands in Wisconsin. It is officially listed as a meteor, but Deep Throat tells Mulder otherwise.

11. EVE

Director: Fred Gerber. *Teleplay:* Kenneth Biller and Chris Brancato. *Broadcast:* 12/10/93.

Mulder and Scully investigate the bizarre death of a man found on a swing, drained of blood. The trail leads them to an identical murder, at the same time, across the country in California.

12. FIRE

Director: Larry Shaw. *Teleplay:* Chris Carter. *Broadcast:* 12/17/93.

Mulder — who has a childhood fear of fire — investigates the strange deaths of British lords who spontaneously burst into flame. Mulder is assisted by an old "flame" from Oxford but it is Scully who deciphers the clues.

13. BEYOND THE SEA

Director: David Nutter. *Teleplay:* Glen Morgan and James Wong. *Broadcast:* 1/7/94.

A death row inmate may have psychic information about a kidnap victim. Heavy on atmosphere, the story delves into the personal life of Scully, who loses her father at the start of the episode and seems to be seeing him as a ghost throughout. Noteworthy for how it explores the Mulder-Scully dynamic.

14. GENDERBENDER

Director: Rob Bowman. *Teleplay:* Larry Barber and Paul Barber. *Broadcast:* 1/21/94.

Mulder and Scully investigate a murder that seems to have been committed by a man who can change into a woman.

15. LAZARUS

Director: David Nutter. *Teleplay:* Alex Gansa and Howard Gordon. *Broadcast:* 2/4/94.

What if someone you know — and love — seems to be someone else? That concept is at the heart of this episode, which delves into Scully's past. Her former lover, FBI agent Jack Willis, and a bank robber, Warren James Dupre, are gunned down. Although Dupre apparently dies, a revived Willis seems to have the personality of the thief.

16. YOUNG AT HEART

Director: Michael Lange. *Teleplay:* Scott Kaufer and Chris Carter. *Broadcast:* 2/11/94.

John Barnett, a ruthless murderer Mulder had captured and put in prison, is apparently back and stalking Mulder — even though he reportedly died years before.

17. E.B.E.

Director: William Graham. *Teleplay:* Glen Morgan and James Wong. *Broadcast:* 2/18/94.

Mulder pursues an "extraterrestrial biological entity." The episode introduces a pivotal part of the series' "mythology": the Lone Gunmen, a paranoid trio who help Mulder in times of need. It also introduces the idea, popular in conspiracy literature, of a shadow government operating outside the law.

18. MIRACLE MAN

Director: Michael Lange. *Teleplay:* Howard Gordon and Chris Carter. *Broadcast:* 3/18/94.

A faith healer seems to be causing people to die.

19. SHAPES

Director: David Nutter. *Teleplay:* Marilyn Osborn. *Broadcast:* 4/1/94.
A werewolf is on the prowl at a Native American reservation.

20. DARKNESS FALLS

Director: Joe Napolitano. *Teleplay:* Chris Carter. *Broadcast:* 4/15/94.

A semi-remake of "Ice," the episode finds the agents investigating the disappearance of loggers at a Washington logging camp. The authorities suspect it's the work of "eco-terrorists" but the clues point elsewhere. The chief one: a corpse, drained of blood, found in a strange cocoon.

21. TOOMS

Director: David Nutter. *Teleplay:* Glen Morgan and James Wong. *Broadcast:* 4/22/94.

A sequel to "Squeeze," reintroducing Eugene Victor Tooms, the man who can squeeze into the oddest places and rips out human livers as a tasty treat. The episode hints at the FBI's plans to close down the X-Files and is notable for the introduction of a semi-regular character, Assistant Director Walter Skinner, and the first lines delivered by the Cigarette-Smoking Man.

22. BORN AGAIN

Director: Jerrold Freeman. *Teleplay:* Alex Gansa and Howard Gordon. *Broadcast:* 4/29/94.

Mulder and Scully investigate a strange death: a police officer, interviewing a young girl, is hurled through a window. The child claims there was someone in the room with her, but an artist's rendering of the suspect is the image of an undercover cop who had been killed eight years before.

23. ROLAND

Director: David Nutter. *Teleplay:* Chris Ruppenthal. *Broadcast:* 5/6/94.

Someone is killing off the scientists at a top-secret research project. The clues point to a dead man.

24. THE ERLENMEYER FLASK

Director: R.W. Goodwin. *Teleplay:* Chris Carter. *Broadcast:* 5/13/94.

Mulder and Sully tap into their biggest case yet — actual proof of the existence of extraterrestrials. The X-Files are closed down at the story's end.

25. LITTLE GREEN MEN

Director: David Nutter. *Teleplay:* Glen Morgan and James Wong. *Broadcast:* 9/16/94.

The second season opener finds the X-Files shut down and Mulder and Scully separated: he is reduced to wiretap surveillance of mobsters while she is teaching FBI agents the basics of autopsies. Nonetheless, Mulder is summoned by his Washington sponsor, Senator Richard Matheson, to investigate a government listening post which may have picked up signs of alien life. Mulder gets evidence of a close encounter with an alien but, once again, loses it in the end.

26. THE HOST

Director: Daniel Sackheim. *Teleplay:* Chris Carter. *Broadcast:* 9/23/94.

Introducing the scary flukeman, a human-sized, humanoid worm creature created out of nuclear waste from Chernobyl and brought to the U.S. by a Russian freighter.

27. BLOOD

Director: David Nutter. *Teleplay:* Glen Morgan and James Wong. *Broadcast:* 9/30/94.

Residents of a suburban farming community in Pennsylvania begin killing people after seeing "KILL 'EM ALL" digital readouts on appliances.

28. SLEEPLESS

Director: Rob Bowman. *Teleplay:* Howard Gordon. *Broadcast:* 10/7/94.

Mulder investigates the deaths of Vietnam vets who seem to have been killed by phantoms from their dreams. This time, he is partnered with Alex Krycek, a new FBI agent who apparently has a lot of enthusiasm for Mulder's beliefs but is actually working for the Cigarette-Smoking Man. This episode also features the first appearance of "X," the replacement for the slain Deep Throat, who acts as a deus ex machina and source of information for Mulder.

29. DUANE BARRY

Director: Chris Carter. *Teleplay:* Chris Carter. *Broadcast:* 10/14/94.

Close encounters of the terror-filled kind. In this installment, we meet Duane Barry, a frequent alien abductee and former FBI agent who thinks the aliens are coming back for him. Confined to a mental institution, he manages to break out and hold a doctor and other personnel hostage. His hope: take one of the hostages to the site of his first abduction and give the hostage up to the aliens in his place. In the end, he manages to escape with Scully as his prisoner.

30. ASCENSION

Director: Michael Lange. *Teleplay:* Paul Brown. *Broadcast:*10/21/94.

Part II of "Duane Barry" finds Mulder, as a man obsessed (again), this time determined to stop Barry from turning over Scully to the aliens. Alex Krycek is revealed as a spy, and strange ties are hinted at between him and the Cigarette-Smoking Man. Assistant Director Skinner takes a more prominent role and sides with Mulder by reopening the X-Files.

31. 3

Director: David Nutter. *Teleplay:* Chris Ruppenthal, Glen Morgan, and James Wong. *Broadcast:* 11/4/94.

With the X-Files reopened, Mulder, still at an emotional low ebb after the loss of Scully, investigates a series of vampire-like murders in Hollywood. But he soon finds himself falling in love with the prime suspect.

32. ONE BREATH

Director: R.W. Goodwin. *Teleplay:* Glen Morgan and James Wong. *Broadcast:* 11/11/94.

An excellent episode, moving, affecting, thoughtful, yet full of action. Scully is mysteriously returned to a Maryland hospital, but she is comatose and not expected to live. Mulder is bent on revenge for what has been done to his partner, seeking information from X, Skinner, and the Cigarette-Smoking Man (CSM to Mulder: "If people knew what I knew, things would fall apart."). This is a key episode in cementing the bond between the protagonists, linking Mulder's sister and Scully by their abductions. It also gets deeply into the feelings and personal histories of Scully, her family, and, to a lesser extent, into the motivations of Skinner, X, and CSM. Mulder is shown to have doubts about himself.

33. FIREWALKER

Director: David Nutter. *Teleplay:* Howard Gordon. *Broadcast:* 11/18/94.

Mulder and Scully investigate the death of a scientist who is studying an active volcano.

34. RED MUSEUM

Director: Win Phelps. *Teleplay:* Chris Carter. *Broadcast:* 12/9/94.

The agents look into the connection between a Wisconsin religious cult and the disappearance of a number of teenagers.

35. EXCELSIUS DEI

Director: Stephen Surjik. *Teleplay:* Paul Brown. *Broadcast:* 12/16/94.

An unseen force seems to be responsible for the rape and murder of several patients and orderlies at the Excelsius Dei nursing home in Massachusetts.

36. AUBREY

Director: Rob Bowman. *Teleplay:* Sara Charno. *Broadcast:* 1/6/95.

Mulder and Scully explore the possibility of genetic memory transference while investigating an unsolved murder dating to 1942.

37. IRRESISTIBLE

Director: David Nutter. *Teleplay:* Chris Carter. *Broadcast:* 1/13/95.

A psychopath, who collects hair and fingernails from the dead, eventually kidnaps and attempts to kill Scully.

38. DIE HAND DIE VERLETZT

Director: Kim Manners. *Teleplay:* Glen Morgan and James Wong. *Broadcast:* 1/27/95.

Mulder and Scully come face-to-face with a secret occult religion cult in New Hampshire.

39. FRESH BONES

Director: Rob Bowman. *Teleplay:* Howard Gordon. *Broadcast:* 2/3/95.

Mulder and Scully versus voodoo in a Haitian refugee camp in North Carolina.

40. COLONY

Director: Nick Marck. *Teleplay:* Chris Carter, from a story by David Duchovny and Chris Carter. *Broadcast:* 2/10/95.

Introducing the alien bounty hunter, a shape-shifting character who will play a prominent role in the later conspiracy episodes. Mulder and Scully are drawn into a case concerning the arson deaths of three doctors who seem to be identical twins but who have no past and no connection, besides the fact that they worked in abortion clinics. (The bounty hunter assumes the guise of a CIA agent, Ambrose Chapel — a name lifted from Hitchcock's second version of *The Man Who Knew Too Much*.) Meanwhile, Mulder's sister seems to have been returned — but is it her?

41. END GAME

Director: Rob Bowman. *Teleplay:* Frank Spotnitz. *Broadcast:* 2/17/95.

The exciting conclusion of "Colony," which resolves little. Skinner shows his stuff, fighting X in a memorable scene in an elevator as he tries to get information. Mulder again searches for Scully.

42. FEARFUL SYMMETRY

Director: James Whitmore Jr. *Teleplay:* Steven DeJarnatt. *Broadcast:* 2/24/95.

The agents investigate apparent alien abductions of zoo animals.

43. DÖD KALM

Director: Rob Bowman. *Teleplay:* Howard Gordon and Alex Gansa. *Broadcast:* 3/10/95.

On a trip to Norway, Mulder and Scully encounter a mysterious force that causes rapid aging of man and machine.

44. HUMBUG

Director: Kim Manners. *Teleplay:* Darin Morgan. *Broadcast:* 3/31/95.

A semi-comic episode, with Mulder and Scully examining death at a freak show. The story plays on the conventions of the horror movie, inverting them; the point-of-view shot of the creepy character approaching the two kids in the swimming pool turns out to be their father. (There is also a homage to 1948's *Lady from Shanghai*, as Scully shoots out some mirrors in the fun house.) For a change, the oddness is normal, and "normal" Mulder and Scully seem out of place.

45. THE CALUSARI

Director: Michael Vejar. *Teleplay:* Sara Charno. *Broadcast:* 4/14/95.

The X-Files meets *The Exorcist* (1973) when the agents encounter a young boy who seems to be possessed by an evil spirit bent on murder.

46. F. EMASCULATA

Director: Rob Bowman. *Teleplay:* Chris Carter and Howard Gordon. *Broadcast:* 4/28/95.

Mulder and Scully try to stop the spread of a plague that has already killed ten people.

47. SOFT LIGHT

Director: James Contner. *Teleplay:* Vince Gilligan. *Broadcast:* 5/5/95.

A scientist's shadow is the prime suspect in a number of possible kidnapping/murder cases.

48. OUR TOWN

Director: Rob Bowman. *Teleplay:* Frank Spotnitz. *Broadcast:* 5/12/95.

Mulder and Scully investigate the disappearance of a federal food inspector who disappeared in a town with a terrible secret.

49. ANASAZI

Director: R.W. Goodwin. *Teleplay:* Chris Carter, from a story by David Duchovny and Chris Carter. *Broadcast:* 5/19/95.

This exciting episode, first of three parts, is the most involved plotline yet. What is that strange, alien-like corpse that comes out of the hidden railroad boxcar in the New Mexican desert? Why is Mulder feeling ill and acting so strange? What is the secret his father needs to tell him? The story starts with a computer hacker obtaining secret defense department documents which purportedly prove the existence of extraterrestrials. The story twists and weaves with breathtaking speed, ending with Mulder apparently burning to death in a boxcar full of what appear to be alien skeletons.

50. THE BLESSING WAY

Director: R.W. Goodwin. *Teleplay:* Chris Carter. *Broadcast:* 9/22/95.

Mulder is apparently dead in the third season opener, and Scully meets the Well-Manicured Man at Mulder's father's funeral. The CSM is seen to be part of a syndicate that predicts the future by making it. Again, a fully stocked episode, this time tinged with a bit of new age/Native American mumbo jumbo as a near-death Mulder is called back from the beyond (in a cheesy-looking outer space sequence) by Native Americans who invoke "The Blessing Way." Scully's sister is shot instead of her; and WMM paraphrases Max Von Sydow's warning to Robert Redford in *Three Days of the Condor*, telling Scully how someone close to her will attempt to assassinate her. That leads to the terrific Mexican standoff between Scully and Skinner in Mulder's apartment.

51. PAPER CLIP

Director: Rob Bowman. *Teleplay:* Chris Carter. *Broadcast:* 9/29/95.

In the third part of this involved three-parter, Mulder learns more about the involvement of his father in the conspiracy; Skinner deals the duo back into the FBI; and Mulder and Scully discover a huge cataloging/filing system (used for government testing involving former Nazi scientists who were attempting human-alien hybrids). Mulder sees a spaceship; Scully sees what look like aliens; and there are enough tantalizing hints of answers to make viewers want to tune in for more. The series is at its peak here; endlessly inventive, taking old ideas and restructuring them into something unique.

52. D.P.O.

Director: Kim Manners. *Teleplay:* Howard Gordon. *Broadcast:* 10/6/95.

The agents travel to Oklahoma to investigate a teenage boy who can apparently control lightning.

53. CLYDE BRUCKMAN'S FINAL REPOSE

Director: David Nutter. *Teleplay:* Darin Morgan. *Broadcast:* 10/13/95.

A blackly comic episode features Peter Boyle as Clyde Bruckman, an insurance salesman who has the gift —curse?— of second sight. Mulder and Scully enlist his aid in the search for a serial killer.

54. THE LIST

Director: Chris Carter. *Teleplay:* Chris Carter. *Broadcast:* 10/20/95.

A death row inmate in Florida is apparently back from the dead and seeking revenge against five people.

55. 2SHY

Director: David Nutter. *Teleplay:* Jeffrey Vlaming. *Broadcast:* 11/3/95.

A serial killer seems to be preying on overweight women and leaving their liquefied corpses behind.

56. THE WALK

Director: Rob Bowman. *Teleplay:* John Shiban. *Broadcast:* 11/10/95.

Bizarre murders at a military base in Maryland lead Mulder to suspect that a bedridden, quadruple amputee may be responsible.

57. OUBLIETTE

Director: Kim Manners. *Teleplay:* Charles Grant Craig. *Broadcast:* 11/17/95.

A young girl's abduction resonates with Mulder who employs an "empath"—a woman who can mystically feel what the abductee feels—to track down the kidnapper and his victim.

58. NISEI

Director: David Nutter. *Teleplay:* Chris Carter, Howard Gordon, and Frank Spotnitz. *Broadcast:* 11/24/95.

Paranoia runs rampant in the first of a very exciting, intriguing two-parter. The agents investigate a video of an alien autopsy that Mulder gets through a mail order house. He believes it's the real thing; an investigation finds the man who made it has been murdered, and there is a kickboxing Japanese national on the scene. The trail leads the two to a rail car containing what looks like an alien, and a conspiracy that seems to involve the governments of the U.S. and Japan and a group of war criminal scientists. The mythology gets darker and darker.

59. 731

Director: Rob Bowman. *Teleplay:* Frank Spotnitz. *Broadcast:* 12/1/95.

Part II doesn't let up in the action department, as Mulder gets on board a train that appears to be a ticking time bomb and faces off with a mysterious killer who piano-wires his victims to death. There's also intrigue tied in to Scully's previous abduction: she meets a group of women who all seem to know her from the "place of the white light." The episode also features mass executions of what could be aliens and X telling Scully about an implant she finds in her neck: "It holds more than I could ever tell you. Maybe everything you need to know." Mulder later says, "I want an apology for the truth." The truth in the series is hard to grasp, hard to decipher, constantly changing depending on your point of view.

60. REVELATIONS

Director: David Nutter. *Teleplay:* Kim Newton. *Broadcast:* 12/15/95.
Mulder and Scully encounter a young boy in Ohio who can seemingly perform miracles.

61. WAR OF THE COPROPHAGES

Director: Kim Manners. *Teleplay:* Darin Morgan. *Broadcast:* 1/5/96.
A semi-comic episode finds Mulder and Scully encountering panic in a small Massachusetts town because of a purported invasion by cockroaches.

62. SYZYGY

Director: Rob Bowman. *Teleplay:* Chris Carter. *Broadcast:* 1/26/96.
Two high school girls seem to be responsible for a series of unusual deaths.

63. GROTESQUE

Director: Kim Manners. *Teleplay:* Howard Gordon. *Broadcast:* 2/2/96.
An evil spirit, a sculptor, and a serial killer all figure in a bizarre investigation that brings Mulder to the brink of insanity.

64. PIPER MARU

Director: Rob Bowman. *Teleplay:* Frank Spotnitz and Chris Carter. *Broadcast:* 2/9/96.
Exciting episode that adds more to the mythology of aliens; this time, there was apparently an alien spacecraft that crashed in the ocean in the 1940s and an American submarine that encountered it. The plot is fast-paced and complicated, involving a number of threads from previous episodes, as Mulder and Scully investigate a radiation-burned French salvage ship.

65. APOCRYPHA

Director: Kim Manners. *Teleplay:* Frank Spotnitz and Chris Carter. *Broadcast:* 2/16/96.
The second part finds the Syndicate upset with the Cigarette-Smoking Man for ordering the shooting of Skinner and an oily alien on the loose. Action-packed, intriguing, typically raising more questions than it answers.

66. PUSHER

Director: Rob Bowman. *Teleplay:* Vince Gilligan. *Broadcast:* 2/23/96.
The agents encounter a man who can talk people into killing themselves.

67. TESO DOS BICHOS

Director: Kim Manners. *Teleplay:* John Shiban. *Broadcast:* 3/8/96.
The unearthing of an ancient Ecuadorian urn leads to deaths which Mulder attributes to an evil spirit.

68. HELL MONEY

Director: Tucker Gates. *Teleplay:* Jeffrey Vlaming. *Broadcast:* 3/29/96.
A bizarre but deadly game involving death and the Chinese spirit world brings Mulder and Scully to Chinatown in San Francisco.

69. JOSE CHUNG'S *FROM OUTER SPACE*

Director: Rob Bowman. *Teleplay:* Darin Morgan. *Broadcast:* 4/12/96.
Amusing, black comedy installment of the series (by resident black comedy writer Darin Morgan), that pokes fun at the whole mythology/alien terrestrial idea. It involves a government conspiracy, aliens who aren't aliens (and some who may be), and a lot of kooky stuff, topped by an out-there performance by Charles Nelson Reilly as a novelist/reporter.

70. AVATAR

Director: James Charleston. *Teleplay:* Howard Gordon and David Duchovny. *Broadcast:* 4/26/96.
Assistant Director Skinner becomes the subject of a murder investigation, which involves a dream-like woman in a red cloak.

71. QUAGMIRE

Director: Kim Manners. *Teleplay:* Kim Newton. *Broadcast:* 5/3/96.
Mulder and Scully go after their own Loch Ness–style monster: a lake creature known by the Georgia locals as Big Blue, said to be responsible for a series of murders.

72. WETWIRED

Director: Rob Bowman. *Teleplay:* Mat Beck. *Broadcast:* 5/10/96.

Mulder and Scully encounter a conspiracy involving television mind control.

73. TALITHA CUMI

Director: R.W. Goodwin. *Teleplay:* Chris Carter, from a story by David Duchovny and Chris Carter. *Broadcast:* 5/17/96.

An epic third season finale to the series. Mulder and Scully investigate a diner shooting and a man who reportedly brought the dead back to life. A lot of mythology information in this one, including a secret meeting between the Cigarette-Smoking Man and Mulder's mother: is he Mulder's real father? (This episode was partly inspired by "The Inquisitor" in Dostoyevsky's *The Brothers Karamazov*, and there is a sequence clearly based on it when the CSM debates the nature of freedom with the "messiah" figure, Jeremiah Smith, a soft-spoken, shape-shifting alien with healing powers.)

74. HERRENVOLK

Director: R.W. Goodwin. *Teleplay:* Chris Carter. *Broadcast:* 10/4/96.

The season-opener for Season 4, and part 2 of 2, resolves some issues that were set up in the previous installment, hinting that "the plan" being prepared by the alien-human conspiracy has something to do with tagging and cataloging everyone on earth through smallpox vaccinations. Jeremiah Smith, who claimed that he could answer all of Mulder's questions, here answers none but poses a few by his actions: why does he take Mulder to a bee farm tended by clones of his sister and a young boy? It was important enough for Smith to want to detour Mulder from his mother, apparently to give him information that would help him stop "the plan." But what information?

75. UNRUHE

Director: Rob Bowman. *Teleplay:* Vince Gilligan. *Broadcast:* 10/27/96.

A killer's psychotic fantasies of the future come true — and appear in photographs before they happen.

76. HOME

Director: Kim Manners. *Teleplay:* Glen Morgan and James Wong. *Broadcast:* 10/11/96.

Incest and murder are among the issues that confront Mulder and Scully when they investigate a strange family living outside the rural community of Home, Pennsylvania.

77. TELIKO

Director: James Charleston. *Teleplay:* Howard Gordon. *Broadcast:* 10/18/96.

Someone or something is killing African-American males and draining them of their pigment.

78. THE FIELD WHERE I DIED

Director: Rob Bowman. *Teleplay:* Glen Morgan and James Wong. *Broadcast:* 11/3/96.

While attempting to prevent a mass suicide at a religious cult, Mulder encounters evidence of a previous life he may have lived.

79. SANGUINARIUM

Director: Kim Manners. *Teleplay:* Valerie Mayhew and Vivien Mayhew. *Broadcast:* 11/11/96.

Mulder and Scully investigate murder among plastic surgeons, witchcraft, and a doctor who may have made a deal with the devil.

80. MUSINGS OF A CIGARETTE-SMOKING MAN

Director: James Wong. *Teleplay:* Glen Morgan. *Broadcast:* 11/17/96.

A "biography" that may or may not be true about the mysterious Cigarette-Smoking Man, linking him to assassinations, bad novels, and losing sports franchises.

81. PAPER HEARTS

Director: Rob Bowman. *Teleplay:* Vince Gilligan. *Broadcast:* 12/15/96.

Mulder reopens the case of a convicted child killer when the murderer offers evidence that he knows the whereabouts of the agent's missing sister.

82. TUNGUSKA

Director: Kim Manners. *Teleplay:* Frank Spotnitz and Chris Carter. *Broadcast:* 11/24/96.

Convoluted mythology episode, in which a mysterious black oil is introduced as something that came from an extraterrestrial rock; it crawls its way under the skin and causes pain, discomfort, even coma. Traitorous agent Alex Krycek is back, and he leads Mulder on a chase to Russia in search of answers.

83. TERMA

Director: Rob Bowman. *Teleplay:* Frank Spotnitz and Chris Carter. *Broadcast:* 12/1/96.

Part II of "Tunguska": more murders, more hints about the black oil, and an explanation of sorts—the conspirators are trying to create a vaccine.

84. EL MUNDO GIRA

Director: Tucker Gates. *Teleplay:* John Shiban. *Broadcast:* 1/12/97.

Migrant workers in southern California are being murdered and some transformed by a mysterious yellow rain.

85. KADDISH

Director: Kim Manners. *Teleplay:* Howard Gordon. *Broadcast:* 2/16/97.

In a version of the "Golem" legend of Jewish mythology, Mulder and Scully encounter a strange force that is killing members of an anti–Semitic gang.

86. NEVER AGAIN

Director: Robert Bowman. *Teleplay:* Glen Morgan and James Wong. *Broadcast:* 2/2/97.

Jodie Foster provides the voice of a sexy tattoo which holds sway over its wearer, giving him orders to kill. A solo case for Scully, who becomes emotionally involved with the killer.

87. LEONARD BETTS

Director: Kim Manners. *Teleplay:* Vince Gilligan, John Shiban, and Frank Spotnitz. *Broadcast:* 1/26/97.

In an unusually bizarre case, the agents investigate a headless corpse that seems to have walked out of a hospital morgue.

88. MEMENTO MORI

Director: Rob Bowman. *Teleplay:* Chris Carter, Vince Gilligan, John Shiban, and Frank Spotnitz. *Broadcast:* 2/9/97.

Scully discovers she has cancer and Mulder desperately searches for a cure among the Syndicate of conspirators who seem to be responsible for it.

89. UNREQUITED

Director: Michael Lange. *Teleplay:* Howard Gordon and Chris Carter. *Broadcast:* 2/23/97.

A vengeful Marine Corps ex–POW seems to have gained the power to make himself invisible.

90. TEMPUS FUGIT

Director: Rob Bowman. *Teleplay:* Chris Carter and Frank Spotnitz. *Broadcast:* 3/16/97.

While investigating the crash of Flight 549, Mulder and Scully find evidence that aliens and Max Fenig, the abductee they encountered and lost in "Fallen Angel," seem to have been involved.

91. MAX

Director: Kim Manners. *Teleplay:* Chris Carter and Frank Spotnitz. *Broadcast:* 3/23/97.

In Part II of "Tempus Fugit," Mulder and Scully get closer to proving aliens were involved in the crash of Flight 549.

92. SYNCHRONY

Director: James Charleston. *Teleplay:* Howard Gordon and David Greenwalt. *Broadcast:* 4/13/97.

Several murders seem to be the work of a time traveler attempting to rewrite history.

93. SMALL POTATOES

Director: Cliff Bole. *Teleplay:* Vince Gilligan. *Broadcast:* 4/20/97.

In a semi-comic episode, *X-Files* scribe Darin Morgan plays Eddie Van Blundht, a man with the remarkable ability of being able to imitate various men and impregnate their women.

94. ZERO SUM

Director: Kim Manners. *Teleplay:* Howard Gordon and Frank Spotnitz. *Broadcast:* 4/27/97.

Assistant Director Skinner makes a deal with the Cigarette-Smoking Man in an attempt to save Scully's life.

95. ELEGY

Director: James Charleston. *Teleplay:* John Shiban. *Broadcast:* 5/4/97.

A mentally disabled man who sees strange visions is the prime suspect in a series of strange murders of young women in Washington, D.C.

96. DEMONS

Director: Kim Manners. *Teleplay:* R.W. Goodwin. *Broadcast:* 5/11/97.

During blackouts that have given him new insights into his sister's abduction, Mulder may have murdered two people.

97. GETHSEMANE

Director: R.W. Goodwin. *Teleplay:* Chris Carter. *Broadcast:* 5/18/97.

In the fourth season finale, Mulder seems to have killed himself after evidence surfaces which rocks the agent's beliefs: Michael Kritschgau, a Defense Department operative, offers proof that all the alien abductions were part of a massive government disinformation campaign.

98. UNUSUAL SUSPECTS

Director: Kim Manners. *Teleplay:* Vince Gilligan. *Broadcast:* 11/16/97.

The story of how the Lone Gunmen, the trio of eccentric conspiracy theorists who often assist Mulder, came together in 1989. Guest-starring Richard Belzer, in an unusual cross-network guest-starring stint as Detective John Munch, his role on NBC's *Homicide: Life on the Street*.

99. REDUX

Director: R.W. Goodwin. *Teleplay:* Chris Carter. *Broadcast:* 11/2/97.

In Part II of a trilogy begun with "Gethsemane," Mulder fakes his own death to shake off surveillance by his enemies. Undercover, he searches for a cure for Scully's cancer.

100. REDUX II

Director: Kim Manners. *Teleplay:* Chris Carter. *Broadcast:* 11/9/97.

The conclusion finds Mulder penetrating the heart of the conspiracy — only to find disillusionment — and Scully facing a radical cure that her partner has supplied.

101. DETOUR

Director: Brett Dowler. *Teleplay:* Frank Spotnitz. *Broadcast:* 11/23/97.

En route to an FBI Creative Team Seminar in Florida, Mulder and Scully stumble across a murder committed by near-invisible forest creatures with glowing red eyes.

102. CHRISTMAS CAROL

Director: Peter Markle. *Teleplay:* Vince Gilligan, John Shiban, and Frank Spotnitz. *Broadcast:* 12/7/97.

While visiting her family for Christmas, Scully seems to be getting phone calls from her dead sister, Melissa, asking her to help a sick child.

103. THE POST–MODERN PROMETHEUS

Director: Chris Carter. *Teleplay:* Chris Carter. *Broadcast:* 11/30/97.

In an offbeat black-and-white episode, the agents encounter a modern-day Victor Frankenstein and a strange boy who could be responsible for strange goings-on in a rural town.

104. EMILY

Director: Kim Manners. *Teleplay:* Vince Gilligan, John Shiban, and Frank Spotnitz. *Broadcast:* 12/14/97.

Emily, the little girl Scully helped in "Christmas Carol," turns out to be the agent's biological daughter and is dying. Meanwhile, Mulder discovers that the child plays a pivotal role in the ongoing conspiracy.

105. KITSUNEGARI

Director: Daniel Sackheim. *Teleplay:* Vince Gilligan and Tim Minear. *Broadcast:* 1/4/98.

Robert Modell, the man who could manipulate minds in "Pusher," escapes prison and seems to be out for revenge against Mulder.

106. SCHIZOGENY

Director: Ralph Hemecker. *Teleplay:* Jessica Scott and Mike Wollaeger. *Broadcast:* 1/11/98.

A man with an ax, teenagers in trouble, and murderous foliage all figure in a bizarre case that initially seems to center on child abuse.

107. CHINGA

Director: Kim Manners. *Teleplay:* Stephen King and Chris Carter. *Broadcast:* 2/8/98.

Horrormeister Stephen King co-wrote this story about a typical subject: an autistic girl with a murderous doll that terrorizes a New England hamlet.

108. KILL SWITCH

Director: Rob Bowman. *Teleplay:* William Gibson and Tom Maddox. *Broadcast:* 2/15/98.

In a variation of *The Avengers*' "The House That Jack Built" concept, the agents encounter a cybernetic life form that has learned how to kill.

109. BAD BLOOD

Director: Cliff Bole. *Teleplay:* Vince Gilligan. *Broadcast:* 2/22/98.

In a small town, Mulder insists that a series of serial killings are the work of a coven of vampires. This comic episode has echoes of Akira Kurosawa's 1950 film *Rashomon* with the story told in flashback from Mulder's and Scully's differing points of view.

110. PATIENT X

Director: Kim Manners. *Teleplay:* Chris Carter and Frank Spotnitz. *Broadcast:* 3/1/98.

Mulder, disillusioned and disbelieving in aliens, encounters Cassandra Spender, a woman who claims to have been abducted. Meanwhile, Scully is drawn to a dangerous rendezvous with murderous extraterrestrials.

111. THE RED AND THE BLACK

Director: Chris Carter. *Teleplay:* Chris Carter and Frank Spotnitz. *Broadcast:* 3/8/98.

In another dense mythology episode, many of the plot threads from "Patient X" are continued; new characters are introduced; and, in a reversal, Scully's recent adventure has caused her to believe in aliens while Mulder is now the skeptic. Disillusioned, he searches for alternative answers.

112. TRAVELERS

Director: Bill Graham. *Teleplay:* John Shiban and Frank Spotnitz. *Broadcast:* 3/29/98.

Darren McGavin (whose series, *Kolchak: The Night Stalker*, was one of the inspirations for *The X-Files*) guest stars as retired FBI agent Arthur Dales, who tells Mulder a tale of murder and conspiracy set in the 1950s.

113. MIND'S EYE

Director: Kim Manners. *Teleplay:* Tim Minear. *Broadcast:* 4/19/98.

Mulder and Scully's only lead to a series of murders is a blind woman who appears to be able to see through the serial killer's eyes.

114. ALL SOULS

Director: Allen Coulter. *Teleplay:* Frank Spotnitz and John Shiban, from a story by Billy Brown and Dan Angel. *Broadcast:* 4/26/98.

Scully's late daughter, Emily, plays a role in a case involving a disabled woman killed while praying.

115. THE PINE BLUFF VARIANT

Director: Rob Bowman. *Teleplay:* John Shiban. *Broadcast:* 5/3/98.

Mulder goes undercover to trap a gang of terrorists.

116. FOLIE A DEUX

Director: Kim Manners. *Teleplay:* Vince Gilligan. *Broadcast:* 5/10/98.

A terrifically terrifying episode, a combination of ideas from zombie and alien possession movies, finds Mulder and Scully investigating claims that a giant, invisible insect is sucking the life out of office workers. Great moments: Mulder in bed, menaced by the shadowy suggestion of a giant bug which only he can see; and Scully's meeting with the zombie nurse.

117. THE END

Director: R.W. Goodwin. *Teleplay:* Chris Carter. *Broadcast:* 5/17/98.

In the fifth season finale, Mulder and Scully seem to be on the verge of finding answers to all the questions they have posed in the past. The key is Gibson Praise, a child chess prodigy who appears to have the power to read minds.

118. THE BEGINNING

Director: Kim Manners. *Teleplay:* Chris Carter. *Broadcast:* 11/8/98.

The follow-up to "The End," and also to the *X-Files* movie which opened between the series' fifth and sixth seasons. Although banished from the X-Files, Mulder and Scully still hunt for a murderous alien creature who is on the loose in Phoenix. Once again, child prodigy Gibson Praise is a key clue.

119. DRIVE

Director: Rob Bowman. *Teleplay:* Vince Gilligan. *Broadcast:* 11/15/98.

In a variation on the film *Speed* (1994), Mulder is a hostage in a high-speed car chase with a twist: his captor's head could explode at any moment.

120. TRIANGLE

Director: Chris Carter. *Teleplay:* Chris Carter. *Broadcast:* 11/22/98.

A terrifically entertaining episode with a couple of technical wrinkles: it is shot in the letterbox format (meaning the top and bottom of the screen are blacked out to give a different aspect ratio), and employs a "one-take" roving camera (much in the style of Hitchcock's 1948 film, *Rope*). The story finds Mulder, lost in a time warp in the Bermuda triangle that has thrown him back to 1939 and a ship full of Nazis and Britons battling for supremacy (some of them, *Wizard of Oz*–like, are played by *X-Files* regulars).

121. DREAMLAND

Director: Michael Watkins. *Teleplay:* Vince Gilligan, John Shiban, and Frank Spotnitz. *Broadcast:* 11/29/98.

Following a close encounter with an alien spacecraft, Mulder and another man switch identities.

122. DREAMLAND II

Director: Kim Manners. *Teleplay:* Vince Gilligan, John Shiban, and Frank Spotnitz. *Broadcast:* 12/6/98.

Mulder tries to find a way to switch back to his own body, while Scully becomes suspicious of her "partner."

123. TERMS OF ENDEARMENT

Director: Rob Bowman. *Teleplay:* David Amann. *Broadcast:* 1/3/99.

A normal suburban couple seems to have given birth to a demonic child.

124. THE RAIN KING

Director: Kim Manners. *Teleplay:* Jeffrey Bell. *Broadcast:* 1/10/99.

The town drunk seems to have gained the ability to control the weather.

125. HOW THE GHOSTS STOLE CHRISTMAS

Director: Chris Carter. *Teleplay:* Chris Carter. *Broadcast:* 12/13/98.

On Christmas Eve, Mulder and Scully encounter a pair of murderously clever ghosts.

126. TITHONUS

Director: Michael Watkins. *Teleplay:* Vince Gilligan. *Broadcast:* 1/24/99.

Teamed with a new partner, Scully investigates a crime photographer who can apparently predict the time of someone's death.

127. S.R. 819

Director: Daniel Sackheim. *Teleplay:* John Shiban. *Broadcast:* 1/17/99.

In a variation on the noir classic *D.O.A.* (1950), Assistant Director Skinner contracts a deadly disease and Mulder, Scully, and Skinner himself frantically search for a cure.

128. TWO FATHERS

Director: Kim Manners. *Teleplay:* Chris Carter and Frank Spotniz. *Broadcast:* 2/7/99.

Abductee Cassandra Spender (from "Patient X") returns with information about the alien conspiracy for world domination.

129. ONE SON

Director: Rob Bowman. *Teleplay:* Chris Carter and Frank Spotniz. *Broadcast:* 2/14/99.

In the sequel to "Two Fathers," Mulder and Scully uncover many of the conspiracy's secrets, while attempting to thwart alien domination of the planet.

130. ARCADIA

Director: Michael Watkins. *Teleplay:* Daniel Arkin. *Broadcast:* 3/7/99.

Mulder and Scully go undercover as a married couple named Rob and Laura Petrie (the husband and wife in *The Dick Van Dyke Show*) to investigate the mysterious disappearances of residents at an upscale suburban homeowners association.

131. AGUA MALA

Director: Rob Bowman. *Teleplay:* David Amann. *Broadcast:* 2/21/99.

In the middle of a deadly hurricane in Florida, Mulder and Scully search for a dangerous creature that is working its way through a small town's water system.

132. MONDAY

Director: Kim Manners. *Teleplay:* Vince Gilligan and John Shiban. *Broadcast:* 2/28/99.

Mulder and Scully become trapped in a time loop in which they repeat the same actions leading up to their deaths at a bank robbery.

133. ALPHA

Director: Peter Markle. *Teleplay:* Jeffrey Bell. *Broadcast:* 3/28/99.
Mulder and Scully hunt a wolf-like creature from China.

134. TREVOR

Director: Rob Bowman. *Teleplay:* Jim Guttridge and Ken Hawryliw. *Broadcast:* 4/11/99.

Violent murders seem to be the work of an escaped prisoner who can apparently walk through walls.

135. MILAGRO

Director: Kim Manners. *Teleplay:* Chris Carter, from a story by John Shiban and Frank Spotnitz. *Broadcast:* 4/18/99.

A young writer, in love with Scully, seems to have the power to make his murderous fantasies real.

136. THREE OF A KIND

Director: Bryan Spicer. *Teleplay:* Vince Gilligan and John Spotnitz. *Broadcast:* 5/2/99.

A comic episode in which the Lone Gunmen, the conspiracy-obsessed trio that often helps Mulder, goes on a fishing trip that turns deadly.

137. THE UNNATURAL

Director: David Duchovny. *Teleplay:* David Duchovny. *Broadcast:* 4/25/99.

Mulder discovers that a famous ballplayer from the 1940s was an extraterrestrial.

138. FIELD TRIP

Director: Kim Manners. *Teleplay:* Vince Gilligan and John Shiban. *Broadcast:* 5/9/99.

Trapped and unconscious inside a cave, Mulder and Scully have strange fantasies.

139. BIOGENESIS

Director: Rob Bowman. *Teleplay:* Chris Carter and Frank Spotnitz. *Broadcast:* 5/16/99.

Mulder contracts a deadly disease, thanks to an extraterrestrial artifact that may hold the key to all earthly life.

140. THE SIXTH EXTINCTION

Director: Kim Manners. *Teleplay:* Chris Carter. *Broadcast:* 11/7/99.

In the follow-up to "Biogenesis," Scully searches for the meaning of the symbols on a spacecraft found on an African coast.

141. THE SIXTH EXTINCTION II: AMOR FATI

Director: Michael Watkins. *Teleplay:* David Duchovny and Chris Carter. *Broadcast:* 11/14/99.

The concluding part of the complex trilogy begun in "Biogenesis" finds the Cigarette-Smoking Man telling Mulder, "I am your father," while Scully finds answers to her questions.

142. HUNGRY

Director: Kim Manners. *Teleplay:* Vince Gilligan. *Broadcast:* 11/21/99.

A creature who passes for human reluctantly kills people so that he can eat their brains.

143. MILLENNIUM

Director: Thomas J. Wright. *Teleplay:* Vince Gilligan and Frank Spotnitz. *Broadcast:* 11/28/99.

Mulder and Scully team up with criminal profiler Frank Black (from the canceled series *Millennium*) to stop a fanatical group from staging a mystical Armageddon.

144. RUSH

Director: Robert Lieberman. *Teleplay:* David Amann. *Broadcast:* 12/5/99.

The hand is quicker than the eye when Mulder and Scully encounter a murderous teenager who moves too quickly to be seen.

145. THE GOLDBERG VARIATION

Director: Thomas J. Wright. *Teleplay:* Jeffrey Bell. *Broadcast:* 12/12/99.

A comic episode finds the agents investigating a man bedeviled by good luck.

146. ORISON

Director: Rob Bowman. *Teleplay:* Chip Johannessen. *Broadcast:* 1/9/00.

The agents must cope with a minister who seems to have hypnotic powers and an escaped prisoner out to kill Scully.

147. THE AMAZING MALEENI

Director: Thomas J. Wright. *Teleplay:* Vince Gilligan, John Shiban, and Frank Spotnitz. *Broadcast:* 1/16/00.

The agents investigate the death of a second-rate magician whose death by decapitation wasn't part of the act.

148. SIGNS AND WONDERS

Director: Kim Manners. *Teleplay:* Jeffrey Bell. *Broadcast:* 1/23/00.
In rural Tennessee, snakes seem to be killing heretics.

149. SEIN UND ZEIT

Director: Michael Watkins. *Teleplay:* Chris Carter and Frank Spotnitz. *Broadcast:* 2/6/00.

In the first of a two-parter, Mulder sees a paranormal cause for the disappearance of a five-year-old girl.

150. CLOSURE

Director: Kim Manners. *Teleplay:* Chris Carter and Frank Spotnitz. *Broadcast:* 2/13/00.

In the conclusion to "Sein und Zeit," Mulder finds an answer to the disappearance of his sister.

151. X-COPS

Director: Michael Watkins. *Teleplay:* Vince Gilligan. *Broadcast:* 2/20/00.

This episode, shot as though it were an episode of TV's cinema verité show *Cops*, finds the agents hunting for a modern-day werewolf. The amusing style hides the lack of substance.

152. FIRST PERSON SHOOTER

Director: Chris Carter. *Teleplay:* William Gibson and Tom Maddox. *Broadcast:* 2/27/00.

A virtual reality game turns deadly when participants end up as corpses.

153. THEEF

Director: Kim Manners. *Teleplay:* Vince Gilligan, John Shiban, and Frank Spotnitz. *Broadcast:* 3/12/00.

Magic spells play a role in the brutal murders of a doctor's family.

154. EN AMI

Director: Rob Bowman. *Teleplay:* William B. Davis. *Broadcast:* 3/19/00.

The Cigarette-Smoking Man offers Scully the cure for cancer — if she takes a secret trip with him.

155. CHIMERA

Director: Cliff Bole. *Teleplay:* David Amann. *Broadcast:* 4/2/00.

Quoth the raven nevermore: the black bird is a precursor to death by demon.

156. ALL THINGS

Director: Gillian Anderson. *Teleplay:* Gillian Anderson. *Broadcast:* 4/9/00.

A failed love affair comes back to haunt Scully in an episode that opens with an ambiguous teaser, never explained: Scully seems to have been sleeping with Mulder.

157. BRAND X

Director: Kim Manners. *Teleplay:* Steven Meeda and Greg Walker. *Broadcast:* 4/16/00.

The case: a cigarette company conspiracy, death-dealing beetles, a man whose touch means death, and Mulder on the brink of dying.

158. HOLLYWOOD A.D.

Director: David Duchovny. *Teleplay:* David Duchovny. *Broadcast:* 4/30/00.

A parody of *The X-Files* mystique with a Hollywood screenwriter offering his take on the Scully-Mulder relationship as he observes them for a movie he is making: "You're both crazy. You're crazy for believing what you believe, and you're crazy for not believing him." More interested in in-jokes and homages than telling a good horror story, the episode features amusing performances by Gary Shandling and Tea Leoni as the movie versions of "Mulder" and "Scully."

159. FIGHT CLUB

Director: Paul Shapiro. *Teleplay:* Chris Carter. *Broadcast:* 5/7/00.

A pair of twin women create havoc whenever they come near each other.

160. JE SOUHAITE

Director: Vince Gilligan. *Teleplay:* Vince Gilligan. *Broadcast:* 5/14/00.

In another comic episode, a genie grants each of her "masters" three wishes, which always end up with disastrous results.

161. REQUIEM

Director: Kim Manners. *Teleplay:* Chris Carter. *Broadcast:* 5/21/00.

Returning to the scene of their first case together seven years before, the agents have a close encounter that ends with a cliffhanger: Mulder disappears.

162. THE X FILES: FIGHT THE FUTURE (Feature Film)

Director: Rob Bowman. *Teleplay:* Chris Carter and Frank Spotnitz. *Release*: 1998.

Mulder and Scully make their big-screen debut, continuing their fight against the alien invasion. Bigger and longer does not necessarily mean better, although there are some wonderful special effects.

Chapter Notes

1: THE DETECTIVE

1. Quoted in Albin Krebs, "Erle Stanley Gardner, the Author of Perry Mason Mystery Novels, Is Dead at 80," *New York Times*, March 12, 1970, p. 1.
2. *Charlie Chan in Egypt* (1935), screenplay by Robert Ellis and Helen Logan.
3. Jeff Siegel, *The American Detective: An Illustrated History* (Dallas: Taylor, 1993), p. 7.
4. Edgar Allan Poe, *Tales of Mystery and Imagination* (London: Oxford University Press, 1967), p. 112.
5. Poe, *Tales*, p. 113.
6. Poe, *Tales*, p. 94.
7. Krebs, *New York Times*, p. 1.
8. Poe, *Tales*, p. 138.
9. Vincent Starrett, *The Private Life of Sherlock Holmes* (New York: Pinnacle, 1975), p. 132.
10. Sir Arthur Conan Doyle, *The Adventures of Sherlock Holmes* (London: Leopard, 1996), p. 18.
11. Quoted in Peter Haining (ed), *The Sherlock Holmes Scrapbook* (New York: Clarkson N. Potter, 1974), p. 7.
12. Sir Arthur Conan Doyle, *A Study in Scarlet* (London: Leopard, 1996), p. 25.
13. Doyle, *Study*, p. 25.
14. Sir Arthur Conan Doyle, *The Memoirs of Sherlock Holmes* (New York: Berkley Medallion, 1968), p. 27.
15. William K. Everson, *The Detective in Film* (Secaucus, NJ: Citadel, 1972), p. 15.
16. Everson, *Detective*, p. 34.
17. Quoted in William Vivian Butler, *The Durable Desperadoes* (London: Macmillan, 1973), p. 132.
18. Quoted in Butler, *The Durable Desperadoes*, p. 124.

19. Quoted in Burt Barer, *The Saint: A Complete History in Print, Radio, Film and Television of Leslie Charteris' Robin Hood of Modern Crime, Simon Templar, 1928–1992* (Jefferson, N.C.: McFarland, 1993), p. 113.
20. Butler, *The Durable Desperadoes*, p. 125.
21. Quoted in Burt Barer, *The Saint*, p. 243.
22. Siegel, *American Detective*, p. 77.
23. Quoted in William L. DeAndrea, *Encyclopedia Mysteriosa: A Comprehensive Guide to the Art of Detection in Print, Film, Radio, and Television* (New York: Prentice Hall, 1994), p. 55.
24. Earl Derr Biggers, *Charlie Chan Carries On* (New York: Pyramid Books, 1969), p. 148.

2: THE TOUGH GUY

1. Quoted in Phil Hardy (ed.), *The Overlook Encyclopedia: The Gangster Film* (Woodstock: The Overlook Press, 1998), p. 7.
2. Marilyn Bardsley, "Al Capone," *The Crime Library* (http://www.crimelibrary.com/capone/caponemain.htm, c. 1999).
3. Hardy, *Gangster*, p. 30.
4. Hardy, *Gangster*, p. 40.
5. Hardy, *Gangster*, p. 41.
6. Todd McCarthy, *Howard Hawks: The Grey Fox of Hollywood* (New York: Grove Press, 1997), p. 137.
7. Hardy, *Gangster*, p. 49.

3: THE ROMANTIC

1. Elizabeth Kendall, *The Runaway Bride: Hollywood Romantic Comedy of the 1930s* (New York: Knopf, 1990), pp. xiv–xv.
2. Quoted in Lee Lourdeaux, *Italian and Irish Filmmakers in America: Ford, Capra, Coppola, and Scorsese* (Philadelphia: Temple University Press, 1990), p. 133.
3. Philip Dunne, quoted in Joseph McBride, *Frank Capra: The Catastrophe of Success* (New York: Simon & Schuster, 1992), p. 291.
4. Graham Greene, *Graham Greene on Film* (New York: Simon & Schuster, 1972), p. 96.
5. Ray Carney, *American Vision: The Films of Frank Capra* (Middletown, Conn.: Wesleyan University Press, 1996), p. 7.
6. McBride, *Frank Capra*, p. 238.
7. McBride, *Frank Capra*, p. 260.
8. Gerald Weales, *Canned Goods as Caviar: American Film Comedies of the 1930s* (Chicago: University of Chicago Press, 1985), p. 163.
9. Quoted in McBride, *Frank Capra*, p. 214.
10. Carney, *American Vision*, p. 51.
11. From interview with the author, December 1999.

4: Ballad of a Thin Man

1. Quoted in James Kotsilibas-Davis and Myrna Loy, *Myrna Loy: Being and Becoming* (New York: Knopf, 1987), p. 90.
2. Tony Goodstone (ed.), *The Pulps: Fifty Years of American Pop Culture* (New York: Chelsea House, 1970), p. ix.
3. DeAndrea, *Encyclopedia Mysteriosa*, p. 150.
4. Quoted in DeAndrea, *Encyclopedia Mysteriosa*, p. 153.
5. Quoted in James Vinson (ed.), *Great Writers of the English Language: Novelists and Prose Writers* (New York: St. Martin's, 1979), p. 525.
6. Raymond Chandler, *Later Novels and Other Writings* (New York: Library of America, 1995), pp. 988–89.
7. Quoted in Richard Layman, *Shadow Man: The Life of Dashiell Hammett* (San Diego: Harcourt Brace Jovanovich, 1981), p. 131.
8. Quoted in Vinson, *Great Writers*, p. 526.
9. Quoted in Layman, *Shadow Man*, p. 142.
10. Quoted in Tom Soter, "Ballad of a Thin Man," *Video*, July 1986, p. 79.
11. Quoted in Joseph Hurley, "Nora on Nick: Myrna Loy Talks About Her Co-Star," *Films in Review*, October 1982, p. 467.
12. Quoted in Charles Francisco, *Gentleman: The William Powell Story* (New York: St. Martin's, 1985), p. 118.
13. Quoted in Lawrence J. Quirk, *The Films of Myrna Loy* (Secaucus, N.J.: Citadel, 1980), p. 20.
14. Kotsilibas-Davis, *Myrna Loy*, p. 48.
15. Kotsilibas-Davis, *Myrna Loy*, p. 75.
16. Kotsilibas-Davis, *Myrna Loy*, p. 52.
17. Kotsilibas-Davis, *Myrna Loy*, p. 54.
18. Kotsilibas-Davis, *Myrna Loy*, p. 88.
19. David Thomson, *A Biographical Dictionary of Film: Third Edition* (New York: Knopf, 1995), p. 454.
20. Kotsilibas-Davis, *Myrna Loy*, p. 89.
21. Kotsilibas-Davis, *Myrna Loy*, p. 89.
22. Kotsilibas-Davis, *Myrna Loy*, p. 89.
23. Pat McGilligan (ed.), *Backstory: Interviews with Screenwriters of Hollywood's Golden Age* (Berkeley: University of California Press, 1986), p. 196.
24. Staton Rabin, "Remembering William Powell," *Films in Review*, October 1982, p. 461.
25. James Harvey, *Romantic Comedy in Hollywood: From Lubitsch to Sturges* (New York: Da Capo Press, 1998), p. 179.
26. Francisco, *Gentleman*, p. 134.
27. Thomson, *Biographical Dictionary*, p. 599.
28. Harvey, *Romantic Comedy*, p. 124.
29. Quoted in Soter, *Video*, p. 80.
30. Quoted in Soter, *Video*, p. 81.
31. Everson, *Detective*, p. 94.
32. Kotsilibas-Davis, *Myrna Loy*, p. 88.
33. Kotsilibas-Davis, *Myrna Loy*, p. 92.

34. Quoted in Hurley, *Films*, p. 467.
35. Hurley, *Films*, p. 464.
36. Quoted in Wendy Lin, "Myrna Loy Dies," New York *Daily News*, December 15, 1993, p. 7.
37. Karyn Kay, *Myrna Loy* (New York: Pyramid Publications, 1977), p. 78. Also, see Loy's comments on the couple in Quirk, *Myrna Loy*, p. 170: "They were both well aware of each other's faults, and they still loved each other in spite of them. And I was hardly the perfect wife in the sense of being the chaste, virginal creature that seemed to be so much admired. Nora of *The Thin Man* was different; she had a gorgeous sense of humor; she appreciated the distinctive grace of her husband's wit; she laughed at and with him when he was funny. What's more, she laughed at herself. Besides having tolerance, she was a good guy. She was courageous and interested in living and she essayed all the things he did. You understand, she had a good time, always."
38. Kotsilibas-Davis, *Myrna Loy*, p. 90.

5: A Humorous Hitch

1. Quoted in Alain Carraze and Jean-Luc Putheaud (ed.), *The Avengers Companion* (San Francisco: Bay Books, 1998), p. 170.
2. William Rothman, *Hitchcock: The Murderous Gaze* (Cambridge, Mass.: Harvard University Press, 1982), p. 6.
3. Quoted in François Truffaut, *Hitchcock* (Touchstone/Simon & Schuster, 1984), p. 103.
4. Rothman, *Murderous*, p. 7.
5. Truffaut, *Hitchcock*, p. 345.
6. Quoted in Sidney Gottlieb (ed.), *Hitchcock on Hitchcock: Selected Writings and Interviews* (Berkeley: University of California Press, 1997), p. 143.
7. Quoted in Robert A. Harris and Michael S. Lasky, *The Films of Alfred Hitchcock* (Secaucus, N.J.: Citadel, 1976), p. 18.
8. Thomson, *Biographical Dictionary*, p. 342.
9. Benedict Nightingale, "'Wanda': From Idea to Reality," *New York Times*, July 17, 1988, p. 23.
10. Terrence Rafferty, "The Current Cinema: Afterglow," *The New Yorker*, July 25, 1988, p. 78.
11. Quoted in George Perry, *Forever Ealing: A Celebration of the Great British Film Studio* (London: Pavilion Books, 1981), p. 7.
12. David Shipman, *The Story of Cinema: A Complete Narrative History from the Beginnings to the Present* (New York: St. Martin's, 1982), p. 803.
13. Shipman, *Story*, p. 897.
14. Quoted in "Guinness Remembers 'Kind Hearts,'" *New York Times*, October 26, 1984, p. 22.
15. Quoted in Perry, *Forever Ealing*, p. 122.
16. Quoted in Ronald L. Smith, *Who's Who in Comedy* (New York: Facts on File, 1992), p. 199.

17. Quoted in *New York Times*, p. 22.
18. Quoted in Jonathan Margolis, *Cleese Encounters: The Unauthorized Biography of Monty Python Veteran John Cleese* (New York: St. Martin's, 1993), pp. 242–43.

6: When a Man Became a Woman

1. From interview with the author, October 1999.
2. Quoted in Patrick Macnee with Dave Rogers, *The Avengers and Me* (New York: TV Books, 1998), p. 15.
3. From interview with the author.
4. "Patrick Macnee on *The Avengers*," *Starburst*, March 1984, p. 12.
5. Patrick Macnee and Marie Cameron, *Blind in One Ear: The Avenger Returns* (San Francisco: Mercury House, 1989), p. 206.
6. Macnee, *Avengers and Me*, p. 19
7. Quoted in Dave Rogers, *The Ultimate Avengers* (London: Boxtree, 1995), p. 7.
8. Quoted in "Look Who's Talking," *On Target*, April 1986, p. 29.
9. From interview with the author, June 2000.
10. From interview with the author.
11. Macnee, *Blind*, p. 221.
12. Macnee, *Avengers and Me*, pp. 32–33.
13. From interview with the author.
14. Macnee, *Blind*, p. 223.
15. From interview with the author.
16. Macnee, *Blind*, p. 213.
17. Quoted in *On Target*, p. 45.
18. From interview with the author.
19. Quoted in *On Target*, p. 45.
20. Macnee, *Avengers and Me*, p. 23.
21. Quoted in David Buxton, *From* The Avengers *to* Miami Vice: *Form and Ideology in Television Series* (Manchester, England: Manchester University Press, 1990), p. 75.
22. Macnee, *Avengers and Me*, p. 38.
23. Macnee, *Blind*, p. 220.
24. From interview with author.
25. Macnee, *Blind*, p. 223.
26. From interview with the author.
27. Quoted in Rogers, *Ultimate,* p. 55.
28. From interview with the author.
29. Quoted in Rogers, *Ultimate,* p. 80.
30. Quoted in Rogers, *Ultimate,* p. 81.
31. From interview with the author.
32. From interview with the author.
33. From interview with the author.
34. From interview with the author.
35. From interview with the author.

36. From interview with the author.
37. From interview with the author.
38. From interview with the author.
39. From interview with the author.

7: M-Appeal

1. Quoted in *On Target*, p. 11.
2. Quoted in *Starburst*, p. 15.
3. From interview with the author.
4. Quoted in *On Target*, p. 45.
5. From interview with the author.
6. Quoted in *On Target*, p. 11.
7. Macnee, *Blind*, p. 237.
8. Quoted in *Starburst*, p. 15.
9. Quoted in *On Target*, p. 47.
10. Quoted in Rogers, *Ultimate*, p. 162.
11. Quoted in Rogers, *Ultimate*, p. 162.
12. Quoted in *On Target*, p. 47.
13. Quoted in *On Target*, p. 30.
14. Quoted in Rogers, *Ultimate*, p. 83.
15. Quoted in Carraze, *Companion*, p. 22.
16. Quoted in *On Target*, p. 30.
17. Quoted in *On Target*, p. 30.
18. Quoted in Rogers, *Ultimate*, p. 170.
19. Quoted in Carraze, *Companion*, p. 21.
20. Quoted in Carraze, *Companion*, p. 21.
21. Quoted in Buxton, *From* The Avengers *to* Miami Vice, p. 75
22. Buxton, *From* The Avengers *to* Miami Vice, p. 97.
23. Buxton, *From* The Avengers *to* Miami Vice, p. 96.
24. Toby Miller, *The Avengers* (London: British Film Institute, 1997), p. 32.
25. Quoted in Miller, *The Avengers*, p. 154.
26. Quoted in *On Target*, p. 31.
27. Quoted in Carraze, *Companion*, p. 169.
28. Macnee, *Avengers and Me*, p. 44.
29. Macnee, *Avengers and Me*, p. 69.
30. Quoted in Rogers, *Ultimate*, p. 176.
31. Buxton, *From* The Avengers *to* Miami Vice, p. 99.
32. Quoted in Buxton, *From* The Avengers *to* Miami Vice, p. 101.
33. Quirk, *Myrna Loy*, p. 13.
34. Quoted in Rogers, *Ultimate*, p. 169.
35. Macnee, *Avengers and Me*, p. 67.
36. Quoted in Miller, *The Avengers*, p. 66.
37. Buxton, *From* The Avengers *to* Miami Vice, p. 101.
38. Paul Cornell, Martin Day, and Keith Topping, The Avengers *Dossier: The Definitive Unauthorized Guide* (London: Virgin Books, 1998), p. 129.

8: Trust No One

1. Walter Kendrick, *The Thrill of Fear: 250 Years of Scary Entertainment* (New York: Grove Press, 1991), p. xix.
2. David J. Skal, *Hollywood Gothic: The Tangled Web of Dracula from Novel to Stage to Screen* (New York: W.W. Norton, 1990), p. 28.
3. Quoted in John McCarty, *The Modern Horror Film: 50 Contemporary Classics* (New York: Citadel, 1990), p. 26.
4. Quoted in Michael J. Murphy, *The Celluloid Vampires: A History and Filmography, 1897–1979* (Ann Arbor, Mich.: Pierian Press, 1979), p. 78.
5. Francis Ford Coppola and James V. Hart, *Bram Stoker's Dracula: The Film and the Legend* (New York: Newmarket Press, 1992), p. 5.
6. Skal, *Hollywood Gothic*, p. 4.
7. Coppola, *Bram Stoker's Dracula*, p. 169.
8. Quoted in Phil Hardy, *The Overlook Film Encyclopedia: Horror* (Woodstock, N.Y.: Overlook Press, 1993), p. xi.
9. Hardy, *Horror*, p. xi.
10. Hardy, *Horror*, p. 79.
11. Chris Steinbrunner and Burt Goldblatt, *Cinema of the Fantastic* (New York: Galahad Books, 1972), p. 221.
12. Quoted in David Kalat, *A Critical History and Filmography of Toho's Godzilla Series* (Jefferson, N.C.: McFarland, 1997), p. 15.
13. Kalat, *A Critical History*, p. 15.
14. From interview with the author, December 1984.
15. Phil Hardy, *The Overlook Film Encyclopedia: Science Fiction* (Woodstock, N.Y.: Overlook Press, 1991), p. 124.

9: The Truth Is Out There

1. Quoted in Paula Vitaris, "*X-Files*: Pushing Horror's Envelope," *Cinefantastique*, October 1995, p. 37.
2. Quoted in Vitaris, *Cinefantastique*, p. 21
3. Quoted in Vitaris, *Cinefantastique*, p. 20.
4. Quoted in Vitaris, *Cinefantastique*, p. 21.
5. Quoted in Vitaris, *Cinefantastique*, p. 22.
6. Quoted in Vitaris, *Cinefantastique*, p. 22.
7. Quoted in Vitaris, *Cinefantastique*, p. 22.
8. Quoted in "X-Cyclopedia: The Ultimate Episode Guide," *Entertainment Weekly*, November 29, 1996, p. 38.
9. Quoted in Vitaris, *Cinefantastique*, p. 30.
10. Quoted in Vitaris, *Cinefantastique*, p. 30.
11. Quoted in Brian Lowry, *The Truth Is Out There: The Official Guide to* The X-Files (New York: HarperPrism, 1995), p. 33.
12. Quoted in "*X-Files*: Episode Guide," *Cinefantastique*, October 1995, p. 58.

13. Quoted in Andy Meisler, *I Want to Believe: The Official Guide to* The X-Files, Volume 3 (New York: HarperPrism, 1998), p. 102.
14. Quoted in Meisler, *Believe*, p. 9.
15. Quoted in Brian Lowry, *Trust No One: The Official Third Season Guide to* The X-Files (New York: HarperPrism, 1996), p. 235.
16. Vitaris, *Cinefantastique*, p. 17.
17. Quoted in Lowry, *Trust*, p. 139.
18. Quoted in Jane Goldman, *The X-Files Book of the Unexplained*, Volume II (New York: HarperPrism, 1996), p. 215.

10: A Man and a Woman

1. Kotsilibas-Davis, *Myrna Loy*, p. 91.
2. From interview with the author.
3. Quoted in "*X-Files*: Episode Guide," *Cinefantastique*, p. 18.
4. From interview with the author.
5. From interview with the author.
6. From interview with the author.
7. Quoted in Kotsilibas-Davis, *Myrna Loy*, p. 69.
8. Quoted in Kotsilibas-Davis, *Myrna Loy*, p. 114.
9. Quoted in Kotsilibas-Davis, *Myrna Loy*, p. 92. Loy and Powell actually appeared in 14 pictures, although in their last, *The Senator Was Indiscreet*, Loy merely had a cameo.
10. Quoted in Kotsilibas-Davis, *Myrna Loy*, p. 88.
11. Quoted in Kotsilibas-Davis, *Myrna Loy*, p. 91.
12. From interview with author.
13. Ken Tucker, "Spooky Kind of Love: An Ode to TV's Most Perfectly Strange Relationship," *Entertainment Weekly*, November 29, 1996, p. 36.
14. Quoted in Kotsilibas-Davis, *Myrna Loy*, p. 185; p. 208.
15. From interview with author.
16. Quoted in Vitaris, *Cinefantastique*, pp. 22, 28.
17. Quoted in Andy Meisler, *Believe*, p. 164.
18. Tucker, *Entertainment Weekly*, p. 36.
19. Quoted in Lowry, *Truth*, p. 16.
20. Tucker, *Entertainment Weekly*, p. 36.

Appendix 1

1. Kotsilibas-Davis, *Myrna Loy*, p. 142.
2. Kotsilibas-Davis, *Myrna Loy*, p. 162.
3. Kotsilibas-Davis, *Myrna Loy*, p. 162.
4. Quoted in Layman, *Shadow Man*, p. 140.
5. Quoted in Kotsilibas-Davis, *Myrna Loy*, p. 185.
6. Quoted in Kotsilibas-Davis, *Myrna Loy*, p. 185.

7. Kotsilibas-Davis, *Myrna Loy*, p. 93.
8. Quoted in Michael Mallory, "The Reluctant Horror Heroine: Phyllis Kirk," *Scarlet Street*, No. 36, Winter 1999, p. 52.

APPENDIX 2

1. From interview with author.
2. From interview with author.

Bibliography

Books

Barer, Burt. *The Saint: A Complete History in Print, Radio, Film and Television of Leslie Charteris' Robin Hood of Modern Crime, Simon Templar, 1928–1992* (Jefferson, N.C.: McFarland, 1993).

Biggers, Earl Derr. *Charlie Chan Carries On* (New York: Pyramid Books, 1969).

Biskind, Peter. *Seeing Is Believing: How Hollywood Taught Us to Stop Worrying and Love the Fifties* (New York: Pantheon Books, 1983).

Brooks, Tim. *The Complete Directory to Prime Time TV Stars* (New York: Ballantine, 1987).

_____, and Earle Marsh. *The Complete Directory to Prime Time Network and Cable TV Shows, 1946–Present* (New York: Ballantine, 1995).

Brosnan, John. *The Primal Screen: A History of Science Fiction Film* (London: Orbit Books, 1991).

Butler, William Vivian. *The Durable Desperadoes* (London: Macmillan, 1973).

Buxton, David. *From* The Avengers *to* Miami Vice: *Form and Ideology in Television Series* (Manchester, England: Manchester University Press, 1990).

Carney, Ray. *American Vision: The Films of Frank Capra* (Middletown, Conn.: Wesleyan University Press, 1996).

Carraze, Alain, and Jean-Luc Putheaud (ed.). *The Avengers Companion* (San Francisco: Bay Books, 1998).

Castleman, Harry, and Walter J. Podrazik. *Harry and Wally's Favorite TV Shows* (New York: Prentice-Hall, 1989).

Chandler, Raymond. *Later Novels and Other Writings* (New York: Library of America, 1995).

Clute, John. *Science Fiction: The Illustrated Encyclopedia* (New York: Dorling Kindersley, 1995).

Conan Doyle, Arthur. *The Adventures of Sherlock Holmes* (London: Leopard, 1996).

_____. *The Memoirs of Sherlock Holmes* (New York: Berkley Medallion, 1968).

_____. *A Study in Scarlet* (London: Leopard, 1996).

Coppola, Francis Ford, and James V. Hart. *Bram Stoker's Dracula: The Film and the Legend* (New York: Newmarket Press, 1992).

Corey, Melinda, and George Ochoa. *A Cast of Thousands: A Compendium of Who Played What in Film*, Vols. I and II (New York: Facts on File, 1992).

Cornell, Paul, Martin Day, and Keith Topping. The Avengers *Dossier: The Definitive Unauthorized Guide* (London: Virgin Books, 1998).

Daly, Carroll John. *The Adventures of Race Williams* (New York: Mysterious Press, 1989).

DeAndrea, William L. *Encyclopedia Mysteriosa: A Comprehensive Guide to the Art of Detection in Print, Film, Radio, and Television* (New York: Prentice Hall, 1994).

Everson, William K. *The Detective in Film* (Secaucus, N.J.: Citadel Press, 1972).

Farrand, Phil. *The Nitpicker's Guide for X-Philes* (New York: Dell, 1997).

Francisco, Charles. *Gentleman: The William Powell Story* (New York: St. Martin's, 1985).

Goldman, Jane. *The X-Files Book of the Unexplained*, Volume II (New York: HarperPrism, 1996).

Goodstone, Tony (ed.). *The Pulps: Fifty Years of American Pop Culture* (New York: Chelsea House, 1970).

Gottlieb, Sidney (ed.). *Hitchcock on Hitchcock: Selected Writings and Interviews* (Berkeley: University of California Press, 1997).

Greene, Graham. *Graham Greene on Film* (New York: Simon & Schuster, 1972).

Haining, Peter (ed.). *The Sherlock Holmes Scrapbook* (New York: Clarkson N. Potter, 1974).

Hammett, Dashiell. *Complete Novels* (New York: Library of America, 1999).

Hanke, Ken. *Charlie Chan at the Movies: History, Filmography, and Criticism* (Jefferson, N.C.: McFarland, 1989).

Hardy, Phil (ed.). *The Overlook Encyclopedia: The Gangster Film* (Woodstock, N.Y.: Overlook Press, 1998).

_____. *The Overlook Film Encyclopedia: Horror* (Woodstock, N.Y.: Overlook Press, 1993).

_____. *The Overlook Film Encyclopedia: Science Fiction* (Woodstock, N.Y.: Overlook Press, 1991).

Harris, Robert A., and Michael S. Lasky. *The Films of Alfred Hitchcock* (Secaucus, N.J.: Citadel Press, 1976).

Harvey, James. *Romantic Comedy in Hollywood: From Lubitsch to Sturges* (New York: Da Capo Press, 1998).

Kalat, David. *A Critical History and Filmography of Toho's Godzilla Series* (Jefferson, N.C.: McFarland, 1997).

Kay, Karyn. *Myrna Loy* (New York: Pyramid Publications, 1977).

Kendall, Elizabeth. *The Runaway Bride: Hollywood Romantic Comedy of the 1930s* (New York: Knopf, 1990).

Kendrick, Walter. *The Thrill of Fear: 250 Years of Scary Entertainment* (New York: Grove Press, 1991).

Kotsilibas-Davis, James, and Myrna Loy. *Myrna Loy: Being and Becoming* (New York: Knopf, 1987).

Layman, Richard. *Shadow Man: The Life of Dashiell Hammett* (San Diego: Harcourt Brace Jovanovich, 1981).

Lourdeaux, Lee. *Italian and Irish Filmmakers in America: Ford, Capra, Coppola, and Scorsese* (Philadelphia: Temple University Press, 1990).

Lowry, Brian. *Trust No One: The Official Third Season Guide to* The X-Files (New York: HarperPrism, 1996).

_____. *The Truth Is Out There: The Official Guide to* The X-Files (New York: HarperPrism, 1995).

McBride, Joseph. *Frank Capra: The Catastrophe of Success* (New York: Simon & Schuster, 1992).

McCarthy, Todd. *Howard Hawks: The Grey Fox of Hollywood* (New York: Grove Press, 1997).

McCarty, John. *The Modern Horror Film: 50 Contemporary Classics* (New York: Citadel, 1990).

McGilligan, Pat (ed.). *Backstory: Interviews with Screenwriters of Hollywood's Golden Age* (Berkeley: University of California Press, 1986).

Macnee, Patrick, and Marie Cameron. *Blind in One Ear: The Avenger Returns* (San Francisco: Mercury House, 1989).

_____, with Dave Rogers. *The Avengers and Me* (New York: TV Books, 1998).

Margolis, Jonathan. *Cleese Encounters: The Unauthorized Biography of Monty Python Veteran John Cleese* (New York: St. Martin's, 1993).

Meisler, Andy. *The End and the Beginning: The Official Guide to* The X-Files, Volume 5 (New York: HarperPrism, 2000).

_____. *I Want to Believe: The Official Guide to* The X-Files, Volume 3 (New York: HarperPrism, 1998).

_____. *Resist or Serve: The Official Guide to* The X-Files, Volume 4 (New York: HarperPrism, 1999).

Miller, Toby. *The Avengers* (London: British Film Institute, 1997).

Murphy, Michael J. *The Celluloid Vampires: A History and Filmography, 1897–1979* (Ann Arbor, Mich.: Pierian Press, 1979).

Parish, James Robert (ed.). *The Great Movie Series* (Cranbury, N.J.: A.S. Barnes, 1971).

_____, and Ronald L. Bowers. *The Golden Era: The MGM Stock Company* (New Rochelle, N.Y.: Arlington House, 1973).

Peary, Danny (ed.). *Omni's Screen Flights/Screen Fantasies: The Future According to Science Fiction Cinema* (Garden City: Doubleday & Company, 1984).

Perry, George. *Forever Ealing: A Celebration of the Great British Film Studio* (London: Pavilion Books, 1981).

Poe, Edgar Allan. *Tales of Mystery and Imagination* (London: Oxford University Press, 1967).

Quirk, Lawrence J. *The Films of Myrna Loy* (Secaucus, N.J.: Citadel, 1980).

Rogers, Dave. *The Ultimate Avengers* (London: Boxtree, 1995).

Rothman, William. *Hitchcock: The Murderous Gaze* (Cambridge, Mass.: Harvard University Press, 1982).

Shipman, David. *The Story of Cinema: A Complete Narrative History from the Beginnings to the Present* (New York: St. Martin's, 1982).

Siegel, Jeff. *The American Detective: An Illustrated History* (Dallas: Taylor, 1993).

Skal, David J. *Hollywood Gothic: The Tangled Web of Dracula from Novel to Stage to Screen* (New York: W.W. Norton, 1990).

Smith, Ronald L. *Who's Who in Comedy* (New York: Facts on File, 1992).

Starrett, Vincent. *The Private Life of Sherlock Holmes* (New York: Pinnacle Books, 1975).

Steinbrunner, Chris, and Burt Goldblatt. *Cinema of the Fantastic* (New York: Galahad Books, 1972).

Thomson, David. *A Biographical Dictionary of Film: Third Edition* (New York: Knopf, 1995).

Truffaut, François. *Hitchcock* (New York, Touchstone/Simon & Schuster, 1984).

Vinson, James (ed.). *Great Writers of the English Language: Novelists and Prose Writers* (New York: St. Martin's Press, 1979).

Von Gunden, Kenneth, and Stuart H. Stock. *Twenty All-Time Great Science Fiction Films* (New York: Arlington House, 1982).

Weales, Gerald. *Canned Goods as Caviar: American Film Comedies of the 1930s* (Chicago: University of Chicago Press, 1985).

NEWSPAPERS/MAGAZINES

Bardsley, Marilyn. "Al Capone," *The Crime Library* (http://www.crimelibrary.com/capone/caponemain.htm, c. 1999).

"Guinness Remembers 'Kind Hearts.'" *New York Times*, October 26, 1984.

Hurley, Joseph. "Nora on Nick: Myrna Loy Talks About Her Co-Star." *Films in Review*, October 1982.

Krebs, Albin. "Erle Stanley Gardner, the Author of Perry Mason Mystery Novels, Is Dead at 80." *New York Times*, March 12, 1970.

Lin, Wendy. "Myrna Loy Dies." New York *Daily News*, December 15, 1993.

"Look Who's Talking." *On Target*, April 1986.

Mallory, Michael. "The Reluctant Horror Heroine: Phyllis Kirk." *Scarlet Street*, No. 36, Winter 1999.

Mandelbaum, Ken. "Nick and Nora: A New Musical." Broadway cast CD liner notes, 1992.

Nightingale, Benedict. "'Wanda': From Idea to Reality." *New York Times*, July 17, 1988.

"Patrick Macnee on *The Avengers*." *Starburst*, March 1984.

Rabin, Staton. "Remembering William Powell." *Films in Review*, October 1982.

Rafferty, Terrence. "The Current Cinema: Afterglow." *The New Yorker*, July 25, 1988.

Soter, Tom. "Ballad of a Thin Man." *Video*, July 1986.

Tucker, Ken. "Spooky Kind of Love: An Ode to TV's Most Perfectly Strange Relationship." *Entertainment Weekly*, November 29, 1996.

Vitaris, Paula. "*X-Files*: Pushing Horror's Envelope." *Cinefantastique*, October 1995.

"X-Cyclopedia: The Ultimate Episode Guide." *Entertainment Weekly*, November 29, 1996.

"*X-Files*: Episode Guide." *Cinefantastique*, October 1995.

Index

After the Thin Man (film) 133, 149–150
Anderson, Gillian 117, 137–138
Annie Hall (film) 27, 28
Another Thin Man (film) 127, 133, 150–151
The Avengers (film) 145
The Avengers (TV series) 65; as live television 77–78; as pop 91–92, 93; as surrealism 90–91; attitude towards women 80–81; Blackman's hiring 70; "The Charmers" 89; compared with *The Thin Man* 79, 80, 94, 96; conversion to film 84; "The Correct Way to Kill" 89; "The Cybernauts" 129; "The Danger Makers" 87; dark humor 131–132; "Dead Man's Treasure" compared with *The Thin Man* 137 "Death of a Great Dane" 88; "The Fear Merchants" 86; "50,000 Pound Breakfast 88–89; "The Frighteners" episode synopsis 66–69; "A Funny Thing Happened on the Way to the Station" 85–86; Hendry's departure 69; "The Hidden Tiger" 93, 125; "The Living Dead" 86; "Mandrake" 129; "Murdersville" 86; plot devices 75–77, 86–88, 90, 92, 134–135; "The Positive-Negative Man" compared with "Squeeze" 136–137; "Quick-Quick-Slow Death" 88; Rigg's effect 84–85; sexual tension 74–75, 83; "The Town of No Return" 81, 85; "What the Butler Saw" 86; "The Winged Avenger" 94; "You Have Just Been Murdered" 85

Biggers, Earl Derr 12, 13
Blackmail (film) 56
Blackman, Honor 70, 72, 75–77, 80–81, 137
Blacula (film) 100
Bram Stoker's Dracula (film) 100–101
Bringing Up Baby (film) 21, 25

Capra, Frank 22, 23, 24
Carter, Chris 114, 115
Cat People (film) 101–102
Catherine Gale (character) 70, 71, 73–74
Charlie Chan (character) 3, 11, 12, 13, 14
Charteris, Leslie 10, 11
Cleese, John 62
Clemens, Brian 54, 86
Clockwise (film) 62

Dana Scully (character) 116–117, 147–148
Dark Shadows (TV series) 100
detectives (in silent films) 8, 9
Dr. Strangelove (film) 84–85
Double Wedding (film) 154

Index

Dracula (character) 99–101
Duchovny, David 116, 137–138

Ealing Film Studios 59–62
Emma Peel (character) 83, 88–89, 93, 147–148
Evelyn Prentice (film) 153

Fail Safe (film) 85
Fierce Creatures (film) 62
A Fish Called Wanda (film) 59, 60, 62, 92
Fox Mulder (character) 116, 147–148
Fleming, Ian 63

gangsters (real life) 15, 16, 18, 19
Gardner, Erle Stanley 3, 5
Get Shorty (film) 61
Godzilla, King of Monsters (Gojira) (film) 104–105
Goldfinger (film) 81
The Great Ziegfeld (film) 153
Guinness, Alec 61

Hammett, Dashiell 30, 31, 32, 33
Hardy, Oliver 9
Hendry, Ian 63, 64
High Sierra (film) 19, 20
Hitchcock, Alfred 54, 63
Holiday (film) 25
Horror of Dracula (film) 100

I Love You Again (film) 154
The Invaders (TV series) 107
It Happened One Night (film) 22, 25, 28

James Bond (character) 78
John Steed (character) 65, 72–73, 78, 93, 147–148

Kalifornia (film) 116
Keaton, Buster 9
The Kennel Murder Case (film) 138
Kind Hearts and Coronets (film) 59, 60, 61
Kolchak: The Night Stalker (TV film) 113

The Lady Eve (film) 29
The Lady Vanishes (film) 56, 57

Laurel, Stan 9
Lewton, Val 101, 102
Libeled Lady (film) 141–142, 153–154
A Life Less Ordinary (film) 28
Little Caesar (film) 16, 17
Love Crazy (film) 154–155
Loy, Myrna 35, 36, 38, 51, 52, 53, 138–142

Macnee, Patrick 64–65, 72–73, 137
Manhattan Melodrama (film) 19, 35, 141, 153
Mask of Fu Manchu (film) 139
Mickey One (film) 106–107
The Missionary (film) 62
Moonlighting (TV series) 142–143, 147
"Murders in the Rue Morgue" (story) 4, 5
My Man Godfrey (film) 21

Newman, Sydney 63
Nick and Nora (play) 156
Nick and Nora (TV film) 156
Nick Charles (character) 33, 45, 51–52, 147–148
Nora Charles (character) 45, 51–52, 147–148
North by Northwest (film) 63
Notorious (film) 57
Notting Hill (film) 29
Nuns on the Run (film) 62

The Palm Beach Story (film) 26
The Parallax View (film) 108
paranoia thrillers 106–108
Pat and Mike (film) 25, 26
Penthouse (film) 37, 140–141
Philo Vance (character) 36, 138
Picnic at Hanging Rock (film) 102–103
Pillow Talk (film) 27
Police Surgeon (TV series) 63, 64, 65
Powell, William 35, 36, 38, 51, 52, 53, 138–139
The Prisoner (TV series) 107–108
The Prizefighter and the Lady (film) 37, 139–140
Psycho (film) 55, 58
The Public Enemy (film) 16, 17, 18

Index

Quatermass and the Pit (film) 106
Quatermass II: Enemy from Space (film) 106
The Quatermass Xperiment (film) 105

The Real Blonde (film) 28
Rear Window (film) 57
Rigg, Diana 81, 83, 137
Rogers, Ginger 138–139
Rope (film) 55
Runaway Bride (film) 28

The Saint (character) 10, 11
Scarecrow and Mrs. King (TV series) 143–144
Scarface, Shame of a Nation (film) 18, 19
The Senator Was Indiscreet (film) 155
The Seventh Victim (film) 102
sexual tension (between characters) 74–75, 83–84
Shadow of a Doubt (film) 57
Shadow of the Thin Man (film) 133, 151
Sherlock Holmes (character) 5, 6, 7, 8, 36
Song of the Thin Man (film) 144, 152
Star of Midnight (film) 138
Star Trek (TV series) 112
Star Trek: The Next Generation (TV series) 114
Strangers on a Train (film) 57
Swing Time (film) 26

Them! (film) 98, 104
The Thing (film) 121
The Thin Man (book) 30, 33, 34, 39, 40
The Thin Man (film): changes from the book 39–40; compared with credits 149; dark humor 131–132; "Dead Man's Treasure" 137; first preview 53; formula 132–133; spontaneity 37–38; synopsis 41–51; women 129
The Thin Man (TV series) 155–156
The Thin Man Goes Home (film) 144, 151–152
The Thirty-Nine Steps (film) 55
Thomas, Howard 63
Three Days of the Condor (film) 109
The Trouble with Harry (film) 61
Twentieth Century (film) 26
The Twilight Zone (TV series) 111–112

Unfaithfully Yours (film) 26
The Upper Hand (TV series) 75, 78

vampires 99–101
Van Dyke, W.S. 30, 34, 37, 38, 39–41, 139–141, 144
Vertigo (film) 57

White, Leonard 64
The Wrong Man (film) 57

The X-Files (TV series) beginnings 115–116; "Clyde Bruckman's Final Repose" 122; dark humor 131–132; "Deep Throat" 118; "Demons" 118; "The Erlenmeyer Flask" 118; horror and science fiction elements 131; "Ice" 121; mythology episodes 119–120, 136; "Nisei" 123, 124; pilot episode 117–118; sex 131; "Squeeze" 119, 136; "Squeeze" compared with "The Positive-Negative Man" 136–137 "Synchrony" 118; "Wetwired" 125; women 129

www.ingramcontent.com/pod-product-compliance
Ingram Content Group UK Ltd.
Pitfield, Milton Keynes, MK11 3LW, UK
UKHW041940140426
5217IPUK00014B/590